THE MOZART MYTHS

THE MOZART MYTHS

A Critical Reassessment

William Stafford

Stanford University Press
Stanford, California
1991

ML
410
M9
S815
1991

Stanford University Press
Stanford, California
© 1991 William Stafford
Originating publisher: The Macmillan Press,
London
First published in the U.S.A. by
    Stanford University Press, 1991
Printed in Hong Kong
ISBN 0-8047-1937-3
LC 91-65301

Contents

Acknowledgments

I am especially grateful to Stanley Sadie for his generous encouragement and invaluable advice at all stages of the preparation of this book. His writings on Mozart first made me aware of the fascinating historical problems of Mozart biography. I am also indebted to Alec Hyatt King for his helpful comments and suggestions. Dr Saskia Roberts patiently and thoroughly discussed the medical aspect with me: without the benefit of her knowledge chapter three would be much poorer. For the most part I have quoted Emily Anderson's generally excellent and reliable translations of the letters, but I have checked them against the standard edition of Bauer, Deutsch and Eibl, making a few small changes where necessary. I have used Helen Mautner's unfortunately rare translation of Niemetschek, and Deutsch's indispensable documentary biography. Cliff Eisen most kindly allowed me to see the manuscript of his substantial and important supplement to Deutsch, to be published by Macmillan in 1991. I have referred to the principal Viennese unit of currency as the gulden, but some of the quoted translations refer to it as the florin. My own translations were carefully checked and improved by Michael Warry. I owe thanks to him, and to the Polytechnic, Huddersfield for enabling and supporting my research in many ways. In particular I must mention the stalwart work of the inter-library loans section; the staff there indefatigably chased up rare and indispensable publications from all over the globe. Pauline Stafford helped me to tighten up and clarify the argument, and Edmund Stafford counted the masons. I have learnt much from the comments of those who listened to earlier drafts of chapters; in particular I must mention George Pratt and his colleagues on the music staff of Huddersfield Polytechnic.

I am also grateful to A & C Black for permission to quote from O E Deutsch *Mozart Documentary Biography* and to the following for permission to reproduce illustrative material. (Every effort has been made to contact copyright holders; I apologise to anyone who may have been omitted.) International Stiftung Mozarteum, Salzburg (figs. 1, 3, 8, 10); Hunterian Art Gallery, University of Glasgow (fig. 2) Musikbibliothek der Stadt Leipzig (fig. 4); Historisches Museum der Stadt Wien, Vienna (fig. 5); The Mansell Collection Ltd, London (fig. 6); Österreichische National-bibliothek, Vienna (fig. 9).

The book is dedicated to my parents.

INTRODUCTION

Chapter I

Melodrama and evidence

Mozart died at five minutes to one a.m. on Monday 5 December 1791, two months before his thirty-sixth birthday. His death fascinated contemporaries and has continued to fascinate posterity. Melodramatic stories were told about it within weeks and have continued to evolve for two hundred years. By way of illustration, here is a narrative stitched together largely verbatim, from anecdotes, memoirs and commonplaces of the Mozart literature.

* * *

During his last year, Mozart was depressed and frequently ill. The heyday of his fame in Vienna was long over, and he had constant money worries. According to Rochlitz,

> As he sat one day sunk in such melancholy phantasies, a carriage drew up and a stranger was announced. Mozart had him brought in. A somewhat ageing, serious, imposing man, of a very respectable appearance, unknown either to Mozart or his wife, entered. The man began:
> I come to you as the messenger of a very distinguished man –
> From whom do you come?
> asked Mozart.
> The man does not wish to be known.
> Good – what does he demand of me?
> A person has died who is and who ever will be very dear to him; he wishes to celebrate the anniversary of her death in a quiet but worthy manner, and for that purpose asks you to compose a Requiem for him.

3

Mozart was deeply affected by this speech, by the mystery which overspread the whole affair, by the solemn tone of the man, and because of his own state of mind, and promised to do as required. The man continued:
Work with all possible diligence: the man is knowledgeable about music –
All the better!
You are not held to a deadline –
Excellent –
Approximately how much time do you require?
Mozart, who seldom bothered to calculate time and money, answered:
Approximately four weeks.
I shall return then for the score. How much do you stipulate as payment?
Mozart casually answered:
A hundred ducats.
Here they are.
said the man: laid the money on the table and left. Mozart sank again in deepest reflection, heard nothing of what his wife said to him, and finally called for pen, ink and paper. He began at once to work on the commission. His interest in it seemed to grow with every bar: he wrote night and day. His body could not stand the strain: on a few occasions he fell fainting over the work.[1]

Niemetschek takes up the story:

Meanwhile Mozart received the honourable and advantageous commission to write the *opera seria* for the Prague coronation of Emperor Leopold. To go to Prague, to compose for his beloved Bohemians, was too attractive a prospect to permit a refusal.

Just as Mozart and his wife climbed into the carriage for the journey, there stood the messenger like a ghost, pulled at his wife's skirts and asked: 'What is the prospect for the Requiem now?'

[1] Friedrich Rochlitz, 'Verbürgte Anekdoten aus Wolfgang Gottlieb Mozarts Leben', *AMZ*, i (1798–9), 149 (5 December 1798)

Mozart excused himself on account of the necessity of the journey, and the impossibility of notifying his unknown patron about it; besides it would be his first task on his return, and it was only a question whether the unknown patron was willing to wait so long. The messenger was entirely satisfied with this.

Already in Prague Mozart was continuously ill and taking medicine; his colour was pale and his expression sad, although his more cheerful mood still frequently broke forth in joyful fun in the company of his friends.

Upon his return to Vienna he immediately took his mass for the dead in hand, and worked on it with much effort and a lively interest; but his illness visibly increased and drove him to gloomy melancholy. His wife observed this with sorrow. One day when she went with him to the Prater, in order to provide him with diversion and uplift, and the two of them were sitting there alone, Mozart began to speak of death, and asserted that he was setting the Requiem for himself. Tears stood in the eyes of this sensitive man. 'I have a strong sense', he continued, 'that I do not have much longer to live: without a doubt, someone has given me poison! I cannot free myself from this thought'.[2]

The state of his mind is revealed by a letter, apparently to his librettist Lorenzo Da Ponte, replying to the latter's suggestion that he should mend his fortune by going to England:

My dear Sir,
I wish I could follow your advice, but how can I do so? I feel stunned, I reason with difficulty, and I cannot get rid of the vision of this unknown man. I see him perpetually; he entreats me, presses me, and impatiently demands the work. I go on writing, because composition tires me less than resting. Otherwise I have nothing more to fear. I know from what I suffer that the hour is come; I am at the point of death; I have come to an end before having had the enjoyment of my talent. Life was indeed so beautiful, my career began under such fortunate auspices; but one cannot change one's own destiny.

---

[2] Franz Niemtschek, *Leben des k. k. Kapellmeisters Wolfgang Gottlieb Mozart, nach Originalquellen beschrieben* (Prague, 1798), 33–4. There is an English translation, as *Life of Mozart*, by Helen Mautner (London, 1956)

> No one can measure his own days, one must resign oneself, it
> will be as providence wills, and so I finish my death-song; I
> must not leave it incomplete.
>   Mozart.
> Vienna, September, 1791.[3]

His wife, seeing that the Requiem was oppressing his mind,
took away the score. His health improved for a while, and he
was able to complete a Masonic cantata which was well
received. This cheered him up, and his wife allowed him to
resume work on the Requiem. But his illness returned, and he
took to his bed. His hands and feet swelled, he was in great
pain and partly paralysed, there was constant vomiting. He
even had to ask them to remove his canary, because the
sound of its singing distressed his nerves. The success of *Die
Zauberflöte* pleased and at the same time saddened him, for
he knew he would not live to enjoy his triumph. In the
evenings, his watch beside him, he followed in imagination
the progress of the opera he would never hear again. He
continued to work on the Requiem, advising Süßmayr as to
its completion. On the very day before his death he held a
rehearsal of the score with a few friends; but when they
reached the Lacrymosa he broke down in tears.

An account of the very end was given by Mozart's sister-in-
law, Sophie:

> I went into the kitchen. The fire was out. I had to light the lamp
> and make a fire. All the time I was thinking of Mozart . . . I
> stared into the flame and thought to myself, 'How I should love
> to know how Mozart is'. While I was thinking and gazing at the
> flame, it went out, as completely as if the lamp had never been
> burning. Not a spark remained on the big wick and yet there
> wasn't the slightest draught – that I can swear to . . . I hurried
> along as fast as I could. Alas, how frightened I was when my
> sister, who was almost despairing and yet trying to keep calm,
> came out to me, saying: 'Thank God that you have come, dear

[3] Dyneley Hussey, *Wolfgang Amadé Mozart* (1928) (London, 2/1933), 302

Sophie. Last night he was so ill that I thought he would not be alive this morning. Do stay with me today, for if he has another bad turn, he will pass away tonight.' . . . I tried to control myself and went to his bedside. He immediately called me to him and said: 'Ah, dear Sophie, how glad I am that you have come. You must stay here tonight and see me die.' I tried hard to be brave and to persuade him to the contrary. But to all my attempts he only replied: 'Why, I have already the taste of death on my tongue'.

Eventually Sophie went for a priest and a doctor was called in.

A long search was made for Dr Closset, who was found at the theatre, but who had to wait for the end of the play. He came and ordered *cold* poultices to be placed on Mozart's burning head, which, however, affected him to such an extent that he became unconscious and remained so until he died. His last movement was an attempt to express with his mouth the drum passages in the Requiem. That I can still hear.[4]

Mozart's widow was prostrated by her loss. His patron, the Imperial minister Baron van Swieten, advised her at this juncture, recommending the cheapest possible funeral. In the words of Joseph Deiner, a local innkeeper:

The night of Mozart's death was dark and stormy; at the funeral too it began to rage and storm. Rain and snow fell at the same time, as if Nature wanted to show her anger with the great composer's contemporaries, who had turned out extremely sparsely for his burial. Only a few friends and three women accompanied the corpse. . . . As the storm grew ever more violent, even these few friends determined to turn back at the Stuben Gate.[5]

[4] Emily Anderson, trans. and ed., *The Letters of Mozart and his Family* (1938) (London, 3/1985), 976–7 [*LMF*]
[5] Thought to be the memoirs of Joseph Deiner, in the Vienna *Morgen-Post* of 28 January 1856: Otto Erich Deutsch, *Mozart: a Documentary Biography* (London, 1965), 565 [*MDB*]

The sexton at the cemetery of St Marx was left to bury the body in a pauper's grave for twenty corpses.

According to a Vienna newspaper, 'The widow of a man to whom so many crowned heads, to whom all Europe accorded unstinted admiration . . . sits sighing on a sack of straw amidst her needy children and under a sizeable burden of debt. An administrative official gave ten Gulden against Mozhart's watch, so that he could be buried.'[6] As for the Requiem, 'he completed it a few days before his death. When his death was known, the servant called again and brought the remaining 30 ducats, did *not* ask for the Requiem, and since then there has been no further request for it'.[7]

The grave was not marked, and could not later be found. A death mask had been taken, but all copies have crumbled away.

* * *

The elements of this melodramatic account are well known and have endlessly been repeated. But most of it is dubious and some of it is demonstrably false. The attentive reader will have noticed contradictions – over when Mozart started work on the Requiem, and over how much he was paid for it (figures have been given ranging from 60 to 400 ducats). Of course the Requiem was not commissioned by a divine or diabolical messenger, but by Count Walsegg for his dead wife. Mozart failed to complete it and his widow had it finished by others; it was collected, and performed by the patron. The authenticity of the alleged letter to Da Ponte cannot be verified. It is by no means certain that he knew he was dying until close to the end. The stories of his instructing Süßmayr about the Requiem, and rehearsing it on the last day,

---

[6] From the MS Vienna newspaper *Der heimliche Botschafter*, 13 December 1791; *MDB*, 424

[7] From the *Zeitung für Damen und andere Frauenzimmer*, Graz, 18 January 1792; *MDB*, 439

are dubious. It was not stormy when Mozart died, nor was there snow and rain together at his funeral. He did not receive a pauper's consecration and burial but, like most Viennese of his day, a third class funeral and burial in a grave to hold five or six coffins.[8] Sophie's highly circumstantial account of the last hours, with all that paraphernalia of precisely remembered conversation, dates from 33 years after the event. The second-hand story of the rehearsal of the Requiem on the last afternoon was recorded in 1827 and the details of the funeral, again second-hand and of uncertain provenance, in 1856.

The stories which have been told about Mozart's death rarely confine their attention to his last few months; very often they explore the relationship of the death to the extraordinary life. Was the death the necessary, inevitable consequence of that life and the manner of its living, or was it an unnecessary, accidental, senseless death? Was it a premature death or not? Did Mozart bring about his own death, or was it brought about in some way by others? These are fascinating questions for the historian. They demand an answer, and many answers have been attempted. They demand an answer, because there is apparently a puzzle about Mozart's life and reputation, and his death is at the heart of that puzzle.

As everybody knows, Mozart was an astonishing child prodigy. The infant was taken around the courts of Europe and quickly became celebrated. As a young adult, his early promise was amply fulfilled, as composer and virtuoso performer. In 1781 Mozart settled in Vienna and enjoyed a few years of renown and success, both artistic and financial. But then it seems his star began to fade and by the time of his death he was out of fashion and neglected, chronically short of money and in considerable debt. His death was the turning-point; immediately after, his fame began to mount. At the time of his death only about one-fifth of his compositions

[8] Mozart's burial is explored in masterly fashion in Carl Bär, *Mozart: Krankheit – Tod – Begräbnis* (Salzburg, 1966, 2/1972)

9

were in print, but by the early 1820s nearly two-thirds of them were published and readily available throughout Europe.[9] With benefit performances and from the sale of unpublished scores the widow was able to put herself quickly into comfortable circumstances, and Mozart's elder son bought an Italian villa and estate with French performing royalties. Today Mozart's genius, his immense natural gifts and his universality as a composer are unquestioned.[10]

Why, then, was the death such a sharp turning-point in his reputation, and what is the connection if any between the death and the period of neglect and despair which apparently preceded it? The evidence does not give clear and definitive answers to these questions and so biographers have regularly gone beyond the evidence, weaving stories about it in an attempt to solve the puzzle.

In the following chapters I shall outline seven of the main stories or types of story that have been told: the murder mystery, the beast and angel story and the related anti-feminist tale, the theory of the eccentric genius, a sociological narrative, a consoling story and the existentialist account. I shall also consider sober theories of the clinical causes of his death.

Before describing and examining these stories in detail, the primary sources on which they are based must be noticed. A full discussion of these would require a book in itself, so here nothing more will be provided than a survey of the most important ones, in the order of their publication. In 1828 Mozart's widow brought out a substantial biography of the composer. It was largely the work of her late second husband, Georg Nikolaus Nissen, and was intended to be the 'official' life. Preparatory to writing, Nissen had assiduously collected a mass of materials, including all the earlier biographies he could find. In his introduction he remarked that

[9] Alexander Hyatt King, *Mozart in Retrospect: Studies in Criticism and Bibliography* (London, 1955), 8, 9, 12
[10] Stanley Sadie, *Mozart* (London, 1965), 164

there were about twenty of these, but seventeen or eighteen simply repeated each other.[11] Only Schlichtegroll, Niemetschek and perhaps the author of *Mozart's Geist* had worked from the sources, in his opinion; this gives us an indication, even if not an entirely reliable one, of where we should start.

Friedrich Schlichtegroll was a teacher, and a scholar with a European reputation, who from 1790–1806 published 34 volumes of a *Nekrolog*, a series of obituaries.[12] His obituary of Mozart, which appeared in 1793 and was reprinted the following year, is not far short of 6000 words in length. As far as we know Schlichtegroll had never met Mozart. As was his custom, he collected his information by correspondence, using a standard list of questions. If he sent his questionnaire to Mozart's widow, she did not respond; Mozart's sister Nannerl was more forthcoming and her reply provided the bulk of the *Nekrolog*. Feeling the need of assistance in her turn, she wrote to Johann Andreas Schachtner, an educated musician and writer who had been a close friend of the Mozart household when Mozart was small.[13]

Schachtner's reminiscences are delightful and have provided some of the best-known anecdotes concerning the infant prodigy. Schlichtegroll took from him the story of Leopold Mozart's tears of joy at the sight of his four-year-old son's first composition, a concerto smeared with inkblots; of the sensitivity of his hearing which enabled him to distinguish one-eighth of a tone from memory and which caused him to swoon when Schachtner blared his trumpet at him; of his affectionate nature, asking Schachtner ten times a day if he loved him. The absolute accuracy of these reminiscences is open to doubt; for example it is unlikely that conversations

[11] Georg Nikolaus Nissen, *Biographie W. A. Mozarts* (Leipzig, 1828), xix
[12] For a discussion of Schlichtegroll, Niemetschek and the biographies they wrote see Georges Favier, ed., *Vie de W. A. Mozart par Franz Xaver Niemetschek précédée du nécrologe de Schlichtegroll* (St Etienne, 1976)
[13] The replies of Mozart's sister and of Schachtner are printed in *MDB*, 451–62.

would be remembered word-for-word after thirty years. But Mozart's sister affirmed that they had awakened her memory; she could vouch for their truth.[14]

Her own contribution was less colourful, but she took the trouble to consult the family correspondence preserved by Leopold and thus was able to give Schlichtegroll a sound chronological framework for the years up to 1781, when Mozart left the family home in Salzburg to settle in Vienna. 'For the events of his later life', she wrote, 'you must make enquiries in Vienna, as I can find nothing from which I could write anything thorough'.[15] Whatever inquiries he made, Schlichtegroll received nothing thorough about Mozart's last Viennese decade, which is covered in the *Nekrolog* in less than a page and a half. Schlichtegroll concluded with an assessment of Mozart the man. The sister's letter has a post-script in an unidentified hand, a postscript which has echoed down two hundred years of Mozart biography:

> Apart from his music he was almost always a child, and thus he remained: and this is the main feature of his character on the dark side; he always needed a father's, a mother's or some other guardian's care; he could not manage his financial affairs. He married a girl quite unsuited to him, and against the will of his father, and thus the great domestic chaos at and after his death.[16]

It has been surmised that this was written by the Salzburger Albert von Mölk, a friend of the sister used by Schlichtegroll as an intermediary, and that he obtained this information by questioning her persistently. This may be, but it is at odds with her assertion in 1800, after reading Niemetschek's biography, that she had not known of his sad situation.[17] Schlichtegroll wrote a favourable assessment of Mozart's

[14] Favier, 45
[15] *MDB*, 461
[16] *MDB*, 462
[17] Favier, 71

wife, but his assessment of the composer followed the postscript, and supplemented it with further information to the same effect drawn from an unnamed and untraced source – including the well-attested fact that Mozart was a keen billiard player possessing his own table, and the unlikely story that his hands had become so adapted to playing the clavier that he had his wife cut his meat so that he should not injure himself.

The *Nekrolog* established a pattern for subsequent biographies. This may testify to the essential truthfulness of Schlichtegroll's picture: alternatively it may be the case that subsequent writers took their cue from him, and remembered selectively in accordance with his account. Its influence upon the next important study, that of Niemetschek, is clear. Franz Xaver Niemetschek was a citizen of Prague, a teacher and writer. He probably witnessed Mozart's performances in Prague in 1787, he met Mozart in 1791 when the latter came to Prague to stage his opera *La clemenza di Tito*, and he knew Mozart's Prague friends such as the Duscheks (Josepha Duschek, a soprano for whom Mozart composed concert arias, and her husband had known Mozart since his Salzburg days). Mozart's son Carl lived happily as a pupil with him from 1792 to 1797, and consequently Niemetschek had dealings with the widow.[18] He records that he obtained information from her and from Mozart's friends. Constanze also supplied him with some documents, including Mozart's own catalogue of his works from 1784 onwards. His important biography, modest in length, was published in 1798.

His account of Mozart's life before 1781 is taken almost entirely from the *Nekrolog*. But the bulk of his biography is concerned with the last, most important decade which Schlichtegroll virtually ignored. Naturally much emphasis is placed upon Mozart's visits to and compositions for Prague.

[18] Favier, 61

But there is information about his life in Vienna too, especially about his operas and the intrigues of the jealous Italians which blighted his career. He is the source of that famous, perhaps apocryphal, remark of Emperor Joseph II about *Die Entführung aus dem Serail*: 'Too beautiful for our ears and an enormous number of notes, dear Mozart'. There is much about his friendship with Joseph Haydn, and about his remarkable methods of composition. Of especial interest to this study, he provides a dramatic and moving account of the commissioning of the Requiem, of the last illness and of the death. His discussion of Mozart's character is very much in the shadow of Schlichtegroll. He insists that Mozart was a delightful and endearing friend, but admits, and attempts to explain and excuse, his faults.

Were we to follow Nissen's opinion about the writings with something new to tell, the ones which are not mere plagiarisms, we would now move on to *Mozart's Geist*. But we would make a bad mistake. Between October 1798 and May 1801 a series of about 40 'authentic anecdotes' (admittedly, in fairness to Nissen, not a biography) appeared in the Leipzig *Allgemeine musikalische Zeitung (AMZ)*. Some are a few lines long; others run to three or four columns. They were the work of Friedrich Rochlitz, the editor of the journal, which was published by Breitkopf & Härtel. Mozart's widow had been negotiating the publication of his works with this firm and had been in touch with Rochlitz about a possible biography. The project aborted, perhaps as a result of Constanze's new relationship with Nissen, who became interested in doing the job himself.[19] But she had already sent some anecdotes for Rochlitz to publish. These can be identified from the covering letters to Breitkopf & Härtel and from Rochlitz's acknowledgement in the journal. They constitute about four of his 50 columns on Mozart. In addition, he recorded, so he says, his own observations, for he was much

[19] Favier, 73

in Mozart's company when the latter visited Leipzig on two occasions in 1789. It seems unlikely, however, that Mozart was in that city for more than a fortnight. Apart from the stories attributed to Constanze and the Leipzig ones there are others whose provenance is obscure. In 1825 Rochlitz published a little additional information, especially about Mozart's method of composition, in his *Für Freunde der Tonkunst*.

Many of Rochlitz's stories have become familiar: for example, the tale of how Mozart galvanized an ageing and lethargic orchestra, bullying them, making them play excessively fast, stamping so hard that his silver shoe buckle broke; or of how he composed a quartet movement in the room where his wife was in labour; of how he interrupted a performance of *Die Entführung* in Berlin by shouting to the second violins, 'Damn it, will you play D!'; and of his remark 'At last, here is something from which we can learn!' when the choir of St Thomas's School in Leipzig sang in his honour Bach's motet *Singet dem Herrn ein neues Lied*. Like Niemetschek, he writes in reply to Schlichtegroll, discussing Mozart's character and finances, adding stories about his freehandedness with money and of how he was cheated by 'friends', patrons, publishers and theatre directors. He adds information about Mozart's high spirits, which sometimes led him into funny but ill-judged satirizing of other musicians. He writes at length about the Requiem and the last illness.

The Rochlitz text raises a major dilemma for the Mozart biographer. Is his testimony credible, or fabricated? A consensus has emerged over time; Niemetschek is almost entirely reliable, whereas Rochlitz is a romancer, almost entirely worthless. This verdict dates back to the first scholarly biography, that of Otto Jahn in 1856:

> I could not fail to observe that those particulars of Mozart's life
> which Rochlitz gives as the result of his own observation . . .
> are peculiar to himself in form and colouring, and that many of

15

the circumstances which he relates with absolute certainty are manifestly untrue . . . But my search led to the further discovery of a parallel (also printed in the *AMZ*) between Mozart and Raphael, giving a detailed account of the circumstances of Mozart's marriage, and with express reference to Mozart's own narrative of the affairs which Rochlitz was supposed to have written down the same night. Now for the period which is here treated of . . . Mozart's entire correspondence is preserved . . . All the statements of Rochlitz as to time, place, persons and events are completely false.[20]

Apparently a devastating critique; but Jahn gives no reference for the article containing the falsities concerning Mozart's marriage. It is in none of Rochlitz's *AMZ* contributions cited in the standard bibliographies. His comparison of Mozart and Raphael says nothing about the marriage.[21] It is not obvious that Niemetschek and Rochlitz inhabit utterly different dimensions where reliability and value are concerned. Niemetschek's work also exhibits a peculiar form and colouring, characterized by Prague patriotism and romantic conceptions of aesthetic productivity. All observers look from a point of view peculiar to themselves and it is methodologically naïve to suppose otherwise. Our suspicions are aroused by anecdotes containing the alleged actual words spoken a decade earlier, but many of our primary sources, including Niemetschek, contain such direct speech. On some occasions Rochlitz can be checked and proved in error; on others, checking confirms his story. For example, he gives the programme of Mozart's concert in Leipzig and narrates how Mozart failed to make any money by it.[22] A surviving handbill confirms the programme and Mozart's letters testify to the financial failure.[23]

---

[20] Otto Jahn, *W. A. Mozart* (1856–9), Eng. trans. (London, 1891), iv

[21] *AMZ*, ii (1799–1800), 641–53 (11 June 1800)

[22] *AMZ*, i (1798–9), 82 (7 November 1798) and 113 (21 November 1798)

[23] *LMF*, 925; *MDB*, 342. Rochlitz's reliability is discussed in Cliff Eisen, *New Mozart Documents: a Supplement to Otto Erich Deutsch's 'Mozart: a Documentary Biography'* (London, 1991); see the end of the first section, on

Both Niemetschek and Rochlitz tell the story of the Requiem and final illness. There are significant similarities and significant differences. The same can be said about the story of Mozart's visit to Berlin in 1789, his favourable reception by the Prussian king and his subsequent thoughts of resigning from imperial service. In this case, not only do the two versions make some of the same points; they are ordered in the same way and they both falsely state that Mozart at this time had no official appointment. Niemetschek then corrects this, and contradicts himself, by recording that Mozart was appointed imperial chamber composer in 1787. Rochlitz's account of Mozart in Berlin is more detailed and colourful, and is the source of the story that the Prussian king offered Mozart a lucrative appointment, a story not confirmed by Mozart's correspondence or the Prussian state archives. How is the relationship between the two texts to be understood?

Is one copied from the other? Rochlitz reviewed Niemetschek's book in the issue of 19 December 1798, indicating in his review that he had only just received it. Since he had already published his anecdotes about the Berlin visit, the Requiem and the final illness, this implies that he did not copy them. Technically it is possible that he was practising a deception; apparently Niemetschek's biography appeared in a few privately printed copies in 1797, and perhaps Rochlitz had got hold of one of them.[24] But this is unlikely. There is information in Niemetschek which is not in Rochlitz and vice-versa. Rochlitz had an unerring eye for colour, but there are sensational details in Niemetschek which he does not mention – for example Mozart's remark to his wife that he had been poisoned. Therefore we must take the two authors at their word, and attribute the similarities in their narratives to a common source. The obvious presumption is that this was Constanze Mozart. But this simply adds to

Mozart's life, where Eisen prints the Rochlitz anecdotes explicitly attributed to Constanze [*NMD*]
[24] Favier, 68

our problems. Rochlitz's stories about the Requiem and the Berlin visit are not among those attributed to Constanze, and they were in fact published before her letters offering anecdotes to Breitkopf & Härtel. Perhaps she met Rochlitz in 1795 when she mounted a Mozart concert in Leipzig and gave him the information then. But, if so, what about the differences between his stories and Niemetschek's? Here are three possible explanations: (1) Constanze told both men the same stories, but Niemetschek treated her testimony with critical caution, and omitted what he found dubious; (2) Constanze told the same stories to both, but Rochlitz embroidered what he was told; and (3) Constanze told different stories to the two men.

There is no way of determining which, if any, of these possibilities is correct; but we cannot escape the conclusion that if there is a question mark over the reliability of Rochlitz as a witness, there is also one over Constanze; a question mark affecting all of the sources recording her testimony, that is to say, those by Niemetschek, Rochlitz, Nissen and the Novellos. We have evidence to suggest that she could be untruthful. The fact that some of the information she gave the Novellos contradicts, for example, Nissen is not too grave; anyone's memories can fade after forty years. But she may have given false information to Niemetschek; for example he states that after Mozart's death the Requiem was given in an incomplete state to the mysterious messenger. In a letter written to Breitkopf & Härtel in 1800 Niemetschek insisted that they should not believe everything that Frau Mozart said.[25] And on 28 August 1798 a notice in a Leipzig newspaper warned that Mozart's widow was selling, as his, works by other composers. To conclude this discussion, it will not do to sort the narrative sources sharply into the reliable and the unreliable; all of them must be subjected to detailed critical scrutiny.

[25] Favier, 69

Mozarts Geist, a little octavo volume of over 450 pages by I.T.F.C. Arnold was published in 1803. Arnold was a writer of, among other things, 'gothic' novels. In spite of Nissen's remark that it is one of the few works to go back to the original sources, the biographical part of it is almost entirely plagiarized from Schlichtegroll, Niemetschek and perhaps Rochlitz, usually word for word. Occasionally Arnold makes mistakes in copying, sometimes he embroiders his sources a little. The discussion of Mozart's works is often perceptive and interesting and apparently his own. There is a long discussion of the cause of Mozart's death which contains no new factual information.

The only biographical information, true or false, not to be found in the earlier works is as follows. Mozart submitted many of his works to Joseph Haydn before publication, and revised the overture to *Don Giovanni* when Haydn found fault with it. He had many affairs with pretty actresses and such smart married and unmarried women; his wife readily forgave him. He could not manage his money but lived from hand to mouth, starving one day, living it up on champagne and tokay on the next when he came into funds. He frequently drank champagne with Emanuel Schikaneder, the writer, actor and impresario who commissioned *Die Zauberflöte*, in the morning and punch with him at night, then sat up working after midnight.[26] Arnold may have gleaned these snippets from an unnamed witness – there is no reason to suppose he ever met Mozart himself – or, with the exception of the Schikaneder story, they may simply be irresponsibly imaginative elaborations of hints in Niemetschek. In any event, they passed into most subsequent biographies.

Nissen is right to remark how many of the subsequent biographies are merely copies, often word for word, often without acknowledgement, of the accounts already surveyed.

[26] [I. T. F. C. Arnold,] *Mozarts Geist* (Erfurt, 1803), 39, 65–6

C.F. Cramer's *Anecdotes sur Mozart* of 1801 are translations of Rochlitz. T.F. Winckler's 'Notice sur Mozart' in the *Magasin encyclopédique* of that year is plagiarized from Cramer, with an excellent translation of Schlichtegroll. Stendhal's *Vie de Mozart* of 1814 is taken from Winckler.[27] The brief life in Hormayr's *Österreichischer Plutarch* and Grosser's life of 1826 contain nothing new. Apart from a long and implausible anecdote, in which Mozart stands up for a modest German soprano against a temperamental Italian prima donna, Schlosser's life of 1828 contains only two or three snippets of information not in earlier texts.

Nissen's biography of 1828 is a substantial work of 700 pages, plus an appendix of 220 pages added by Constanze or her helper J. H. Feuerstein after Nissen's death. He was in a better position than any of his predecessors to write a biography, with the widow at hand, access to Mozart's relatives and friends, and having a mass of original letters and other documents at his disposal. From one point of view it is therefore surprising that this pivotal work has not appeared in an English translation: from another it is not so strange, for the work is rambling and very badly assembled. Nissen did not know how, or did not have the time, to digest his materials into a book. He was a Danish diplomat, not a writer. It is by no means an entirely fresh account of the life, based upon the letters and Constanze's reminiscences. There are elements of this; but much is simply a scissors-and-paste job, which assembles, usually verbatim and without acknowledgment, the bulk of the material furnished by Schlichtegroll, Niemetschek, Rochlitz and Arnold. For example, Nissen relates the well-known story of the composition of the overture to *Don Giovanni* at the last moment during the night, prefacing it with the remark, 'The widow tells the course of events as follows'. But what follows is in fact lifted from Rochlitz, with a final sentence from Niemetschek.[28]

[27] Favier, 49–51
[28] Nissen, 651

Perhaps this manner of proceeding was necessary (though it could have been done with more art and honesty) because memory had faded by this time, and Constanze could claim that part of what was in Niemetschek and Rochlitz was indeed her memories, recorded when they were still fresh. The humble seeker after truth therefore needs to compare Nissen with the earlier writings, in order to sift out what is new – and a good deal is. There is important information about the death and about Mozart's methods of composition. There is much about his character, not always favourable in tone. Constanze and her sister thought that he was unwise in his choice of friends, bringing home for meals low and disreputable persons. There were bloodsuckers among them, including the clarinettist Anton Stadler for whom the Clarinet Concerto and Clarinet Quintet were composed. Apparently he borrowed money from Mozart and did not repay it, kept money entrusted to him in order to redeem pawned articles, and even stole a pawn ticket from Mozart's desk, all of which Mozart forgave. But what about the part of Nissen which is old and borrowed? Can we say that it has been reviewed by Nissen and Constanze, and checked against record and memory? Does it come stamped with the seal of validation? Unfortunately, the Nissen biography confers no such blanket approval.

Sometimes Nissen corrects the chunks he borrows, and occasionally he tells the reader that he has done this. Niemetschek mentions that Mozart had good friends and benefactors, coyly giving only their initials: Nissen lifts the passage and fills in the names. He copies Niemetschek's account of the first performance of *Le nozze di Figaro* in Prague, but corrects the date. He borrows Rochlitz's discussion of the composition of *Idomeneo* which maintains that the work was written under uniquely happy circumstances, but refutes the suggestion that that happiness had anything to do with Mozart's growing love for Constanze – that love began later. He quotes Arnold's remark that the overture to *Don Giovanni* was revised because Haydn found fault with it, and adds, 'The widow knows nothing of this'.[29]

Unfortunately, he does not always correct and revise in this way. Assembling his narrative with scissors and paste, he allows contradictions to creep in. He incorporates Arnold's long argument to the effect that Mozart was not poisoned, backs it up with further points of his own, and then leaves in Niemetschek's hint that he *was* poisoned. In one place we are told that Mozart's favourite opera was *Figaro*, in another that he liked *Idomeneo* and *Don Giovanni* best. He quotes sources indicating that *Così fan tutte* was composed for Prague, and that Da Ponte revised the libretto of *La clemenza di Tito* for him, and does not draw attention to these falsities. He takes unacknowledged Niemetschek's remark that at the time of the visit to Berlin in 1789 Mozart had no official appointment, and then omits Niemetschek's correcting sentence to the effect that Mozart was given an imperial post in 1787. Most astonishing of all, he takes from the same author the statement that soon after Mozart's death the mysterious messenger reappeared, demanded the unfinished Requiem and took it away. Thereafter the widow never saw him again, nor heard anything of the Requiem or the unknown patron. Every statement here is false, and was known to be false by both Nissen and Constanze. Yet the passage is presented as if it were Nissen's own.[30]

The Nissen biography does not only transmit the misinformation of others; it also adds new misinformation. We are told that Mozart left behind no important works, whose publication might profit the widow and her children, apart from the Requiem and *Idomeneo*; the others for the most part had been published many times. The widow did not have disposal of the Requiem because it belonged to the unknown patron.[31] In fact, most of Mozart's works were unpublished

[29] Nissen, 651
[30] Nissen, 566
[31] Nissen, 579

at his death, and Constanze made a lot of money out of them; she did not have disposal of the Requiem, but she set about disposing of it all the same.[32] All of this is most depressing: if there are so many places where we can check Nissen and find him in error, how much reliance can we place on the parts we cannot check?

Nissen's biography published extensive portions of Mozart's correspondence for the first time. Accordingly it is appropriate to digress here to consider this, the most valuable source for the life. Nissen greatly approved of Leopold Mozart's letters, but was less happy with the son's. They contained unbridled and excessive high spirits, and also low, vulgar, tasteless wit.[33] He avowed his decision to publish them selectively, so as not to harm Mozart's reputation. He omitted all the scatological passages. He did not print the letters reflecting the severe and agonized disagreement between Mozart and his father in 1778, nor those giving the details of Mozart's traumatic breach with his employer in 1781. The names of still living persons who might take offence at Mozart's remarks were scored out in the manuscripts themselves. Even if he had wanted to publish the letters in full, Nissen did not have all of the surviving ones in his possession. Further letters, and fuller versions of ones in Nissen, were published during the nineteenth century; but it was not until 1914 that Schiedermair published an almost complete version in four volumes, and Emily Anderson's translation of 1938 was the first to publish every relevant thing then available, including the scatological pasages which Nissen did not like but excluding material written by Leopold Mozart having no bearing upon his son's life. The definitive German edition in seven volumes came out between 1962 and 1975.

---

[32] Richard Maunder, *Mozart's Requiem* (Oxford, 1988), provides a critical discussion of the circumstances surrounding the Requiem.
[33] Nissen, p.xvi

The correspondence is copious; Emily Anderson's original edition was in three volumes, with 1500 pages containing over 600 letters. They are informative, lively and quite delightful. But they have their problems and limitations as a biographical source. When Leopold toured Germany and Europe with his prodigious son he sent detailed letters home, asking that they should be kept; he had thoughts of writing a biography himself. The correspondence is also very full for the tour that Mozart undertook with his mother through Germany to Paris in 1777 and 1778. For this period we have both sides of a correspondence between Mozart and his father, and it is like a good eighteenth-century epistolary novel, full of incident, drama, tragedy, love and conflict. But these letters need to be read with critical attention. Leopold did not always agree with what his son was doing, and consequently the latter may not always have told the truth, the whole truth and nothing but the truth. He deceived his father, for example, about how much he had composed.[34]

After Mozart settled in Vienna in 1781 he wrote much less to his father; he was independent now, and also very busy. And some of his letters to his father were destroyed. His sister opined that this was because they made reference to freemasonry, and Leopold thought they were too dangerous to keep when official opinion turned against the masons. All of his father's letters to him of this period have been lost; consequently we have only one side of the conversation. Some scholars have thought that Constanze destroyed these letters because they contained adverse remarks about herself and her family, but this is implausible. There was no discrimination against Leopold; all letters sent to Mozart after March 1781, including Constanze's, are missing except two, one of which is dubious. Perhaps Mozart did not bother to save letters; perhaps they were lost in the many house movings; perhaps Constanze, after his death, thought that letters by

[34] Alan Tyson, *Mozart: Studies of the Autograph Scores* (London, 1987), 112–3

him were valuable but letters to him worthless. In any event we have lost a body of documents which would have given important indications about what others thought of him.

To return to the narrative sources, in 1829 Vincent Novello, the London music publisher, went with his wife Mary on a 'Mozart pilgrimage', to collect information for a book which in the end was never written. In Salzburg they met Mozart's dying sister and interviewed his wife and sister-in-law. In Vienna they met surviving friends. Their travel diaries were rediscovered, and published in 1955, since when they have been frequently cited by Mozart scholars. Part of their appeal is the reliability of the authors; the Novellos were scrupulous record-keepers. We can confirm this because they wrote up their diaries separately, and one can be checked against the other.[35]

They provide snippets of new information, some of it trivial, such as Mozart's favourite swear-word and the fact that he enjoyed fish and especially trout, some of it more interesting: 'She told us that after their marriage they paid a visit to Salzburg and were singing the Quartet of 'Andrò ramingo' [from *Idomeneo*] when he was so overcome that he burst into tears and quitted the chamber and it was some time before she could console him'.[36] But Constanze's memory was no doubt fading by this time, and contaminated by Nissen's biography, which she had recently seen through the press. Wording, organization and selection indicate that much of the information she gave was derived from the biography rather than from direct recollection. And the Novellos were not skilled interviewers; they often asked for confirmation of what they already knew and were not persistent in their questioning.

[35] *A Mozart Pilgrimage: being the Travel Diaries of Vincent and Mary Novello in the year 1829*, transcribed and compiled by Nerina Medici di Marignano, ed. Rosemary Hughes (London, 1955) [Novello]
[36] Novello, 115

Edward Holmes was a friend of the Novellos; his *Life of Mozart* of 1845 performed for English and other readers the inestimable service of providing the bulk of Nissen's information, translated and reworked into a coherent and readable book. Holmes had read other sources too, and had visited Austria to collect stray oral traditions. The principal difference from Nissen is that Holmes endorses and emphasizes the story that Mozart was persistently unfaithful to his wife.

Mozart's goings-on with pretty women and his jolly tavern life are major themes in the short stories of the journalist J. P. Lyser, which he collected and published with a short biography in J. F. Kayser's centenary *Mozart-Album* of 1856. Lyser's work does not inspire confidence but may contain stray fragments of authentic witness. For his mother had been a friend of Mozart's widow, and he had met members of Mozart's circle, including the sister-in-law Sophie Haibl. He also had access to the oral and documentary evidence assembled by Aloys Fuchs.

Otto Jahn's massive biography of 1856–9 was a milestone, the work of a trained philologist, 'scientific' by the standards of its day. It summed up the work of previous biographers, taking a critical attitude to them. As reworked by Deiters and Abert it remains the standard life, now severely in need of replacement. Jahn, like Holmes, attempted to find surviving witnesses: 'Living testimony as to his life, person, or circumstances was almost extinct, little of what I learnt was from impressions at first hand, and it was generally necessary to guard against such communications as the result of book knowledge distorted by verbal transmission'.[37] Jahn had the deepest admiration for Mozart, but his ideal of scholarship caused him to aim at completeness and scrupulous honesty. Hence he relates anecdotes about Mozart, including those he

[37] Jahn, xiv

finds unflattering to the composer, even when he thinks them unworthy of credence.[38] Through Jahn they have entered the canon, and are regularly cited, sometimes with, sometimes without a question-mark. On occasion Jahn does not cite his sources. Perhaps in such cases he could not do so, because these rumours were oral traditions which had never been written down: in effect his book is the original documentary source for them.

An especially rich crop of anecdotes clusters about Mozart's three visits to Prague. They tell of him making merry in taverns, composing while playing games, waking up an innkeeper late at night and demanding coffee, composing a song for the harpist who entertained the customers. For many years the tavern table was preserved out of which Mozart was alleged to have cut toothpicks. Such stories are attractive but unreliable, and their origins elusive.[39]

The source of at least some of them can be identified today, thanks to the documentary biography by O.E. Deutsch. This invaluable work is intended as a complement to the correspondence, and assembles 600 pages of original documents, from the records of the marriages of Mozart's grandparents to the very last scraps of indirect original testimony, late in the nineteenth century. There are concert programmes, publishers' announcements, diary references, remarks in newspapers and scandal-sheets. From these pages we can glimpse what contemporaries thought of Mozart and his works. Cliff Eisen has tracked down a considerable number of additional documents, to be published in 1991 as a substantial supplement to Deutsch. As he states in his preface, it must be remembered that the 'complete' documentary biography of Deutsch and Eisen prints only a small selection of passages

---

[38] For a discussion of Jahn see Gernot Gruber, 'Die Mozart-Forschung im 19. Jahrhundert', *MJb 1980–3*, 10–17
[39] The Prague stories can be found in Paul Nettl, *Mozart in Böhmen* (Prague, 1938)

from key posthumous biographical writings, such as those of Schlichtegroll, Niemetschek, Rochlitz, Arnold and Nissen.[40]

We can be confident that few new facts remain to be discovered about Mozart's life and death: and thanks to the documentary biography of Deutsch and Eisen, most of the evidence is in the public domain, though not all of it easily accessible to the English reader. A trickle of significant new evidence has come forward in recent years, however, from the autograph scores. Wolfgang Plath's study of the hand-writing has overthrown some previous datings and demonstrated the amount of help Mozart had from his father with his early compositions. Alan Tyson's work on the paper types and watermarks has also provided some revised datings and thrown new light on Mozart's methods of composition. But for the most part it remains true to say that future new work on Mozart's life and death must come from better interpretation of the known evidence; accordingly, it is to interpretation that we now turn.

[40] *NMD*, preface

THE DEATH

THE DEVIL

Chapter II

Was there foul play?

Mozart is – dead. . . . Because his body swelled up after death, some people believe that he was poisoned. . . . Now that he is dead the Viennese will at last realize what they have lost in him. In his life he was constantly the object of cabals, which he at times may well have provoked by his *sans souci* manner.

This, our earliest recorded reference to murder, appeared as a report from a Prague correspondent in a Berlin weekly less than a month after Mozart's death. According to the reminiscences of the author Georg Sievers there was a rumour that he had fallen victim to the Italians.[1] But Sievers's story was not recorded until 1819, and there is no further evidence to show that this rumour was widespread, or widely believed, in the first few years. If the surviving written records are a reliable indication, the murder mystery begins its continuous life in 1798 with the publication of Niemetschek's biography. This contains the story of the outing to the Prater in the autumn of 1791, when he told his wife that he was convinced he was composing the Requiem for himself and that he had been poisoned. The detail of the story – 'the two of them were sitting there alone' – and Niemetschek's acknowledgement of the friendly help of the widow when he was preparing his book make it likely that he obtained this story from Constanze herself.

Her own attitude to the story cannot be determined with certainty. Again according to Niemetschek, 'She had great difficulty in consoling him, and in showing him the groundlessness of his melancholy ideas', and in the biography

[1] *MDB*, 432; *NMD*, no.113

Was there foul play?

prepared with her help by her second husband Nissen much space is given to refuting the murder story. But if she was totally convinced of its groundlessness, why did she put the story about in the first place? Thirty years later she told a related but significantly different story to the Novellos:

> Some six months before his death he was possessed with the idea of his being poisoned – 'I know I must die', he exclaimed, 'someone has given me acqua toffana and has calculated the precise time of my death – for which they have ordered a Requiem, it is for myself I am writing this'.[2]

Once again Constanze referred to this as an 'absurd idea', but in a letter of 1837 she reported her elder son's opinion that 'he does not have, as his father once had, envious people to fear, who strive after his life'.[3] There is ample evidence to suggest that she was convinced there had been a conspiracy against him. Her elder son Karl Thomas wrote but did not publish a memorandum expressing strong suspicion of poisoning: 'Another indicative circumstance is that the body did not become stiff and cold, but remained soft and elastic in all parts, as was the case with Pope Ganganelli and others who died of organic poisons'.[4] Was this entirely his own opinion, or did it represent gossip current within the Mozart family?

The story launched by Niemetschek has persisted on its course right up to the present day.[5] A lengthy discussion, considering fast and slow poisons, acqua toffana and poisoned dust in letters, was published as early as 1803 in Arnold's *Mozarts Geist*. Arnold argued against poisoning, and his discussion was quoted wholesale by Nissen.

[2] Novello, 125
[3] Wilhelm A. Bauer, Otto Erich Deutsch and Joseph Heinz Eibl, *Mozart: Briefe und Aufzeichnungen* (Kassel, 1962–75), iv, 515 [*MBA*]
[4] Johannes Dalchow, Gunther Duda and Dieter Kerner, *Mozarts Tod 1791–1971* (Pähl, 1971), 231
[5] For a catalogue of the early references see O. E. Deutsch, 'Die Legende von Mozarts Vergiftung', *MJb 1964*, 7–18

*

In 1819 the *Allgemeine musikalische Zeitung* pointed the
finger at the Italian musicians in Vienna; a named suspect
appears for the first time in the records in 1823. In the
autumn of that year Salieri lost his reason and attempted to
cut his own throat; from then until his death in May 1825
rumours flew around that he had confessed to the murder.
Beethoven's conversation book is one of several contemporary sources recording the rumours:

> Karl van Beethoven: 'Salieri maintains that he poisoned Mozart'.
> Anton Schindler: 'Salieri is very ill again. He is quite deranged.
> In his ravings he keeps claiming that he is guilty of Mozart's
> death and made away with him by poison. – This is the truth –
> for he wants to make confession of it –, so it is true once again
> that everything has its reward'.[6]

This theory faces a grave problem: what possible motive
could Salieri have had for poisoning Mozart? Salieri held the
post of Imperial Kapellmeister which no doubt Mozart would
have liked. He had a higher salary and more opportunity for
composing and staging operas; as an opera composer he was
at least as highly regarded as Mozart. Mozart had a stronger
motive to kill him. A solution to this problem was provided
by Pushkin in his one-act play *Mozart and Salieri* of 1830.
Salieri, serious and devoted to his art, was overcome by envy
and resentment at the spectacle of this God-inspired genius
who was so manifestly *not* serious.

> O where is justice when the sacred gift,
> Immortal genius, comes not in reward
> For toil, devotion, prayer, self-sacrifice –
> But shines instead inside a madcap's skull,
> An idle hooligan's?[7]

---

[6] *MDB*, 524
[7] Alexander Pushkin, *Mozart and Salieri*, trans. Antony Wood (London, 1982)

33

Pushkin's playlet was turned into an opera by Rimsky-Korsakov in 1898 and forms the basis of the play by Peter Shaffer and the film *Amadeus*. In 1953 a Russian Pushkin scholar, Igor Belza, published a book in which he asserted that a contemporary record of Salieri's confession, stemming from the attending priest, had been found in a Viennese religious archive.

We come now to the darkest and most astonishing series of stories of Mozart's death. *Aus der Mansarde* ('Out of the Attic'), a periodical devoted to polemic, criticism, essays and poetry was edited and largely written by G. F. Daumer. The fourth issue, in 1861, was devoted to the occult and the mysterious. Here is Daumer's tale.

*   *   *

For thousands of years a secret conspiratorial organization has been active in the world; it became especially vigorous in the eighteenth century. 'Human society is occupied and infested by a ghastly and terrible worm, pervaded and imbued by a secret conspiracy, which has turned the ground on which we walk into a volcano, continually threatening eruption and devastation.'[8] It has appeared in many forms – for example, the Freemasons, the Illuminati, the Jacobins and the Carbonari – but its inner esence is hidden, even from the mass of the 'initiated', in the deepest darkness. Its aims are world domination, free love and the worship of nature. It masquerades behind the ideals of freedom and equality, but in truth seeks a new order of power and domination; it has a low view of the common people and of women, wishing to reduce them to a degraded and bestial condition. It is ready to use violent means to attain its ends. It fears only one enemy, namely Christianity. The leading members of the antichrist party – for example Hume, Voltaire, Condorcet and

---

[8] G. F. Daumer, *Aus der Mansarde*, iv (Mainz, 1861), p.xiii

Was there foul play?

Proudhon were all members. At its head is a secret trium-
virate: the God-man or Man-god, and below him the world-
bishop and the world-emperor – perhaps the last is Karl Marx
in London.

Mozart was drawn into the toils of this organization when,
in all innocence, he became a freemason. *Die Zauberflöte* is
manifestly a masonic opera symbolizing the struggle against
Christianity and the Catholic church. But the masonic propa-
ganda of the opera is challenged and subverted by Mozart's
doubts. His nature was deeply religious, and for the duet of
the armed men he smuggled in a Christian chorale. Sarastro is
not unambiguously praised, but appears as a kidnapper.
Mozart had come to be at odds with the masons; this is most
clearly revealed by his plan to found a rival order, *Die Grotte*,
as reported in a letter from Constanze to Breitkopf & Härtel
in 1799.[9] Tragically he took his friend, the clarinettist
Stadler, into his confidence and the latter betrayed him.
Therefore he was poisoned, like Leopold II and Lessing. Most
of his masonic brothers were not involved; it was the work of
those hidden in the inner recesses of the order, perhaps using
Stadler as their agent to administer the poison. His estrange-
ment from the order is revealed, however, by the fact that
they did not help Constanze with the funeral expenses, but
allowed him to be buried like a dog.

* * *

Daumer's theme was repeated in 1910 by Hermann Ahlwardt
in his book *Mehr Licht*; he introduced the Jews as the power
behind the scenes. This became central to the story as related
by Mathilde Ludendorff, a neuropsychiatrist and General
Ludendorff's wife. The General himself argued in 1926 that
the masons and Jews had poisoned Mozart.[10] His wife, who

[9] Arthur Schurig, *Konstanze Mozart: Briefe, Aufzeichnungen, Dokumente
1782–1842* (Dresden, 1922), 23
[10] Paul Nettl, *Mozart and Masonry* (New York, 1970), 85

35

wrote books with such titles as *Triumph of the Deathless Will* and *The Soul of the Volk and the Forms of its Power*, published in 1928 *The Unatoned Crime against Luther, Lessing, Mozart and Schiller*. The Mozart chapter was later enlarged and published in 1936 as *Mozart's Life and Violent Death*. Although she cites Daumer's article as proving that Mozart was murdered by the masons, her *Weltanschauung* differs significantly from his. He identifies a primordial conspiracy, directed against religion, and makes no mention of the Jews. She by contrast detects a Jewish-Christian, or rather Jewish-Roman conspiracy, spearheaded by such organizations as the Jesuits, the masons (whose aim was to build the temple of Solomon, that is to say, Jewish domination) and the Jacobins (those true sons of Jacob). Its intention is to establish a cosmopolitan Jewish world-state, and therefore it seeks to destroy every vestige of national pride. She spins the following web.

* * *

The young Mozart was dragged around Europe by his father, whose only concern was to exploit him for monetary gain. Mozart was protected from the enormous moral and physical danger of these tours only by his genius and good-heartedness. He loved his homeland and was homesick. In early manhood he was persuaded by his father, who was already an Illuminatist and freemason, to join the Salzburg lodge *Zur Fürsicht*. His employer, Archbishop Colloredo, also a member of the lodge, persecuted Mozart because he wanted to be a German musician rather than composing in the cosmopolitan Italian style. At first he was happy in Vienna, working for Emperor Joseph who wished to replace Italian opera with German. But his patriotism posed a threat to the aims of his brother masons. 'The German People would for ever more be able to draw strength from his immortal works; and so Mozart earned the hatred of all those who wish "to detach the people from their roots, their nation and their language" and would like to force them into a Jewish or Jewish-Christian world-empire.'[11] They therefore used all their influence to ensure that he became neglected and impoverished.

Mozart was not yet aware of the criminality of the order; but, as was the case with many other noble-minded and unsuspecting masons, his eyes were opened by the French revolution, when he witnessed 'the bloody race-hatred of the Jews in their massacre of the blonde nobility of Paris'. He was especially shocked to hear it said in the lodges that Marie Antoinette would be condemned to death for the crime of her mother, the Empress Maria Theresa, who had banned the masons in Austria. For as a child he had met Marie Antoinette at the Viennese court and, when she was kind to him had, in childlike fashion, promised to marry her.

The Viennese Jews trembled before mounting public indignation; in response they ordered Schikaneder, Giesecke (a fellow-mason and actor in Schikaneder's troupe) and Mozart to celebrate the freemasons in an opera. But Mozart wove in his own anti-masonic message. Tamino (Mozart) aims to use the magic flute, which his father (the German Volk) carved from the thousand-year-old German oak, to move the hearts of the evil brothers to release Pamina (Marie Antoinette), daughter of the Queen of Night (Maria Theresa).

Giesecke fled to Dublin: Mozart sought to protect himself by founding a rival organization, *Die Grotte*, devoted only to the noblest purposes. But Stadler betrayed him. When the unknown messenger came, kissed him on the forehead and commissioned a Requiem, Mozart knew that his death sentence had been passed and that he was writing the Requiem for himself.

The masons had him compose a cantata for them, so as to avert suspicion; then they poisoned him with acqua toffana, a

[11] Mathilde Ludendorff, *Mozarts Leben und Gewaltsamer Tod* (Munich, 1936), 141

mixture of arsenic, antimony and lead, possibly using van Swieten to perform the deed. After his death the stranger came, demanded the uncompleted score of the Requiem and took it away; later the masons had it completed and performed. His suspicious death was not investigated, because many lodge brothers were in high official and judicial places, and the Emperor himself was a freemason.

Van Swieten then supervised Mozart's burial according to the Jewish ritual for criminals. Instead of a coffin, he was wrapped in a black cloth. He went unaccompanied to the cemetery and was thrown into a mass grave. At some point his head or skull was removed. Van Swieten prevented Constanze from having a gravestone erected; the masons got rid of the gravediggers and the records, and so the grave was lost. When later a monument was erected on the presumed site it was mutilated, and his last home in Vienna was torn down. Rumours were assiduously spread putting the blame for the shabby funeral on Constanze, but it was not her fault. Nissen, perhaps an innocent member of the outer masonic circle, was manipulated and persuaded to include a refutation of the poisoning theory in his book.

* * *

The gentle reader might be forgiven for supposing that conspiracy explanations of this kind came to an abrupt end in 1945. Not so. The thesis that Mozart was murdered by the masons has been argued in books published in 1966 and 1971 by three German doctors, Dalchow, Duda and Kerner. Dieter Kerner was formerly 'a fanatic in the Ludendorff circle' and the books were published by the Ludendorff press and its successor.[12] The reader will be happy to learn that the Jews are no longer mentioned as puppet-masters; but the story

[12] Deutsch, 'Legende', 13

related below,[13] is in its own way as bizarre as Ludendorff's, and it follows hers in many essentials.

*   *   *

Mozart did not die a natural death. We are pointed towards this conclusion by his manifest good health, revealed in his enormous capacity for work, right up to the end. But the shades began to close around his life in 1786 – the year of *Figaro* which with its social radicalism so much offended his patrons, the Viennese nobility. Society progressively drew away from him, leaving him isolated. He was an awkward customer; relations with Colloredo had broken down dramatically, the nobility were alienated, we may surmise that he antagonized his masonic brethren also. He will have angered them by revealing their secrets in *Die Zauberflöte*. It would be a mistake, however, to think that he was destroyed solely or even primarily as a traitor. He was sacrificed, and his sacrifice was part of the elaborate ceremony surrounding the dedication of a new masonic temple. This is why mercury was chosen; mercury was a substance of great symbolic significance in the alchemical doctrine which is central to masonic ideology and ritual.

The fundamental masonic myth is the story of Hiram. Hiram was the master-mason of Solomon's temple; he was murdered because he refused to reveal craft secrets. His murderers attempted to conceal his body, but a palm tree sprang up over his remains, alerting his avengers. The myth can be thought of as parallel to the story of Christ: a hero is sacrificed for the sake of his followers, the palm tree symbolizes his rebirth. It was the practice of the masons to commemmorate Hiram's death by performing a human sacrifice upon completion of an important building, incorporating the body into the foundations.

[13] Dalchow, Duda and Kerner

Was there foul play?

Die Zauberflöte is indeed a masonic opera, but somewhat ambivalent, poking fun at the pomposity of Sarastro and his priests and revealing them as kidnappers, slave owners and hypocrites who talk of reconciliation at one moment and threaten revenge the next. It is not about the conflict between freemasonry and Catholicism; the struggle between Sarastro and the Queen of Night is a struggle between the higher and lower grades of freemasonry itself. In particular the symbolism and ceremony of the opera is about the eighteenth, Rosicrucian grade. Confidential Viennese masonic files reveal that Mozart had attained the nineteenth grade; he had probably been initiated into the secrets of Rosicrucianism by the mystical mason Count Josef Thun.

Not only is 18 the number of the Rosicrucian grade; it also symbolizes Hiram and sacrifice. The word sacrifice, *Opfer*, appears three times in the opera – and three is an important masonic number. Commentators have been ready to admit that the number 3 crops up repeatedly, but Jahn, Abert and Deutsch have tried to hide the fact that the heart of the opera is the glorification of the eighteenth grade. Sarastro is accompanied by 18 priests; his name is spoken 18 times and sung 18 times. He has 18 spoken sentences and he sings 180 bars. When he first appears, the chorus which accompanies him is 18 bars long. His aria 'O Isis und Osiris' is number 18 in Mozart's own piano reduction. Papagena is 18 years old and the opera lasts 180 minutes! The number 8 is of subsidiary symbolic significance, for it is the alchemist's number for mercury. Sarastro's name has 8 letters and he enters 8 times. Tamino's flute solo in the first act is 8 bars long, and the key words in the initiation trials, 'Feuer, Wasser, Luft und Erden' are sung to eight notes.

Mozart's last completed work, indeed the last thing he worked on, was a little masonic cantata, written – for a temple dedication! The autograph has 18 pages, the first performance was on 18 November, and Mozart was dead 18 days later, at the end of 1791, whose digits add up to 18, in his 36th year (36 = 2 × 18)! He knew that he was condemned to death. This is revealed by his letter to Da Ponte, and also by his remark to Constanze, later reported to the Novellos, 'some one of his enemies had succeeded in administering the deleterious mixture which would cause his death . . . they could already calculate at what precise time it would infallibly take place'. For he knew that the Requiem had been commissioned by the masons; it was an announcement that he had been elected for sacrifice, and it was intended to play a part in the solemn ritual. The unfinished score was collected, and paid for, by Baron Jacobi, servant of the Rosicrucian King of Prussia. Van Swieten organized its completion and performance; Constanze Mozart had nothing to do with it and was kept in the dark. Subsequently the now orthodox story of its commissioning by Walsegg was fabricated. Brother Rochlitz was the first to launch it, without mentioning Walsegg's name; Walsegg himself came forward in *1800*.

That Mozart was poisoned is directly proved by the characteristic mercury finger tremor revealed in the last three bars of the autograph of the little masonic cantata, and also by the swelling up of his body in the last stages. The evidence for this swelling is the newspaper report quoted at the opening of this chapter, and also Karl Thomas Mozart's memorandum:

> Especially worthy of mention in my opinion are the circumstances that a couple of days before death a general swelling set in, to such an extent as to make the smallest movement impossible for the patient, moreover there was a stench, indicating an inner dissolution, which grew stronger after death making an autopsy impossible.[14]

Nothing was normal about the death. All the stories about the burial are lies, elaborately concocted to hide the real truth about what happened to Mozart's body. The whole affair was

[14] Dalchow, Duda and Kerner, 231

carefully managed by van Swieten. He arranged for Constanze to be out of the way and ensured that no-one accompanied the body on its last journey. The ostensible reason for this, the snowstorm, is a pure fiction. No doubt on the following day or days friends and family – perhaps Constanze herself – went out to the cemetery of St Marx to visit the grave. But they did not find it, for Mozart's body was not there. A lie was fabricated to explain the loss of the grave. Constanze was unfairly blamed for negligence. It was later put about that burial in a common grave was normal at the time, and that gravestones marking the spot were not allowed. But in fact quite ordinary people were given individual graves with headstones.

In 1855, in preparation for the centenary of Mozart's birth, an attempt was made to locate Mozart's last resting place. Witnesses came forward, and a consensus emerged about the precise spot in St Marx' cemetery. Their testimony is worthless, perhaps part of the masonic cover-up. What was alleged to be Mozart's skull turned up (it is now in the Salzburg Mozarteum). It is not Mozart's skull but it *is* a carefully contrived symbol for the initiated; it signifies that the real skull is being kept somewhere and used in masonic ceremonies.

The conspiracy is still at work, and has penetrated the Salzburg Mozarteum: 'But we soon saw ourselves confronted by an anonymous power-faction, determined at any price to obstruct our work. It operated in secret, and had fundamentally no interest in the truth.'[15] Journals refused them the right of reply; others which favoured their work suddenly closed down because of loss of subscribers or because the chemical industry stopped placing advertisements. The 'high priest of Mozart research, masonic brother O. E. Deutsch' was their bitterest enemy. Finally the Mozarteum wheeled out Dr

[15] Dalchow, Duda and Kerner, 240

Carl Bär to prove that Mozart died of rheumatic fever. But his argument was demolished by Dr Greither, and now 'the Mozart hierarchy finds itself in a hopeless plight. The 'poisoning legend' can no longer be conjured away . . . one is now fully justified in speaking of that which appears to the Viennese and Salzburg guardians like a nightmare as terrible as a *Götterdämmerung* – the twilight of the Mozart-hierarchy!'[16]

*   *   *

These are the main poisoning stories; are they at all believable? In autumn 1823 Salieri was visited in hospital by his former pupil, the pianist Moscheles. According to his biography, written fifty years later by his widow from his letters and diaries,

> The reunion was a sad one; for his appearance shocked me, and he spoke only in broken sentences of his approaching death; but finally with the words: 'Although this is my last illness, however I assure you in good faith that there is no truth in the absurd rumour; you know what I mean – that I poisoned Mozart. But no, dear Moscheles, tell the world that it is malice, pure malice; old Salieri, who will soon be dead, has told you this'.[17]

In August 1824 an acquaintance of Salieri, Giuseppe Carpani, published a lengthy defence of him in an Italian monthly. He vouched for Salieri's honourable character and claimed that Salieri and Mozart held each other in high regard. More significant, he had obtained and now published the testimony of Dr Guldener von Lobes, Medical Superintendant for Lower

[16] Dalchow, Duda and Kerner, 244
[17] Deutsch, 'Legende', 9

Austria, who declared that he had been in constant touch with the doctors attending the dying Mozart:

> His death aroused general interest, but the very slightest suspicion of his having been poisoned entered no-one's mind. So many persons saw him during his illness, so many enquired after him, his family tended him with so much care, his doctor, highly regarded by all, the industrious and experienced Closset, treated him with all the attention of a scrupulous physician . . . in such a way that certainly it could not have escaped their notice then if even the slightest trace of poisoning had manifested itself. The illness took its accustomed course and had its usual duration . . . This malady attacked at this time a great many of the inhabitants of Vienna, and for not a few of them it had the same fatal conclusion and the same symptoms as in the case of Mozart. The statutory examination of the corpse did not reveal anything at all unusual.[18]

Guldener sent a copy of this letter in English to Sigismund von Neukomm in Paris, who published a defence of Salieri in which he too insisted that the composers had enjoyed friendly and respectful relations. Neukomm's version of Guldener's letter was slightly different from Carpani's; in particular it contained the assertion that Guldener himself had seen Mozart's corpse.[19]

Carpani's defence of Salieri also prints a declaration by the two nurses who attended the sick man. It states that they attended him continuously from the winter of 1823; that no-one else was allowed to see him apart from his doctors; and that at no time did he confess to having murdered Mozart. This declaration is dated 25 June 1824, almost a year before Salieri's death. Imperturbable advocates of the murder thesis have therefore suggested that Salieri could have made a confession *after* the declaration. That gap, however, is appar-

[18] *MDB*, 523
[19] Dalchow, Duda and Kerner, 218–9, 227

ently plugged by a repeat of the declaration, published in 1826 and dated 5 June 1825.[20]

But what about the written record of Salieri's confession, found in a Viennese religious archive? Belza claimed that Professor Guido Adler had found it and told Boris Asaf'yev in 1928; Asaf'yev in turn told Belza. When Belza published the news in 1953, both Adler and Asaf'yev were dead; the document could not be found nor any other witness with whom Adler had shared the discovery.[21]

The case against Salieri as Mozart's murderer therefore collapses utterly. All the evidence against him is hearsay and rumour, and there is good documentary evidence in his defence. The alleged motive invented by Pushkin might convince a panel of poets; it would carry little weight with a jury.

There remains the possibility, on which the Shaffer play and *Amadeus* are based, that Salieri did not poison Mozart but nevertheless contributed to his death by plotting against him and obstructing his career, thereby helping to produce indebtedness, depression and overwork. This cannot absolutely be ruled out. There are some eighteen references in the Mozart family correspondence suggesting strained relations between the two composers.[22] Niemetschek, without naming names, refers to plots and a campaign of malicious gossip, pointing the finger at the Italian musicians. Maybe he got this from Constanze; she accused Salieri in the presence of the Novellos, adding the curious and unbelievable story that

---

[20] In 'Mozart and Salieri', *Harmonicon*, iv, no.46, October 1826: reference from a modern edition of A. W. Thayer's *Salieri*, ed. T. Albrecht (Kansas City, 1989), 159. Curiously, whereas the declaration in Carpani states that the nurses began attendance on Salieri in the winter of 1823, this version gives spring 1824. No doubt the protagonists of poisoning will latch on to this to discredit the declaration, but it could well be seen as strengthening its credibility, suggesting that the declaration was not simply plagiarized and given a new date but rather was looked at again.

[21] Deutsch, 'Legende', 13

[22] Anton Neumayr, *Musik und Medezin am Beispiel der Wiener Klassik* (Vienna, 1987), 92

Was there foul play?

'Salieri's enmity arose from Mozart's setting the *Così fan tutte* which he had originally commenced and given up as unworthy of musical invention'.[23] Moscheles, after defending Salieri against the charge of murder, added 'Certainly he had damaged him morally through intrigues, and thereby poisoned many an hour for him'.[24] According to Jahn,

> But although Salieri occasionally spoke in praise of Mozart in after years, I have heard upon trustworthy authority in Vienna, that Salieri, even in his old age, when among confidential friends, expressed, with a passion that was painful to his hearers, the most unjust judgments on Mozart's compositions. Thayer's attempt to justify Salieri led me to make a searching examination of the facts.

Not only did Salieri disparage Mozart during his lifetime; he also conspired to ensure that the Emperor heard as little of Mozart's music as possible.[25] Any judgment by Jahn about the facts of Mozart's life deserves consideration; but against this should be set the declarations of Carpani, Neukomm, Rochlitz and Lyser that the two men respected each other. The remarks of Constanze to the Novellos, of Moscheles and the witnesses who spoke to Jahn may have been shaped and influenced by Niemetschek's well-known biography.

There is a knock-down argument against all the poisoning theories: it is that the doctors who attended him did not think he had been poisoned. And they would have known. Thomas Closset, Mozart's doctor, consulted his colleague Mathias von Sallaba about his dying patient. Sallaba had a special interest in poisons, and in that very year, 1791, had petitioned for the establishment of a chair of forensic medicine whose teaching duties he would fulfil without salary. The law already prescribed that corpses should be inspected by an independent doctor for foul play. Viennese doctors of the period were

23 Novello, 127
24 Dalchow, Duda and Kerner, 191
25 Jahn, *Mozart*, ii, 205–6

46

familiar with the signs of mercury poisoning; mercury chloride was taken internally for syphilis and overdosing was easy. In an article on the treatment of putrid fever, published in 1783, Thomas Closset describes the cloudy urine and stinking breath and sweat of the mercury victim.[26] Acqua toffana, the other poison mentioned in connection with Mozart, would also produce unmistakeable symptoms: the arsenic would give a severe burning pain in the mouth and throat, scalding tears, abdominal pain and muscle spasms, while the lead would cause a blue line on the gum, foot-drop and wrist-drop.[27]

A point-by-point refutation of Daumer, Ludendorff and the three doctors would be easy, but largely a waste of time. They uncritically accept the most vulgar gossip against the masons, such as the tale of the burial of human sacrifices in the foundations. Their stories will find credit only with readers whose minds are attuned to conspiracy theory. No countervailing arguments would convince such readers: they would simply assume that the critic was himself part of the conspiracy. It will be sufficient, therefore, to note a few factual errors and to comment on the methods and nature of stories of this type.

Ludendorff's story of Leopold Mozart, already a mason and member of the Illuminati, pressing his son to join the Salzburg lodge *Zur Fürsicht*, can only be based on the work of Richard Koch. He claimed he had seen a list, giving Colloredo as a member, and Mozart, his father and Schikaneder as guests. No such list can now be found. The lodge *Zur Fürsicht* was founded in 1783; in that year Mozart visited Salzburg for the last time. But he and his father could have been admitted as guests only if they had already been masons. The Viennese records demonstrate that Mozart was admitted in December 1784, and his father in 1785.

[26] Bär, 75–6
[27] Peter J. Davies, 'Mozart's Illnesses and Death – 2', *Musical Times*, cxxv (1984), 559

47

Ludendorff's attempt to blame Leopold for Wolfgang's membership therefore collapses; it was in fact Wolfgang who persuaded his father to join.[28]

Other key elements in her story – for example, that the French Revolution opened his eyes to the criminal plans of the masons, that in the lodges it was said that Marie Antoinette should be condemned to death, that the unknown messenger who commissioned the Requiem kissed him on the forehead and that he was betrayed by Stadler – are supported by no documentary evidence whatsoever. Her notion that freemasonry was part of a Jewish conspiracy is fantastic; membership lists prove that very few Jews gained entry, and indeed Viennese Jewry was powerless because of distrust and unofficial discrimination. The credulous have long believed that the masons murdered their enemies, but the notion is ludicrous; as Deutsch remarked in 1964, 'The fact that Dr Ludendorff still lives at a great age allows us to conclude that Lodge murder has become less common'.

Ludendorff cites Daumer as an authority; the reader, hungry for proof of her strange tale, turns to *Aus der Mansarde*. Alas, this also is a dry place, where no water is. There is no new evidence here; his whole case, as far as Mozart is concerned, rests upon a strained interpretation of *Die Zauberflöte* and the elusive reference in Constanze's correspondence to Mozart's desire to found a secret order called *Die Grotte*.

The case is quite different with Dalchow, Duda and Kerner; they have assiduously mastered the primary and secondary sources. The problem is rather their remarkably unscholarly and uncandid use of them. They accept highly dubious documents capable of being interpreted to fit their theory, and reject more reliable ones which contradict it. For example,

---

[28] Richard Koch, *Br. Mozart: Freimaurer und Illuminaten* (Bad Reichenhall, 1911); Jacques Chailley, *La flûte enchantée, opéra maçonnique* (Paris, 1968), Eng. trans. (London, 1972), 12. For the documented facts about Mozart and the masons, see O. E. Deutsch, *Mozart und die Wiener Logen* (Vienna, 1932)

they accept the rumour in the Berlin newspaper of late 1791, and the memorandum of Karl Thomas Mozart, which together support the contention that Mozart's body swelled up before and after death, and reject the evidence to the contrary, such as the declaration of Dr Guldener von Lobes. They reject the irresistible weight of evidence demonstrating that the Requiem was commissioned by Walsegg. This evidence includes the pamphlet by Abbé Maximilian Stadler, who had witnessed the transactions from Constanze's end, and the memorandum of Anton Herzog, who had witnessed them from Walsegg's end. They argue, on the basis of no evidence worthy of the name, that the Walsegg story is an elaborate masonic fabrication and that Walsegg, Stadler, Herzog, Nissen and van Swieten were involved in the conspiracy. But the evidence does not even show that key figures such as Nissen and van Swieten were ever masons.

There is no good reason whatsoever for accepting their theory that Mozart's death in general and *Die Zauberflöte* in particular have to be understood in terms of the symbolism of the eighteenth, Rosicrucian grade. There is no evidence that the lodge to which Mozart belonged had higher grades. On the contrary, the evidence reveals the Viennese lodges as orthodox St John's lodges, with three grades only. Accordingly, Mozart could and did progress no higher than the third grade of Master Mason. We are told that confidential Viennese files reveal that he had attained the nineteenth grade. But if they are confidential, how do Dalchow, Duda and Kerner know their contents, and if they do know their contents, why have they not published the crucial documentation?

The charge that Mozart's remains were treated disrespectfully – that he was not given a proper funeral nor accompanied to the cemetery, that he was not given an individual grave and headstone but either buried in a mass grave, or his remains dispersed or stolen – plays a key role in the stories told by Daumer, Ludendorff, Dalchow, Duda and Kerner. The thesis of disrespectful treatment was widely accepted in the nineteenth century and the first half of the twentieth. Dr Carl Bär's research has dispelled the myths.[29]

Viennese citizens in 1791 could choose from three classes of funeral ceremony, at different set prices; there was in addition a free pauper's funeral. Class one was largely reserved for the aristocracy; even Beethoven, who was mourned with great pomp, was done second class. Mozart received a third-class funeral, the most common type. After the consecration at St Stephen's Cathedral, which according to much later reports was attended by friends and professional colleagues, the coffin rested in a sidechapel. The regulations decreed that in winter the body could not be taken to the cemetery until six o'clock in the evening; the purpose of this regulation was to put a stop to the practice of parking hearses, with coffins on board, outside taverns in the middle of the day.

The register records Mozart's funeral on 6 December; we now know that the weather was still and mild on that day. Apparently therefore the story, first documented in the 1840s and 50s but apparently supported by several independent witnesses, that some of the mourners accompanied the corpse to the Stuben gate and then turned back because of a storm is falsified. But the regulations required 48 hours to elapse between death and burial, there being great fear of burying people alive. It seems likely, therefore, that the register entry is a mistake, and that Mozart' funeral took place on December 7. That evening, a strong wind got up; the roads around Vienna were notorious for their dust storms on windy days. Given that the cemetery was outside the city and more than four kilometres from the cathedral, the mourners can hardly be blamed for not accompanying the coffin through the windy night. Because of the darkness the coffin was

---

[29] Bär, 126–157

probably kept at the cemetery overnight and interred the following day.

The official regulations governing funerals and burials were the product of enlightened Josephinian utilitarianism. The emperor found the traditional ceremony and expense quite irrational. He had attempted, and failed, to ban the use of coffins; corpses should be put in linen sacks, and consigned to the earth with quicklime so as to speed up the process of decomposition. By 1791 this regulation no longer applied; but most bodies were buried not in a mass grave but in a shaft grave containing five or six coffins. These graves were cleared and re-used after nine years. The limited amount of cemetery space in proportion to the population made this essential. In order to save space, headstones were not permitted; memorial tablets could be affixed to the perimeter wall. There were some family vaults, and individual graves could be obtained by special dispensation. But Mozart's unceremonious burial was normal for that rationalist time. By the standards of his day, his obsequies were not neglected, and he was not 'buried like a dog'.

The innocent reader, reviewing the story as told by the three doctors, is likely to experience just a little amazement. Their narration is not quite as clear as I have made it. Nevertheless the impression is conveyed that Mozart cooperated in his own ritual sacrifice, carefully and knowingly preparing three works to that end, *Die Zauberflöte*, the Requiem and the cantata *Laut verkünde unsre Freude*, filling and surrounding them with symbols of sacrifice and mercury. At one point our authors appear to get cold feet: 'It would be an error to presume that this was, as far as he was concerned, a move towards oblivion and disappearance from the scene, completely abandoned and unaccompanied to the grave. No, it was much more a thoroughly strange coming-together of events before the last road to the deathbed.'[30] On reflection,

---

[30] Dalchow, Duda and Kerner, 74

this is even more amazing. To suppose that Mozart played his part so well, but unknowingly and unintentionally, conveys an impression of supernatural control and manipulation. Is this what the authors mean?

Their argument about numbers cannot fail to produce wonderment in the mind of the reader. Given enough things to be counted (and an opera contains a great many notes) coincidence will produce plenty of recurrences. The frequency of a particular number – say 18 – can easily be increased, given sufficient determination, by carefully selecting what to include and what to exclude. For example, are two half-bars counted as one or two? By such tactics the recurrence of other numbers could easily be 'demonstrated'. Ever since the origins of Western philosophy in ancient Greece numbers have fascinated those who long to find patterns in events. They love to 'find' what they have themselves imposed.

Our authors are not innocent of disreputable tactics in argument. They don the mantle of medical expertise, and deny the right of others to gainsay them.

> Apart from the dermatologist A. Greither and the dentist C. Bär our opponents have been for the most part historians of medicine, who must therefore be judged professionally out-of-touch, since they have long lost contact with the sick and bedridden. Their arguments are therefore without exception just as amateur as out-of-date and moreover for the most part medically false.[31]

There are in fact more pages of solid medical discussion in the little book by that mere dentist, Dr Carl Bär. They also smear their chief opponent, 'the high priest of Mozart research, O. E. Deutsch', referring to him as a masonic brother; Deutsch has declared that he has never belonged to any lodge.[32]

[31] Dalchow, Duda and Kerner, 23–4
[32] Deutsch, 'Legende', 18

The theory put forward by the three doctors is a perfect specimen of a closed system with built-in strategies to protect itself against scientific testing. They are not made downhearted by the absence of documentary proof of the nefarious activities of the masons; for them it is axiomatic that the masons represent an occult conspiracy which takes care never to leave documentary evidence. The very absence of the evidence proves the depth and danger of the secret.

*

Apart from Salieri and the masons, one further suspect poisoner deserves to be mentioned – Mozart himself. In 1969 it was surmised, by Katner and, surprisingly, by Kerner, that Mozart may have treated himself for syphilis with mercury, and miscalculated the dose.[33] The only scrap of evidence for this, obscure, ambiguous and worthless, is contained in Suard's plagiarized *Anecdotes sur Mozart*:

> I have heard it said that he wrote *La flûte enchantée* only to please a woman of the theatre with whom he had fallen in love, and who had offered him her favours at this price. It is added that his triumph had very cruel consequences, and that he contracted from it an incurable disease of which he died shortly after. This fact seems to me to be very unlikely; *La flûte enchantée* is not the last of his operas, and when he composed it, his health was already seriously impaired.[34]

There is no reliable evidence to suggest that Mozart had caught syphilis or was treating himself with mercury. Deutsch's sarcasm is surely justified: 'In order to save Salieri's honour, I should like to point out to Dr Kerner that in the

---

[33] P. J. Davies, 'Mozart's Illnesses and Death', *Journal of the Royal Society of Medicine*, lxxvi (1983), 783; Deutsch, 'Legende', 18
[34] *MDB*, 498

official inventory of the dwelling of the dead Mozart no barometer is mentioned. Obviously he had emptied it'.[35]

One recent commentator has opined that Mathilde Ludendorff was mad.[36] Conspiracy theories, however, cannot be dismissed on such grounds. Manifestly sane people have believed in them, including a former British Prime Minister, Benjamin Disraeli. They respond to a deeply felt human need to weave a pattern into events, eliminating chance, accident and contingency, and finding a human meaning, however sinister. They represent the story-telling impulse in unusually pure form. Their development is dependent upon certain conditions being met. They flourish in the context of a manichean mentality, which sees the world dominated by a conflict between sharply polarized forces of good and evil, hence their appearance during acute religious and political conflicts. That side of romanticism which was fascinated by everything out-of-the-ordinary, mysterious, occult and satanic gave them a new lease of life: Disraeli and Daumer belong here.

At the level of personal psychology, conspiracy theory can appeal to individuals who have difficulty coming to terms with certain aspects of their experience. A classic example is to be found in Hitler's *Mein Kampf*. He relates how from an early age his deepest conviction was nationalism, a love of the German people – the *Volk*, a term which suggests the common people, the mass. But when he met labouring people in Vienna he was deeply troubled, for they did not live up to his image of them. They were feckless and disorderly, influenced by socialism and Marxism and therefore antinational. Gradually, he tells us, he came to understand the reason; these basically good but simple Germans had fallen under the influence of the Jews, which spread like a poison through society. This insight restored his faith in his fellow-countrymen. General Ludendorff solved a similar personal

[35] Deutsch, 'Legende', 18
[36] Davies, 'Mozart's Illnesses and Death – 2', *Musical Times*, cxxv (1984), 559

problem in a similar way. In spite of his better knowledge, he came to explain the defeat of the glorious German army in 1918 in terms of a 'stab in the back' by the civilians back home – those civilians of course including socialists and Jews.[37]

This chapter can come to a firm conclusion: Mozart died a natural death. The poisoning legend collapses in ruins when scrutinized. According to the proverb, it is impossible to touch pitch without being defiled; the material considered here leaves the reader with a slight sense of defilement. But there is the consolation that Mozart himself was not defiled by this. He continued to be a loyal mason, even when the freemasons fell from favour. No anti-semitic utterance by him is known to us. He had more contacts with Jews than was usual, and his Jewish former landlord stood godfather to his first child.[38] Even his last recorded encounter with Salieri was amicable:

> At six o'clock I called in the carriage for Salieri and Madame Cavalieri – and drove them to my box. . . . You can hardly imagine how charming they were and how much they liked not only my music, but the libretto and everything. They both said it was an *operone*, worthy to be performed for the grandest festival before the greatest monarch, and that they would certainly often go to see it, as they had never seen a more delightful or beautiful show. He listened and watched most attentively and from the overture to the last chorus there was not a single number that did not call forth from him a bravo! or bello! It seemed as if they could not thank me enough for my kindness.[39]

[37] F. Fischer, *Germany's Aims in the First World War* (London, 1967), 627–8, 637
[38] Volkmar Braunbehrens, *Mozart in Wien* (Munich, 1986), 12, 76, 78; Eng. trans. *Mozart in Vienna 1781–1791* (New York, 1989)
[39] *LMF*, 970

Chapter III

The medical history

But what did he actually die of? Mozart's medical history is like an inverted pyramid: a small corpus of primary documentation supports a large body of secondary literature. There is a small quantity of direct eye-witness testimony concerning the last illness and death, and a larger quantity of reporting of what eye witnesses are alleged to have said. Altogether it would not cover ten pages; some of it is vague, and some downright unreliable. All too often later writers have used this data uncritically to support pet theories. They have even invented new symptoms, nowhere recorded in the primary sources.

Medical experts have discussed Mozart's final illness in the light of his medical record from childhood onwards. A fair amount is known about this; Leopold wrote long letters home when he and his son were on tour, anxiously describing each illness. He was an excellent observer and reporter, and consequently present-day doctors can often make confident diagnoses. Hence we know that the child suffered a series of life-threatening illnesses: smallpox, abdominal typhoid, streptococcal angina (a bacterial infection of the tonsils with danger of choking) and rheumatic fever. Posterity can count itself lucky that he survived childhood, but the early ailments may have caused permanent damage. After he left the parental home, the record becomes poorer. Mozart was an erratic correspondent, many of his letters are lost, and he described his illnesses much less precisely than his father had done.

Mozart took to his bed on or about 20 November 1791; 'From information received from Vienna he died on 5 December (55 minutes after midnight)'.[1] It is curious and revealing that we owe this precise information to Mozart's sister Nannerl, far away in Salzburg. He was attended by Dr Thomas Closset, one of the most esteemed physicians in Vienna. At some point Closset brought in for a second opinion his up-and-coming young friend and colleague, Dr Mathias von Sallaba.[2] The first piece of testimony stems, presumably, from Closset, namely the cause of death recorded in the death register. It is given as 'Hitziges Frieselfieber' – a severe fever with a rash. For twentieth-century doctors, as indeed for Closset and Sallaba, this is not a specific diagnosis nor in itself a potential cause of death; it is merely a record of some of the symptoms. No other direct testimony from the attending doctors is known.

Contemporary newspapers repeated 'Hitziges Frieselfieber'. The Berlin weekly which reported the rumour of poison at the very end of the year was quoted in the previous chapter. Of relevance to this chapter, it also said that 'he was said to be dropsical . . . his body swelled up after death'.[3] A Speyer newspaper reported on 28 December 1791 that he had died of a 'dropsy of the heart'.[4]

For several years no further information was recorded, as far as we know; then in 1798 some scraps were served up by Niemetschek and Rochlitz, presumably based in part upon information from Constanze. Niemetschek, apart from his hints at poisoning, remarks that Mozart was conscious to the end and died calmly. 'The doctors were not agreed on the diagnosis of his illness.' This little sentence has been meat and drink to the enthusiasts for poisoning. Carl Bär suggests that

[1] *MDB*, 461
[2] We can be fairly but not absolutely certain who attended Mozart; see Bär, *Mozart: Krankheit – Tod – Begräbnis*.
[3] *MDB*, 432
[4] *MDB*, 428

it could simply reflect Constanze's misunderstanding of an overheard debate between the doctors, sprinkled with technical vocabulary in Latin, about the appropriate treatment for a deteriorating patient.[5] Niemetschek also says that Mozart was pale and ill in Prague in September, and taking medicine. This illness is confirmed by the Coronation Journal published in 1791.[6] Both Niemetschek and Rochlitz convey a strong impression of an overworked composer, suffering occasionally from depression and irritability, reacting irrationally to the Requiem commission as if it were an announcement of doom. Rochlitz is the first source for a further piece of information:

> His exertions were often so great that he not only became oblivious to the whole world about him, but also sank back utterly exhausted, and had to be put to bed . . .
> Often when in the grip of his genius, indifferent to day and night, he sank in exhaustion and semi-unconsciousness lasting for several minutes over this opera [*Die Zauberflöte*]. . . .
> [when working on the Requiem] His body could not stand the strain: several times he sank in a swoon over the work.[7]

The next document of importance, partly quoted in the previous chapter, is the declaration of Dr Guldener von Lobes, supplied to Carpani in 1824 in refutation of the poisoning rumours. Apart from the entry 'Hitziges Frieselfieber' in the death register, it is the only testimony, indirect testimony at that, which we have from the doctors:

> He fell sick in the late autumn of a rheumatic and inflammatory fever, which, being fairly general among us at that time, attacked many people. I did not know about it until a few days later, when his condition had already grown much worse. I did not visit him for some reason, but informed myself of his condition through Dr Closset, with whom I came in contact

---

[5] Bär, 44
[6] Niemtschek, *Leben*, 34, 37; *MDB*, 405
[7] *AMZ*, i (1798–9), 148, 150 (5 December 1798)

almost every day. The latter considered Mozart's illness to be dangerous, and from the very beginning feared a fatal conclusion, namely a deposit on the brain. One day he met Dr Sallaba and he said positively, 'Mozart is lost, it is no longer possible to restrain the deposit'. Sallaba communicated this information to me at once, and in fact Mozart died a few days later with the usual symptoms of a deposit on the brain.[8]

Together with this should be grouped the draft reply by Mozart's son Karl Thomas, also quoted in the previous chapter, which suggested the likelihood of poisoning and asserted the swelling and internal putrefaction of the body both before and after death.

Nissen's biography of 1828 reprints much of the above, but adds important new material furnished by Constanze's sister Sophie and presumably by Constanze herself. It is curious that most of Nissen's new information comes from Sophie rather than the widow. Did Sophie have a better memory? Did Nissen think her more reliable? Was Constanze in such a state in the dying embers of 1791 that later her memories were confused? Or was it simply the result of Nissen's incompetent method of working? Sophie had sent her recollections in a long letter, and Nissen perhaps found it easier to stitch in the ready-prepared words than to compose his own account synthesizing all the material at his disposal. Apart from Sophie's report, Nissen provides a mere quarter-of-a- page:

> His final illness, during which he was bedridden, lasted 15 days. It began with swelling in hands and feet, and an almost complete inability to move: this illness, which later was followed by sudden vomiting, is called a heated miliary fever. He remained fully conscious until two hours before his end.[9]

Part of Sophie's vivid letter was quoted above in Chapter 1. In addition she reported that at one point in the illness he felt better and spoke of getting up, also:

[8] *MDB*, 522–3
[9] Nissen, *Biographie*, 572

> When Mozart fell ill, we both made him a night-jacket which could be put on frontways, since on account of the swelling he was unable to turn in bed. Then, as we didn't know how seriously ill he was, we also made him a quilted dressing gown.

Nissen adds:

> The sister-in-law thinks Mozart was not effectively enough looked after in his illness, for instead of bringing out the spots yet more by other methods, they bled him and applied cold compresses to his head . . . Even in his serious illness he never became impatient, and only at the end his fine ear and feeling became sensitive to the song of his pet, a canary, which even had to be moved from the next room, because it put too much strain on him.[10]

Sophie tells how on the very last evening Mozart discussed with Süßmayr how he should complete the Requiem after his death. The lengthy appendix which Constanze added to the biography after Nissen's death contains the well-known story of the rehearsal of the Requiem on the penultimate day, with Mozart singing alto.

Nissen's notes contain information provided by Constanze which he chose not to use:

> He asked his wife what the physician Closset had said. She answered comfortingly. He contradicted: that's not true, and was very depressed: now I must die, when I could care for you and the children. *Ach*, now I must leave you unprovided for. Suddenly he began to vomit – it spat out of him in an arch – it was brown, and he was dead.[11]

The sisters spoke about Mozart's death to the visiting Novellos in 1829. According to Constanze, 'his death was at last sudden, but a few moments before he had spoken so gaily, and in a few moments after he was dead – she could not

[10] *LMF*, 975; Nissen, 575
[11] H. C. Robbins Landon, *1791: Mozart's Last Year* (London, 1988), 168

believe it'. He gave Süßmayr instructions about the completion of the Requiem and rehearsed it with Süßmayr and her a short time before his death.

It was about six months before he died that he was impressed with the horrid idea that someone had poisoned him with acqua toffana – he came to her one day and complained that he felt great pain in his loins and a general languor spreading over him by degrees.

Sophie told them that he had been writing a part of the Requiem on the very day that he died, that his arms and limbs were much inflamed and swollen, and that 'the Doctor persisted in his orders and Madame Haibl accordingly applied a damp towel to his forehead. Mozart immediately gave a slight shudder and in a very short time afterwards he expired in her arms'.[12]

Some miscellaneous references remain to be quoted. In 1816 Dr Carl von Bursy wrote in his diary, on the occasion of a visit to Vienna:

The most distinguished doctor of the town considered Mozart's illness to be inflammatory and ordered bloodletting. The catarrh developed into a nervous fever, which was prevalent at that time.

In 1825 the composer Joseph Eybler recorded in his autobiography that

I had the good fortune to enjoy Mozart's unbroken friendship up to his death, so that during his painful last illness I helped to lift him up, lay him down and nurse him.

In 1840 Ignaz von Seyfried, a piano pupil of Mozart's, wrote:

On the evening of 4 December Mozart lay hallucinating, imagining that he was listening to *Die Zauberflöte* at the

[12] Novello, 97, 126, 127, 128

Theater auf der Wieden; almost the last words he whispered to his wife were: 'Quiet! quiet! now Hofer is taking the high F; – now my sister-in-law is singing her second aria: "Der Hölle Rache"; how powerfully she hits the B flat and holds it: "Hört! hört! hört! der Mutter Schwur!" '[13]

In 1856 J. P. Lyser wrote that Sophie Haibl had told him that

That part of the instrumentation [of the Requiem] which he could no longer write himself, because his hands were crippled, he dictated to Süßmeyer up to the day of his death.[14]

Finally, there is the report in the Vienna *Morgen-Post* of 1856, allegedly of the memoirs of the innkeeper Joseph Deiner, who had died in 1823, already quoted in Chapter 1. It is the sole source for the claim that 'At 12 o'clock in the night Mozart raised himself in his bed, his eyes staring, then he sank back with his head towards the wall, and seemed to fall asleep again'. It also states that on 28 November Drs Closset and Sallaba held a consultation on Mozart's condition.[15] This highly dubious source completes the survey of the documentation: in this and the preceding chapters the reader has been provided with all of the documentary evidence on which a medical diagnosis can be based.

*

The fundamental modern study is the little book prepared for the Internationale Stiftung Mozarteums by the Swiss dentist Dr Carl Bär, published in 1966 and in an enlarged version in 1972. Not only is it a thorough medical discussion: it is also a

---

[13] Bär, 32–3, 39, 42
[14] Johann Friedrich Kayser, *Mozart-Album* (Hamburg, 1856), 64
[15] *MDB*, 564–5

model of historical inquiry. Bär was the first to interpret the evidence in the context of the medical knowledge and practice of the late eighteenth century. By consulting the works of Closset and Sallaba, and of their teacher Dr Maximilian Stoll, he was able to establish the extent of the ability of the doctors to recognize and distinguish different illnesses. He also revealed the medical theory which shaped their thinking. Stoll and his disciples followed Hippocrates' doctrine that the health of the body depended upon the correct balance in the body of the four humours – blood, phlegm, yellow and black bile. Different illnesses were caused by different imbalances in the body, and treatment was aimed at restoring the balance. Twentieth-century doctors writing about Mozart ignore this context at their peril, running the risk of reading the documents anachronistically.

During the course of two hundred years many different diagnoses have been proffered – consumption, typhoid, Graves's disease, meningitis. These can be dismissed. Today, the debate revolves around two theories. One of them proposes that he died of a long-standing kidney complaint. The other directs attention to the attacks of rheumatic fever he had as a child, arguing that in 1791 he died as a consequence of this: either suffering a fresh bout of rheumatic fever, which directly or indirectly brought about his death; or dying of a heart disease to which the earlier rheumatic fever had made him liable. The case for rheumatic fever has been argued by Bär, and recently by Professor Dr Anton Neumayr.[16]

Even today the mechanism of rheumatic fever is not perfectly understood. It is a secondary illness, occurring two or more weeks after the primary infection, commonly of the upper air passages, for example the tonsils, by streptococci (chain-form bacteria). It produces fever with much sweating and attacks tissues of a certain kind, initially in the joints,

[16] Neumayr, *Musik und Medizin*

especially of the hands, knees and feet. These become swollen, inflamed and terribly painful – so painful that the patient cannot bear to be touched or to have the joints covered. The agony makes it impossible to move. In spite of the pain, the affliction of the joints is neither lasting nor dangerous. The danger of the illness derives from the fact that in the majority of cases it also attacks the heart, causing permanent damage to the valves, especially when it recurs. It is primarily an illness of those aged between 5 and 19; only rarely does it occur for the first time in older persons. But immunity is not acquired; rather the reverse is the case, and those who have had it in childhood are susceptible as adults. In the West today the disease is rare and no longer a killer: but it did kill both children and adults in the eighteenth and nineteenth centuries. The reasons for this change are not certain. It is surmised that the disease may have evolved into a less virulent form, or that better standards of nutrition and hygiene may have increased resistance. It is rarely experienced in untreated form. Children who are susceptible are given antibiotics against the bacteria which trigger it so as to prevent dangerous recurrences.

It is not immediately obvious that the entry in the death register – 'Hitziges Frieselfieber' – is consistent with this diagnosis. Rheumatic fever produces an elevated temperature but only rarely a rash. But in the unhygienic conditions of the eighteenth century, the sweating could have caused a rash.[17] There is strong evidence for this diagnosis. According to Nissen the illness began with swelling in the hands and feet and near immobility. Sophie reported that they made him a night-shirt which could be put on from the front – he could not move because of the swelling. She told the Novellos that his arms and limbs were much inflamed and swollen, and Lyser that his hands were crippled. Eybler reported that he had helped to lift and lower Mozart during his painful illness.

[17] Neumayr, 90

Finally we know that Mozart had had at least two bouts of rheumatic fever as a child, at the ages of six and ten. But if this was indeed Mozart's last illness, what was the immediate cause of death? Rheumatic fever is survivable. Neumayr thinks that the clue lies in Guldener von Lobes's reiterated reference to a 'deposit on the brain'. Accounts of the illness from the nineteenth century, when it was still lethal, refer to 'cerebral rheumatism' – a deterioration of the patient with heightened fever as the illness attacked the central nervous system and brain.[18] Bär directs attention instead to the heart, probably damaged in childhood by the attacks of rheumatic fever.

An obvious objection here is that the adult Mozart showed no sign of a weak heart. He could work phenomenally hard, as in 1784 and 1791. He loved dancing. For several years he was much in demand as a virtuoso performer – though the Viennese fortepiano, with its light touch, did not require as much physical exertion as a modern pianoforte. In any case, damaged heart valves may produce no symptoms for many years, until suddenly some exertion, or infection, brings on a heart attack.

At this point, the methods of treatment employed by Mozart's doctors become highly relevant. They thought that rheumatic fever was produced by an imbalance, an excess of black bile, which went to the joints. When a patient deteriorated, they believed this was caused by the *materia morbifica*, the illness-producing excess, migrating to the chest or the head – this is the correct interpretation of the expression 'a deposit on the brain'.[19] They thought such migration could cause the death of the patient. They therefore sought to prevent it from happening by removing the excess from

[18] Neumayr, 110

[19] Bär, from whom this discussion derives, shows that 'deposit on the brain' does not signify a diagnosis of meningitis. Stoll distinguished meningitis, 'wahre Phrenitis', and the deterioration caused by the alleged deposit on the brain, 'zufällige Phrenitis' (see Bär, 72).

the body. To this end they administered emetics and a course of bloodletting by venesections.

We know from their writings and those of Stoll that this was their treatment for rheumatic fever. Can we be sure that they inflicted these 'remedies' on Mozart? Nissen refers to sudden vomiting, and Constanze mentioned the vomit spitting out of him in an arch. There are two references to bloodletting, from Sophie Haibl and Dr von Bursy. The doctors thought that rheumatic fever required, and could stand, a lot of bloodletting – Sallaba describes the case of one patient from whom he took five litres of blood in a week. The man survived!

Bearing all this in mind, a horrific possible scenario opens up for Mozart's case. The doctors inflicted emetics on a man for whom every movement was agonizing. They bled him, and when he got worse bled him even more. He was unable to spare so much blood, for he was a small man and his heart was already in trouble. It may be that the doctors, the best doctors in Vienna, conscientiously attending their patient, unwittingly killed Mozart. For their medical theory was false, and they lacked knowledge of the central place of the functioning of the heart in the course of serious illness. The stethoscope, which could have revealed any heart anomaly, was not invented until almost thirty years later.

Recently another possible cause of death, related to his history of rheumatic fever, has been proposed, namely infective endocarditis.[20] With this disease, an infected blood clot grows usually upon a heart valve, spreading infection through the body, damaging the valve and perhaps perforating it. In the absence of modern treatment with antibiotics it is usually fatal. The disease is secondary to an infection elsewhere in

---

[20] The case for bacterial endocarditis is argued by Willem Boissevain, 'Neue Erklärung der Todesursache Mozarts: "Hitziges Frieselfieber" war bakterielle Herzklappenentzündung', *Mitteilungen der internationalen Stiftung Mozarteum*, xxxviii (July 1990)

the body; to a streptococcal infection such as tonsilitis, or to infection introduced into the bloodstream, for example during dental work. It could easily be started by bloodletting in non-sterile conditions, and so, once again, Mozart's doctor could have been the unwitting cause of his death.

Patients whose heart valves are abnormal, because of heredity or a prior attack of rheumatic fever, are especially prone to this disease; the infection lodges on the damaged valve. It can produce the symptoms Mozart is known to have had; fever, inflamed and swollen joints in hands and feet, immobility, vomiting and spots on the skin. Even today it can be difficult to distinguish by observation alone between infective endocarditis and a severe attack of rheumatic fever.

There are two sorts of infective endocarditis, chronic and acute. A patient suffering from the chronic form is ill for weeks or months. It begins with low-grade fever, with fatigue and weight-loss. The patient, progressively deteriorating, may experience slight remissions but never feels well. Apparently this would accord with the narrative sources, such as Niemetschek and Rochlitz, which tell of his ailing throughout the second half of 1791. But in reality it would be incompatible with the hard work and productivity of that period, and with his late letters filled with high spirits and zest for life. The acute form, which can kill within days or weeks, would therefore be more likely.

This new diagnosis is not superior to that of rheumatic fever. Its strength is that it readily accounts for the spots on the skin; but, as Bär argues, they could have been a sweat rash. These are early days for the new diagnosis, and the medical Mozartians need to give it more thought. But it is a real candidate, and this underscores a vital point: with the limited evidence at our disposal, the best we can do is indicate possible causes of Mozart's death. Many proposed runners can be eliminated, but there will never be an out-and-out winner. Indeed, Mozart could have had both rheumatic fever and infective endocarditis. He could have started with the former. Then, when his doctor treated it in the usual way with bleeding, the latter may have been introduced.

The diagnosis of kidney failure was first proposed by Barraud in 1905.[21] His article is full of mistakes. It gives Mozart and Constanze three children instead of six, cites the overture to *Figaro* as the one composed in a single night before the première instead of that to *Don Giovanni*, and states that Mozart fainted every time he saw the mysterious stranger who commissioned the Requiem. A colourful picture of poverty is borrowed from Nohl's romantic biography: 'The day after their marriage the newlyweds had not a florin in their pockets. They offered bread and coffee, which Constanze prepared in her wedding dress because she had no other clothes, as a complete meal to one of their friends.' Barraud's diagnosis of inflammation of the kidneys occupies no more than the last ten lines of the article. It traces the complaint back to an attack of scarlet fever when he was 6 – but medical commentators are now agreed that the illness in question was erythema nodosum, not scarlet fever at all. Barraud backs up his diagnosis by citing Mozart's rapid loss of weight, but in fact there is absolutely no evidence for this.

A more thorough and informed case for kidney failure has been presented in a series of articles by Dr Aloys Greither. Inflammation of the filtering mechanism of the kidney can occur as a secondary illness following a streptococcal infection. Greither thinks that in Mozart's case repeated attacks caused cirrhosis, permanent scarring, of the kidney tissues; complications ensued, including pyelitis (inflammation of that part of the kidney where the urine collects before passing to the bladder) and perhaps kidney stones. This chronic condition led to a collapse of kidney functions late in 1791. Mozart's kidneys ceased to separate urine from his blood, his body swelled with water retention, finally there was uraemic coma and death. Greither maintains that the final collapse

[21] J. Barraud, 'A quelle maladie a succombé Mozart?', *Chronique médicale*, xxii (1905), 737–44

could be sudden, and therefore his diagnosis is compatible with apparent good health and unimpaired activity for much of 1791.[22]

Greither traces Mozart's alleged chronic kidney condition back to known earlier illnesses. In 1819 Mozart's sister Nannerl wrote about portraits of her brother to Joseph Sonnleithner, an imperial civil servant who collected composers' portraits, mentioning an otherwise undocumented illness in 1772: 'the one that was painted when he came back from the Italian journey is the oldest, he was then just 16 years old, but as he had just got up from a serious illness, the picture looks sickly and very yellow'.[23] This brief reminiscence of events almost half a century earlier is a flimsy support for any diagnosis; but for what it is worth, inflammation of the kidneys does not produce conspicuous yellowing. A diagnosis of jaundice caused by yellow fever or, more likely, viral hepatitis is appropriate.[24] Then in 1784 Mozart contracted an illness, about which Leopold wrote to Nannerl:

> My son has been very ill in Vienna. At a performance of Paisiello's new opera he perspired so profusely that his clothes were drenched and in the cold night air he had to try to find his servant who had his overcoat . . . He writes as follows: 'Four days running at the very same hour I had a violent attack of colic, which ended each time in violent vomiting. I have therefore to be extremely careful. My doctor is Sigmund Barisani, who since his arrival here has visited me almost daily.'[25]

In 1787 Barisani made a versified entry in Mozart's album, in which he stated that he had served and saved the composer twice.[26] From these two pieces of evidence it has been

---

[22] Aloys Greither, 'Mozart und die Ärzte, seine Krankheiten und sein Tod', *Acta mozartiana*, iii (1956), 4
[23] *MDB*, 520
[24] Neumayr, 100
[25] *LMF*, 883
[26] *MDB*, 289

inferred that Barisani twice treated Mozart for a kidney complaint.[27] But this is a blatant instance of the marshalling of evidence to fit a preconceived theory. Nothing is known of the second serious illness treated by Barisani. The 1784 illness could have been inflammation of the kidneys; it could also have been a gastro-enteritis, and Leopold's assertion that a number of other people had suffered from it at the same time makes the latter more likely. Evidence for longstanding kidney disease, therefore, is entirely lacking.

But does Mozart's history in 1791 support the hypothesis of kidney failure? Constanze's remark to the Novellos that six months before his death he complained of great pain in his loins and a general languor could point to kidney inflammation and uraemic contamination of the blood; but as evidence it is isolated and inconclusive. There is little evidence for a progressive loss of consciousness ending in uraemic coma. Seyfried's 1840 story of Mozart imagining in a delirium that he was attending a performance of *Die Zauberflöte* is contradicted by the repeated insistence of Constanze and Sophie that he remained fully conscious until the end, or until the last couple of hours. Seyfried's story could simply be an embroidered version of the Rochlitz anecdote that tells of Mozart, on his death bed, following the performance of *Die Zauberflöte* in imagination with the aid of his watch.[28]

Greither supposes that Mozart's inability to move on his death bed was caused by dropsy, general swelling of the body resulting from water retention as a consequence of kidney failure. But the evidence for *general* swelling is not strong: a couple of reports in newspapers, neither of them Viennese, one of them containing gossip about poisoning and the false statement that the Requiem had been performed at his funeral; and the memorandum by his son Karl Thomas, written in or after 1824, referring to swelling and a stench. Did Karl witness the deathbed? He was seven years old at the

[27] Greither, 'Mozart und die Ärzte', 5
[28] *AMZ*, i (1798–9), 149 (5 December 1798)

time. Certainly the hands and feet were swollen; could the child see the rest of the body? There was vomiting, and rheumatic fever causes sour-smelling sweat. The smell of the sick room will not have been pleasant. Did an impressionable, frightened child later build these unpleasant memories into the horrific image of a bloated, stinking body? In fact, general swelling at the very end is compatible with Bär's diagnosis of rheumatic fever. If Mozart's heart went into failure, that could cause water retention and swelling, either directly or indirectly through consequent kidney failure.

Greither's diagnosis falls down, however, because it cannot account for the *inflamed* swelling of the hands and feet. He attempts to discredit the evidence for this, and for the pain; but the attempt is not convincing.[29] Finally and conclusively, Bär has demonstrated that the doctors were clearly aware of the difference between the swellings produced by rheumatic fever and the generalized swelling produced by the illness attributed to Mozart by Greither. Sallaba called the latter 'Hydrops' or 'Hydrops urinosus'.[30]

Dr Peter J. Davies has proposed an alternative version of the kidney theory, which corresponds rather better to the recorded symptoms, namely Henoch-Schönlein syndrome.[31] Like rheumatic fever, this is a secondary illness which may follow a streptococcal infection or viral illness, usually after one to four weeks. It is thought to be caused when bonded-together fragments of the bacteria and antibodies enter and damage certain tissues. This occurs under the skin of buttocks, legs and arms, producing a purple rash. Joints are affected too – ankles, knees, sometimes hands, becoming warm, swollen and tender. The bowel wall may suffer,

[29] A. Greither, 'Noch einmal: Woran ist Mozart gestorben?', *Mitteilungen der internationalen Stiftung Mozarteum*, xix/3–4 (1971), 25–7
[30] Bär, 123
[31] Peter J. Davies, 'Mozart's Illnesses and Death', *Journal of the Royal Society of Medicine*, lxxvi (1983), 776–85; 'Mozart's Illnesses and Death', *Musical Times*, cxxv (1984), 437–41, 554–61. His theory is repeated in Peter J. Davies, *Mozart in Person. His Character and Health* (New York and London, 1989)

causing abdominal pain. In a minority of cases there is kidney inflammation which normally heals but occasionally progresses to kidney failure.

Davies argues that Mozart suffered a series of attacks, progressively damaging his kidneys. He points first of all to the illness of 1784, already mentioned in connection with Greither's theory. This in itself is a problem, for the syndrome usually affects schoolchildren and young adults, rarely occurring for the first time in a 28-year old patient. He suggests that the second illness treated by Barisani, perhaps in 1787, was a second attack. But as argued above, the 1784 illness was probably gastro-enteritis and nothing is known about the second. Mozart was ill between April and August 1790, and Davies suspects yet further attacks. This is convincing only if one *starts* with the assumption that the final illness was Henoch-Schönlein, for Mozart's descriptions of his symptoms do not suggest that illness:

> My head is covered with bandages due to rheumatic pains . . .
> My toothache and headache are still too painful and altogether I still feel very unwell . . .
> I am absolutely wretched today. I could not sleep all night for pain. I must have got overheated yesterday from walking so much and then without knowing it have caught a chill.[32]

The evidence for the period up to and including 1790, therefore, provides no independent support for Davies' diagnosis.

It looks as if his case really rests upon Mozart's medical history in 1791. Davies thinks that by this date Mozart's kidneys were so impaired that he was suffering from high blood pressure. As evidence for this he cites the 'mental symptoms' of 1791 – headaches, depression, delusions about poisoning and the occult commissioning of the Requiem,

---

[32] *LMF*, 937, 938, 941

fainting fits. This looks like an impressive supporting catalogue: when scrutinized it is rather less strong. No headaches
are documented for 1791. Mozart's own letters bubble with
cheerfulness; the only exception is the passage where he
writes of emptiness and longing, but this could simply be
longing for Constanze, away at Baden: 'You cannot imagine
how I have been aching for you all this long while'.[33] To be
sure, Niemetschek and Rochlitz paint a vivid picture of irritability, depression, obsession and strange moods. Mozart may
well have been in a nervous state in 1791, but there is no
need to invoke high blood pressure to explain it. He was just
beginning to emerge from a bad period of worry about
money and his wife's health, and he was working far too hard.
As for the blackouts, Rochlitz is the primary source of evidence, and he was not an eye-witness. His tendency to
embroider his information has often been remarked. It is not
certain that anything more is at issue here than bouts of
exhaustion after phenomenal exertion. Nevertheless the
fainting is also mentioned by Nissen. On one occasion the
reference is a straight lifting from Rochlitz, in the second it is
not. Nissen's second remark reads like a working-together of
passages from Rochlitz and Arnold; but it may represent
information independently given to him by Constanze.
Perhaps then the blackouts should be taken seriously. But
high blood pressure caused by kidney failure is not the only
possible explanation. Damage to the aortic valve of the heart
following the childhood attacks of rheumatic fever could also
produce them.[34]

Henoch-Schönlein syndrome fits the final illness in that it
would explain the rash, the swollen, inflamed joints and the
vomiting. Davies says the vomiting occurred especially at
night, but there is no evidence for this. Constanze's solitary

[33] *LMF*, 963
[34] The passages in Rochlitz are *AMZ*, i (1798), 148 and 150 (5 December 1798)
and 178 (19 December 1798), and Nissen, 548, 624

remark about brown vomit could indicate blood in the sto-
mach, consonant with the lesions caused by Henoch-
Schönlein. The documentary evidence for the rash is the
entry in the death register: 'Hitziges Frieselfieber'. Sophie and
Nissen referred to the final illness by this title, but no eye-
witness directly described a rash. As already remarked, a rash
could have been caused by sweating and poor hygiene, or by
bacterial endocarditis complicating rheumatic fever. The
vomiting could be explained, as Bär explains it, as a consequence of the treatment administered by the doctors.

Henoch-Schönlein would not of itself cause inability to
move or death. Davies's hypothesis is that it further damaged
his kidneys, exacerbating the high blood pressure. This in
turn caused a stroke, a brain haemorrhage and paralysis of
one side of his body. Davies appears to be suggesting that this
occurred 'after a week in bed'. But Nissen says that the
swollen hands and feet and an almost complete inability to
move were evident at the beginning of the illness. If Mozart
had a stroke leading to partial paralysis at the outset, it is
difficult to believe that Constanze and Sophie could have
thought for so long that his illness was not mortal, that they
set about making him a quilted dressing-gown ready for his
recovery, and that he himself spoke of getting up shortly.[35]
Davies backs up his case by arguing for a further stroke at the
very end:

> Then, an hour later, he attempted to sit up, opened his eyes
> wide and then fell back with his head turned to the wall. His
> cheeks were puffed out. These symptoms suggest paralysis of
> conjugate gaze, and facial nerve palsy. They are consistent with
> a massive haemorrhage in either one of the frontal lobes or
> brain stem.[36]

This story, which contradicts Sophie's account of the very
end, is based solely on the 'Joseph Deiner' memoirs of 1856,

[35] *LMF*, 975
[36] Davies, *Journal of the Royal Society of Medicine*, 784

which are so dubious that no argument can reasonably be built upon them.

The kidney failure theory, therefore, is not compelling. Much of the evidence cited in its support is unreliable or ambiguous. Some of the evidence contradicts it. There seems to be no reason to prefer it to the diagnoses of rheumatic fever or infective endocarditis, which are supported by more and better evidence. The kidney theorists have not really appreciated the force of Bär's reading of the documents in the light of late eighteenth-century medical theory and practice.

So is the conclusion warranted that this issue is broadly resolved? Can it be concluded with some confidence that Mozart's doctors diagnosed, and treated him for, rheumatic fever; and that Mozart did indeed have that, or infective endocarditis which his doctors would have been unable to distinguish from rheumatic fever? Bär's argument makes considerable use of the testimony of Dr Guldener von Lobes in his letter of 1824. On his own admission he did not visit Mozart during his final illness, but relied on reports by the attendant doctors, both of whom had died by 1824. How reliable was von Lobes's memory? Did he have notes to consult when he wrote his letter?

He writes that the rheumatic and inflammatory fever 'being fairly general among us at that time, attacked many people'.[37] In the version of the letter sent to Neukomm in Paris he wrote: 'In the autumn of 1791 he fell ill of an inflammatory fever, which at that season was so prevalent that few persons entirely escaped its influence'.[38] So widespread an epidemic of rheumatic fever, in the modern sense of the term, is inconceivable; von Lobes must here be using it, as it was used by Stoll and by lay persons, to refer to a wide range of feverish illnesses, rather as we use the term 'flu' today. Therefore we do not have direct evidence that the

[37] *MDB*, 522–3
[38] Bär, 59

doctors diagnosed rheumatic fever in the modern, specific sense. But Sallaba did in fact use the term as a twentieth-century doctor would, and his description of the symptoms could come from a present-day text book. In the preface to his book on diseases (1791) he asserted that his opinions coincided with those of its dedicatee, his mentor Thomas Closset.[39] Von Lobes's description of the course of the disease in Mozart's case, communicated to him by Closset and Sallaba, corresponds with Sallaba's account of the progress of rheumatic fever. Mozart's medical history and the eye-witness accounts furnished to Nissen and the Novellos offer further support.

When, therefore, Von Lobes writes 'This malady attacked at this time a great many of the inhabitants of Vienna, and for not a few of them it had the same fatal conclusion and the same symptoms as in the case of Mozart', the likeliest interpretation is that there was a widespread infection, which in some cases led on to complications such as Mozart suffered and death. On the evidence at our disposal, therefore, and in the present state of medical knowledge, rheumatic fever and/or infective endocarditis are the best candidates for Mozart's final illness.

There will always be question marks hanging over Mozart's last illness and death. The puzzles, contradictions and uncertainties to be discussed in the remainder of this chapter have given comfort to those who wish to find something sinister. The entry in the death register 'Hitziges Frieselfieber' is a puzzle. As already remarked the doctors would not have regarded this as a specific diagnosis. Out of 656 male deaths recorded in November or December Mozart's is the only one for which this cause of death is given. Official documents give 6 December as the date of burial, but that date would contravene the regulation requiring a lapse of 48 hours between death and burial. Bär has therefore argued that the entry is a

[39] Bär, 66

mistake: Mozart was taken from the city to the cemetery on December 7, a stormy evening, as a number of reports testify. But we cannot be absolutely certain that the official documents are in error. Earlier burial was permitted if the deceased had a contagious disease, or if the state of the corpse made hasty burial desirable.

The documents we must use to reconstruct Mozart's last days are neither consistent nor entirely trustworthy. The unreliability of the 'Joseph Deiner' story, or of the newspaper rumours, even of Rochlitz, is not fundamentally troubling. Much more serious are the doubts hanging over the reports from the key witnesses, Constanze and Sophie. Apart from any information Constanze may have given to Niemetschek and Rochlitz, their testimony dates from 1825–9, half a lifetime after the events in question. Nissen reports that Mozart was unconscious for two hours before he died, and Sophie's testimony refers to a period of unconsciousness. But two statements from Constanze say that he died a few minutes after speaking to her.

Grave doubts crowd round the story, put about by Constanze and Sophie, of Mozart's working on the Requiem right up to the last day. It is not compatible with a hypothesis of rheumatic fever causing immobility and ending in heart failure or an attack on the central nervous system. Nor will it square with paralysis of one side of the body as a result of a stroke. It is difficult to see how it can accord with immobility caused by water retention and uraemic poisoning. Sophie told the Novellos 'on the very day that he had died he had been writing a part of the Requiem'.[40] This cannot be right. All of Mozart's own handwriting in the autograph score is clear and firm and must have been written at a desk, before he took to his bed. It is contradicted by her statement to Lyser that he dictated to Süßmayr, his hands being crippled.

[40] Novello, 214

Nor is the story of the rehearsal on the penultimate day, Mozart singing alto, really credible. It is attributed to Schack, the first Tamino in *Die Zauberflöte*, but it is not his own testimony for it appeared in his obituary in 1827. Intrinsically it is implausible: why would Schack have sung the soprano line instead of Constanze, who sang in benefit concerts after Mozart's death?[41] The claim that the rehearsal ended because Mozart appropriately broke down in tears at the 'Lacrymosa' cannot be right: the autograph score reveals that the dying composer actually stopped work early in that movement.

Sophie and Constanze later insisted that the dying Mozart had discussed the Requiem with Süßmayr and given him precise instructions about its completion. This too is suspicious. If it were so, why did Constanze first draw up a contract with Eybler to complete it? Eybler contributed some orchestration, and so apparently did Mozart's composition pupil Freystädtler,[42] before the score was finally handed to Süßmayr. Constanze's later explanation, 'That I proposed to Eybler that he should complete it came about because I was (I do not know why) angry with Süßmayr' conveys an impression of one attempting to deceive.[43] Maunder has argued that, whereas Mozart's high regard for Eybler is documented, Constanze's own account suggests that he did not think much of Süßmayr as a composer. The whole story supposes a romantic and implausible deathbed scene in which Mozart knew he was dying but was still able to give instructions.

Constanze appears to have lied to Niemetschek about the Requiem:

---

[41] Maunder, *Mozart's Requiem*, 14. Maunder's first chapter is an excellent critical discussion of the sources for the story of the composition of the Requiem, to which I am much indebted.
[42] Landon, 150
[43] Maunder, 15

Immediately after his death the messenger presented himself, demanded the work, unfinished as it was, and received it. From that moment on the widow never saw him again, and heard nothing at all, neither of the mass for the dead, nor about the patron . . . The author narrates the events, as he has often heard them from the mouth of the widow.[44]

It is not difficult to think of motives for this deception. Constanze had the Requiem completed, and delivered to the patron, because she wished to obtain the second half of the payment and did not want to refund the first half. The patron might have been unwilling to pay for a work by a nonentity, and so it was necessary to put it about that Süßmayr was little more than an amanuensis.

Another, more subtle, motive is possible. Gradually a legend crystallized about the Requiem. Constanze played her part in creating it, but she was ably abetted by Niemetschek, Rochlitz, Arnold and others. It is a familiar legend and can be briefly summarized. In his last months, Mozart was increasingly ill and depressed, troubled with thoughts of death. There were sorrowful partings from Haydn and his friends in Prague. As his body weakened, his spirit intensified, his genius burned ever brighter; he worked as one possessed. In this state, the Requiem, and the mysterious manner of its commissioning, overwhelmed him. Feverishly he laboured at it, composing and rehearsing on his deathbed up to the very end. In Rochlitz's words:

> I will confess that Mozart was firmly convinced that the man with the noble appearance was a quite extraordinary being, standing in close contact with another world, perhaps even sent to announce his death. He therefore resolved all the more earnestly to leave a worthy monument to his name. With these ideas he worked on, and therefore it is no wonder that so perfect a work was created. In the course of this labour he sank

[44] Niemtschek, 35 and footnote

more often in complete exhaustion and fainting. Even before the end of four weeks he was finished – and he was dead.[45]

This was perfect publicity. It conferred a special aura upon the Requiem, which is abundantly evident in nineteenth-century writing on Mozart. It is impossible to measure how much Constanze gained financially as a result, but it is reasonable to suppose that it aided her benefit concerts and sale of scores. It need not be supposed that it is all lies with no basis in fact; rather, the facts have been woven and embroidered into a good story. Nor should it be thought that she consciously set about manufacturing a story for publicity purposes and that it is all her own work; others helped because it was so tempting, so romantic. The first documented beginnings of it are amazingly early, in a Salzburg newspaper of 7 January 1792: 'So Mozart had to write it, which he did, often with tears in his eyes, constantly saying: I fear that I am writing a Requiem for myself'. This report is the earliest source for the story that Mozart had tried in vain to evade the commission by asking an inflated price: its unreliability is proved when it tells the demonstrable falsities that Mozart completed the Requiem, and that the patron paid for but did not collect the score. The beginnings of the legend are also to be found in the Graz *Zeitung für Damen und andere Frauenzimmer* of 18 January 1792.[46]

It would probably be a mistake to think that Constanze herself, or Sophie, saw through the story, distinguishing fact from fiction. In spite of romantic nineteenth-century paintings and novels, Mozart's deathbed scene cannot have been noble, tranquil and sentimental. It will have been sordid, characterized by pain and fear. Far better to remember it through a myth which gave it spiritual and artistic significance.

[45] *AMZ*, i (1798–9), 178 (19 December 1798)
[46] *NMD*, no.119; *MDB*, 439

A recurrent theme in the writings of medical authorities about Mozart's death has been the connection between the final, fatal illness and the preceding life history. One example will suffice as illustration, taken from Carl Bär. As we have already seen, rheumatic fever primarily affects children, and recurrences become rarer with maturity. But in the case of adults, 'especially unaccustomed stresses can lead to an increased frequency of this kind of streptococcal infection. Under bad living conditions rheumatic fever can even become as common [with adults] as with children'.[47] In other words, there may have been a link between the debts and worries of 1790, the overwork of 1791 and the tragedy of November. Furthermore, the series of childhood illnesses which prepared the ground have often been blamed upon the exhausting travels around Europe, perhaps with reason. Joseph Yorke wrote to his brother, the second Earl of Hardwicke, from the Hague in 1765:

> We have got the little German Boy here who plays upon the Harpsichord like Handel, & composes with the same facility, he is really a most extraordinary effort of Nature, but our Professors in Physick don't think he will be long lived.[48]

The medical history of Mozart's death, therefore, in no way precludes the possibility of explaining that death in terms of the life as a whole. To put it another way, the life, more often than not, has been told as a coherent drama leading up to and culminating in that death. Such stories group into a number of distinct narrative types. The following chapters will consider them in turn.

[47] Bär, 106–7
[48] *NMD*, no.13

THE DEATH
IN THE CONTEXT
OF THE LIFE

Chapter IV

Beast and angel

According to this story, Mozart was Caliban and Prospero rolled into one, *homme supérieure* and *Erdenkind*:

> In *Die Zauberflöte* this double life is brought to clearest expression. Mozart is Tamino, who strives for Pamina, the symbol of the highest humanity. But at the same time he is Papageno, the natural man, the Pantagruel . . . The fundamental idea of the whole is the conflict between the earthly and heavenly powers in men, hence the problem we investigate in Amadeus's double life.[1]

The thesis of the split personality is the major theme of Schurig's biography. First published in 1913, it was to have a considerable influence. Its image of a man constantly wrestling with inner contradictions seemed a salutary counter to sickly-sweet nineteenth-century portrayals. Saint Mozart could only be shallow as a man and an artist: Schurig's Mozart had aesthetic and psychological profundity. Einstein's well-known study of 1945 follows Schurig: 'There is a strange kind of human being in whom there is an eternal struggle between body and soul, animal and god, for dominance. In all great men this mixture is striking, and in none more so than in Wolfgang Amadeus Mozart'.[2]

The books by Schurig and Einstein are noteworthy because they work this theme out so thoroughly; but the theme itself goes back to the first obituary. In Mozart's case, supreme musical genius was housed, so it was said, in a human being

[1] A. Schurig, *Wolfgang Amadé Mozart* (1913) (Leipzig, 1923), ii, 89, 345
[2] Alfred Einstein, *Mozart: his Character, his Work* (1946) (London, 1971), 13

who was undistinguished, indeed flawed and inadequate: a pearl in an oyster. His inadequacy manifested itself in several areas which will be considered in turn: he was physically unprepossessing; he was always a child; he was addicted to the pleasures of low company and strong drink; he never learnt how to handle money; as a professional musician he was irregular and unreliable; and he was utterly incompetent in professional relationships, completely lacking in tact and worldly wisdom. Where women were concerned he was a philanderer and a fool. His relations with women is a large issue and will accordingly be treated separately in the next chapter. His faults were notorious and ruined his career. His debauchery brought him to debt, despair and death. 'He became wild in the pursuit of pleasure; whatever changed the scene was delightful to him, and the more extravagant the better . . . It was . . . lighting the candle at both ends.'[3] 'No need for poison here, nor for a secret messenger, nor for fine dust in a letter, nor for a Requiem – his powers were worn out, his constitution destroyed.'[4]

*

Already in 1793, in Schlichtegroll's obituary, is to be found a description of Mozart the genius whose appearance was anything but that of a genius:

> Mozart was not distinguished by an especially striking physical appearance . . . He was small, thin, pale, and his features betrayed nothing out of the ordinary. His body was in constant motion; he always had to be doing something with his hands or feet . . . Even his face did not stay constant.[5]

Niemetschek adds that 'The insignificance of his outer appearance, the small growth of his body resulted from his

[3] Edward Holmes, *Life of Mozart* (1845) (London, 1912), 241, 242n
[4] Arnold, *Mozarts Geist*, 66–7
[5] Schlichtegroll, *Mozarts Leben*, 29–31

early mental exertions, and from the lack of free movement in the time of his childhood'.[6] Here was ample material for anyone wishing to weave a sensational story of a divided being. Stendhal seized the opportunity: 'He exhibited a mannerism which is normally a sign of stupidity: his body was in perpetual movement . . . The body was of the least possible significance in that astonishing compound known as Mozart.'[7]

Nissen copied Niemetschek's remarks and added a few more, perhaps from Constanze, which could be incorporated into the picture of the ugly genius. His eyes were prominent, and his head was too large for his body. He was once referred to in the *Morgenblätter* as the enormous nosed Mozart.[8] Michael Kelly, the Irish tenor who sang in the first performance of *Figaro*, recorded that 'He was a remarkably small man, very thin and pale, with a profusion of fine fair hair, of which he was rather vain'. He also describes Mozart coming on stage with his crimson pelisse and gold-laced cocked hat.[9] The inventory of Mozart's effects at the time of his death reveals that he spent a good deal on fine and fashionable clothes. There is also a curious letter to Baroness von Waldstätten in which he drops a heavy hint about his infatuation with a red coat with jewelled buttons. 'I should like all my things to be of good quality, genuine and beautiful'. Apparently the Baroness was willing to oblige.[10] Many have inferred that Mozart sought to compensate for his insignificant appearance by dressing like a butterfly. Schurig goes so far as to suggest that he had an effeminate taste in clothes, adding in a footnote that he did not need to shave until he was twenty-two.[11]

[6] Niemtschek, *Leben*, 44
[7] Stendhal, *Vie de Mozart* (1814), *Oeuvres complètes* (Paris, 1970), 284, 333
[8] Nissen, *Biographie*, 622–3
[9] *MDB*, 530, 533
[10] *LMF*, 823–4
[11] Schurig, ii, 397–400

Doubts cannot but arise about this important building-block in the story of Mozart, beast and angel. All subsequent biographers are heavily indebted to Schlichtegroll, Niemetschek and Nissen; and Nissen plagiarized Niemetschek who in turn plagiarized Schlichtegroll. Where then did Schlichtegroll, who never saw Mozart as far as we know, get his information? The anonymous postscript to Nannerl's letter to him was crucial, containing the remark that 'Wolfgang was small, thin, pale in colour, and entirely lacking in any pretensions as to physiognomy and bodily appearance'. We simply do not know who told Schlichtegroll that Mozart was distracted and nervy; he combined this with a stray remark of Nannerl's, 'As soon as he sat down at the clavier he was absolutely the master', to produce the beguiling image of a man who behaved like an idiot, then underwent a total transformation when he turned to music.[12] All this was meat and drink to later writers; but was it true? The posthumous memoirs of the poet and critic Ludwig Tieck, published in 1855, record an impression of him as 'small, rapid of movement, restless, and with a stupid expression on his face: an unprepossessing figure in a grey overcoat'.[13] Is this a confirmation of the early biographies, or a memory shaped by them?

In his diary for 1790 Wilhelm Backhaus, who was singing in the Mannheim première of *Figaro*, recorded his embarassment when he discovered that the man to whom he had forbidden entrance, taking him for a journeyman tailor, was none other than Mozart himself. But other scraps of information are less scathing about his appearance. Niemetschek copies Schlichtegroll's remark about his unsteady, absent-minded glance but in the preceding sentence contradictorily mentions his large intense eyes as a sign of his genius.[14] An English visitor remembered:

[12] *MDB*, 462
[13] *MDB*, 562
[14] *NMD*, no.104; Niemtschek, 44

I was surprised, when he rose to find him of not more than about five feet and four inches in height and of very slight build. His hand was cold but his grip was firm. His face was not particularly striking, rather melancholy until he spoke, when his expression became animated and amused.

Mozart's piano pupil Johann Nepomuk Hummel describes his pleasant and friendly countenance, his melancholy graveness, his large bright blue eyes. Kelly remembered his animated countenance lighted up with the glowing rays of genius.[15] To be sure, this favourable account of his appearance is no more to be accepted uncritically than its rival; perhaps Hummel and Kelly are serving up clichés rather than authentic memories. Nissen is utterly contradictory. He tells us that his eyes were large and fiery, and in the next sentence that they were more dull than fiery. He had an excellent, faultless profile: his nose was too big and he had bulging eyes.[16] This is just what one might expect in a biography prepared with scissors-and-paste.

Nissen is the sole original source of information about Mozart's left ear, which the portraits suggest he carefully covered with hair. Nissen's biography reproduces a drawing of the ear of Mozart's younger son, which apparently was the same. The ear was malformed, completely lacking the conch or outer convolution – a feature, incidentally, often associated with malformed heart valves. This ear has furnished the strangest twist to the beast and angel story. It has been said that such an ear is characteristic of lower races.[17] A late nineteenth-century paper in a medical journal remarked:

In Mozart's ear we have to do with a malformation of a kind which, besides being unsightly relates to a low stage of physical

[15] *NMD*, no.62; *MBD*, 527, 533
[16] Nissen, 622–3
[17] Otto Keller, *Wolfgang Amadeus Mozart: sein Lebensgang nach den neuesten Quellen geschildert* (Berlin and Leipzig, 1926), 214–5

development; whereas his *inward ear* meanwhile had reached the highest point of human development possible.[18]

*

That Mozart was always a child – not merely direct and childlike, but also childish – has echoed through the literature. Once again we return to that fateful postscript in Nannerl's letter to Schlichtegroll: 'Apart from his music he was almost always a child, and thus he remained: and this is a main feature of his character on the dark side; he always needed a father's, a mother's or some other guardian's care'.[19] Schlichtegroll broadcast this judgment to the wide world, adding that he could not govern himself, that he was not reasonable and moderate in his choice of pleasures, and that he was easily distracted from serious concerns.[20] It is just possible that these unfavourable additions are an unwarranted transposition of Schachtner's memoirs about the child (which Schlichtegroll had before him) to the man. According to Schachtner:

> He was of a fiery disposition, no object held his attention by more than a thread. I think that if he had not had the advantageously good education which he enjoyed, he might have become the most wicked villain, so susceptible was he to every attraction, the goodness or badness of which he was not yet able to examine.[21]

Wherever he got it from, true or false, it became part of the canon. Niemetschek was critical of this verdict, but by answering the charge he gave it circulation.[22] It may be that he could not entirely shake off the influence of Schlichtegroll

[18] Quoted in E. J. Breakspeare, *Mozart* (London, 1902), 234
[19] *MBD*, 462
[20] Schlichtegroll, 30
[21] *MDB*, 452
[22] Niemtschek, 63

– after all, his personal knowledge of Mozart was restricted to the period of the composer's last, three-week stay in Prague in 1791[23] – or that he felt there was a grain of truth in it all:

> Already as a child and a boy indeed, Mozart devoted himself to all the things and persons his spirit found of interest, with all the warm and lively cordiality of which so sensitively organized a man is capable. This trait continued to be a distinguishing characteristic of the man – and was often his misfortune . . . Mozart had a sincere inclination to the joys of sociability and friendship. Among good friends he was as open as a child, full of cheerful humour.[24]

Niemetschek treated the tale with caution; others latched on to it with delight. Suard's *Anecdotes sur Mozart* of 1804 epitomize the damning verdict:

> His mind, limited to those ideas which concerned music, shed a bright light on all that interested his talent, but shewed little aptitude to occupy itself with other things. He was extremely irritable; his affections were lively, but superficial and of short duration. He was melancholic and dominated by an active and mercurial imagination, which was only feebly kept in check by his reason . . . Mozart was all his life a sort of child. All his sentiments had more violence than depth. Light and inconstant in his affections, he was good and kind, but more from weakness than virtue.[25]

Few subsequent biographies are unaffected by this picture. According to Wyzewa and Saint-Foix, Mozart's was a feminine, impressionable nature, dominated by the musical influence of the moment, taking it up like a new toy, eating and sleeping with it, then, tired of it, throwing it forgotten into the bottom of a cupboard.[26] Kreitmeier thought that he was

---

[23] Favier, 58
[24] Niemtschek, 4, 60
[25] *MDB*, 498
[26] Théodore de Wyzewa and Georges de Saint-Foix, *Wolfgang Amédée Mozart: sa vie musicale et son oeuvre* (Paris, 1912), i, 175

completely turned inwards to the world of his music and consequently dreamy, naive and childlike, helpless in worldly affairs, his character soft as wax.[27] Boschot thought him a divine infant, and for Ghéon he was pure in heart, his bird's brain unaffected by ideas.[28]

Mozart's relish for lavatory humour is a key piece of evidence for the hypothesis of eternal childishness. The best, or worst, examples are contained in his letters, written when he was in his early twenties, to his young Augsburg cousin, Maria Anna Thekla Mozart:

> Well, I wish you good night, but first shit into your bed and make it burst. Sleep soundly, my love, into your mouth your arse you'll shove . . . Oh, my arse is burning like fire! What on earth does it mean? – Perhaps some muck wants to come out? Why yes, muck, I know, see and smell you . . . and . . . what is that? – Is it possible . . . Ye gods! can I believe those ears of mine? Yes indeed, it is so – what a long melancholy note![29]

Even from the last year of his life there is a joke letter to Stoll, the choirmaster for whom Mozart composed the *Ave verum*, which he has signed 'Franz Süßmayr, Muckshitter, Shitting-house'.[30] Mozart did not confine such humour to letters. In 1777 he confessed to his father that in the company of the musicians of the Mannheim court he had recited rhymes 'on muck, shitting and arse-licking'. The 'Zorastran riddles' he gave out at the Vienna Carnival of 1786 include one whose solution, apparently, is 'paper':

[27] Josef Kreitmeier, *W. A. Mozart: eine Charakterzeichnung des grossen Meisters nach literarischen Quellen* (Düsseldorf, 1919), 14, 36, 41, 206, 236; see also Ludwig Schiedermair, *Mozart: sein Leben und seine Werke* (Munich, 1922), 21, 160, and Bernhard Paumgartner, *Mozart* (1927) (Zürich, 1945), 23–8

[28] Henri Ghéon, *In Search of Mozart* (London, 1934), 62, 64; Adolphe Boschot, *Mozart* (Paris, 1935), 35, 38–9, 84

[29] *LMF*, 358–9

[30] *LMF*, 966

My death is generally terrifying – painful, and when it happens gently, base and contemptible. Nevertheless, should I die in the last manner at the hand of a beautiful woman, so shall I take that consolation with me to the grave, that I have seen some things which not everyone gets to see.[31]

He enjoyed composing canons to rude texts – for example K231 to *Leck mich im Arsch* ('Lick my arse').

Einstein comments that the nineteenth-century suppression of such letters

> is not an exercise of the same prudence that banishes the erotic etchings of Rembrandt to the secret drawers of the cabinet, and a few of the Roman Elegies of Goethe to 'scientific editions'. . . . There is also a certain not incomprehensible embarrasment. It is difficult to understand how a young man of twenty-two or twenty-three, and above all a Mozart, could write such childish obscenities, such ill-smelling bouquets, to a young girl.[32]

A note of caution needs to be sounded here. The meaning of Mozart's scatalogical turn of mind is not a timeless meaning; it has to be understood in its precise temporal context. Quite early in the nineteenth century there was a sea change in attitudes to such matters, apparently throughout Europe. In the late twentieth century, the wheel has come full circle, and 'Victorian' prudery has been consigned to the dust hole of history. The educated have read Joyce's *Ulysses*, and all have watched television comedians. Mozart's humour no longer seems particularly shocking or strange. The essential point, however, is not how it appeared to the nineteenth or even the twentieth century. How did it strike his contemporaries? Until a definitive history of humour has been written, suffice it to say that such coarse wit was common among adults. We find Nannerl, a twenty-four-year-old maiden, ending a letter with a remark about the sh— —ng and p— —ng of Miss Pimpes, the family dog. And mother Mozart closes with

[31] *LMF*, 373; *NMD*, entry for February 1786
[32] Einstein, 39

'Keep well, my love. Into your mouth your arse you'll shove. I wish you good-night, my dear, but first shit in your bed and make it burst'.[33]

Is there any truth in the notion that Mozart never grew up? One answer to this would be to say that what we have here is a myth, a pure fabrication, set going by Schlichtegroll and his anonymous sources and subsequently embroidered, endlessly enlarged by others. Henickstein the banker told the Novellos in 1829 that Mozart was too gay in his manner. Holmes, who visited Vienna in 1827 to interview eyewitnesses, reported that he 'at times enjoyed such a holiday of sheer animal spirits as could scarcely have been tolerated in an inferior person' and that Van Swieten had counselled Constanze how to manage and guide her wayward spouse. Doris Stock, who sketched his portrait in 1789, remembered that he had paid her the naivest compliments[34]. Perhaps these reminiscences should be regarded as memory shaped and coloured by tradition rather than clear-sighted reporting. The most striking account of childish behaviour, that of Caroline Pichler, will be discussed in Chapter 6, on genius: that chapter will propose an explanation of *why* Schlichtegroll and others were happy to describe Mozart in this way.

What stands in the way of complete acceptance of this defence is the testimony of Mozart's own father. 'I could not let you travel alone at that time, because you were not accustomed to attend to everything yourself or to do this and that without someone's help.' 'Do you think that Wolfgang will now attend to his affairs? I hope he has got accustomed to doing this and that his head is not always full of music.'[35] Parents are often unwilling to admit that their children have grown up, but these remarks offer some support to Schlichtegroll's guess that 'His father was well aware of his

---

[33] *LMF*, 283, 278
[34] Novello, 159; Holmes, *Life of Mozart*, 188, 203; *MDB*, 568–9
[35] *LMF*, 423, 425

lack of self-control, and therefore sent . . . the mother to accompany the son to Paris.'[36] In Mozart's defence it can be said that these letters all date from before Mozart settled in Vienna and stood on his own feet. Most of the adverse comments broadcast by Schlichtegroll appear to stem from Salzburg sources, and Salzburg memories were of him when he was kept in paternal tutelage. Perhaps he grew up after 1781 if he had not done so already.

*

Schlichtegroll's indictment is couched in general terms: he lacked self-control and moderation, he was pleasure-loving and irregular. Later writers quickly filled in the details. The reader can witness the story grow, as scattered remarks in the earliest sources get drawn together, elaborated and over-interpreted. Rumours of extravagance and indebtedness had circulated immediately after his death. Schlichtegroll added sensuality and excess to the brew. Niemetschek reported that he was jolly company with good friends. He also told the famous story of the composition of the overture to *Don Giovanni*: it was written on the evening before the day of the first performance, 'when he had been frivolous long enough'. Rochlitz told this story twice, and in his second version he added that Mozart asked his wife to keep him company as he worked through the night: 'She should make him punch . . . But the punch made him so sleepy'.[37] Rochlitz also told how in Leipzig in 1789 Mozart, at the end of a sociable evening, 'became bitter, drank much strong wine, and spoke thereafter no more rational words'.[38] He also painted a powerful pic-ture of Mozart's destroying his health by *overwork* in the last year of his life. When Suard plagiarized many of these anec-dotes in 1804, this had become 'The nervous irritability

---

[36] Schlichtegroll, 30

[37] Niemtschek, 55; *AMZ*, i (1798–9), 290 (6 February 1799)

[38] *AMZ*, iii (1800–01), 495 (15 April 1801)

which was part of his constitution grew worse owing to the excess of work and pleasure into which he alternately threw himself'.[39]

The story had crystallized already in the previous year in Arnold's little book *Mozarts Geist*, which draws heavily and frankly upon Niemetschek and perhaps upon Rochlitz, though this is less clear. Arnold added his own twist. Mozart was no economist. As a consequence, he fell into debt and his family were often on the verge of starvation. But when a roll of louis d'or came along, the scene changed, Mozart got drunk on champagne and tokay and was soon as badly off as ever. 'It is known how often he endangered his health, how many mornings he drank champagne with Schikaneder, how many nights he spent drinking punch and set to work again after midnight, without allowing his body the slightest chance of recuperation.'

These excesses were the cause of his death. Arnold adds a detail to the *Don Giovanni* overture story. Not only did Constanze supply him with punch as he wrote: he was already drunk on wine and punch when he sat down to write.[40]

The story of Mozart the drunkard and boon companion was now launched: it sailed triumphantly on through the nineteenth century. Nissen incorporated the relevant passages from Arnold word for word. Lyser's short stories, published in the 1840s, depict Mozart in taverns drinking with riff-raff, 'Creti und Pleti', Tom, Dick and Harry. The same story is repeated in Mörike's little novel and in Rau's three-decker. Anecdotes accumulated about Mozart composing in pubs, drinking beer and wine, kissing barmaids, playing skittles and billiards. The following is from the anonymous biography of the composer Gyrowetz of 1848 – it could even be an authentic memory:

[39] *MDB*, 499–500
[40] Arnold, *Mozarts Geist*, 65–7, 148

One evening it so happened that Mozart did not appear right at the beginning of the concert, and everyone had been waiting for him for some time, for he had promised to bring a new song for the lady of the house. Several servants were sent to look for him; at last one of them found him in a tavern . . . Mozart then remembered that he had not yet composed the song; he at once asked the servant to bring him a sheet of music paper – when this had been done, Mozart began to compose the song in the inn itself.[41]

The story of the *Don Giovanni* overture underwent further, contradictory elaboration in a memoir of Anton Genast published by his son in 1862. Mozart, some of the singers and Genast dined with a pleasure-loving priest; the food was good and the Hungarian wines even better. Mozart drank deep. At one in the morning, Genast and a friend escorted Mozart, singing – naturally it was the champagne aria from *Don Giovanni* – back through the streets to his lodging. The singing, the wine and the cold night air caused the composer to pass out: Genast and his friend slept on a sofa. In the middle of the night they were woken by powerful tones; Mozart was at his desk writing the overture.[42]

Jahn elaborated upon the dissipations with Schikaneder:

What he [Schikaneder] wanted in cultivation (he could barely write or reckon) he made up for in mother-wit . . . He was addicted to sensual gratification, a parasite and a spendthrift . . . The pressure of external circumstances, of growing domestic troubles, and the bitter feeling of failure and disappointed hope, combined with his own excitable nature to cause Mozart to seek for distraction and forgetfulness in the whirl of a pleasure-loving life. His wife was at Baden . . . her absence deprived his home life of any comfort, and drove him to take refuge among his theatrical friends. Folly and dissipation were the inevitable accompaniments of such an existence, and these soon reached the public ear, combining with the exaggerated

[41] *MDB*, 558–9
[42] *Acta mozartiana*, xxvii (1980), 83

accounts current of the loose life led by Schikaneder and his associates to cover Mozart's name for several months with an amount of obloquy beyond what he deserved.[43]

Jahn's authoritative account has cast its shadow over biographies right up to the present day. What is the basis of his magisterial pronouncement? He provides no references for the story of Mozart debauching with Schikaneder. Did he rely upon surviving oral traditions? The kind of data he had at his disposal is perhaps illustrated by his story of Mozart receiving wine from his neighbour, the freemason Loibl, while he was composing. Loibl's daughter told the story to Karajan who retailed it to Jahn.[44] Or is his account built upon the questionable tradition already outlined in this chapter? The earliest documentation I have found is Arnold's book of 1803, and we do not know where Arnold got his information. Jahn's portrait of Schikaneder is probably too black. He was indeed suspended from his masonic lodge in Regensburg because of a sexual scandal but he was something better than a dissipated scoundrel. He was a good businessman and organizer, for much of the time very successful. The repertory of his theatrical troupe was by no means entirely low comedy. He put on serious contemporary drama and was famed for his performance as Hamlet. He wrote his own plays and even Singspiels.[45]

Hummel is said to have stated on his deathbed in 1831 'I declare it to be untrue that Mozart abandoned himself to excess, except on those rare occasions on which he was enticed by Schikaneder, which had chiefly to do with the *Zauberflöte*'.[46] Sophie Haibl told Nissen that her brother-in-law drank until he was merry: she had never seen him

---

[43] Jahn, *Life of Mozart*, iii, 283, 285
[44] Jahn, ii, 307
[45] Emil Karl Blümml, *Aus Mozarts Freundes- und Familienkreis* (Vienna, Prague and Leipzig, 1923), 93, 96; Braunbehrens, *Mozart in Wien*, 395–402
[46] Jahn, ii, 271

drunk.[47] According to Kelly, 'He was remarkably fond of punch, of which beverage I have seen him take copious draughts'.[48] Nannerl's diary records that he once bought her punch to celebrate her birthday. In 1790 he wrote to his wife: 'At Regensburg we lunched magnificently to the accompaniment of divine music, we had angelic cooking and some glorious Moselle wine'.[49]

Passing these few and fugitive scraps of evidence in review leads to the conclusion that Mozart most certainly enjoyed a drink: but in spite of the large part drink has played in the Mozart legend, there is no trustworthy support for the notion that he regularly imbibed to excess.

*

There is much more evidence for the charge that Mozart was incompetent in money matters. At first sight the evidence also seems more reliable; certainly it goes back earlier, to the days immediately following his death. Four days later a newspaper was reporting that he had left many debts. And four days after that came the report that:

> Mozhart unfortunately had that indifference to his family circumstances which so often attaches to great minds. . . .This man's widow sits sighing on a sack of straw amidst her needy children and under a sizeable burden of debt. An administrative official gave ten gulden against Mozhart's watch, so that he could be buried.[50]

The sack of straw and the watch were pure fiction, but the debts were real enough. Presumably reports such as this inspired the reference to 'the great domestic chaos at and after his death' in the postscript to Nannerl's letter to

[47] Nissen, 672
[48] *MDB*, 530
[49] *LMF*, 942
[50] *MDB*, 420, 423–4

Schlichtegroll, and Schlichtegroll's own 'He had no capacity for domestic order and the fitting use of money'.[51]

'If the same fairness is exercised towards Mozart, as each man would like to experience towards himself, still the consequence will be that he will not be commemorated as a model of economy and thrift', wrote Niemetschek. He also told the story, which he doubtless heard from Constanze's own lips, that rumour had reached the Emperor that Mozart had died leaving debts of 30,000 gulden. She sought an audience, complained about the lies and rumours, and insisted that 3,000 gulden – still a considerable sum – would suffice to clear the debts.[52]

Rochlitz, partly from his own observations in Leipzig in 1789, built up a picture of a man who was careless about money. Mozart gave lavish tips to a bass singer who had pleased him, and to an old piano-tuner who had supplied him with a few strings. He let the choir in free to a sparsely attended concert, on which he then made no profit. A publisher pirated several of his works; Mozart simply commented, 'He's a rat'. Without naming names, Rochlitz was the first to put into circulation the story of Schikaneder's chicanery over *Die Zauberflöte*. The agreement was that Mozart would receive no fee, but would have sole right to sell the score to other houses. Schikaneder quietly sold the score himself.[53] He wrote things gratis for friends and even for poor travelling musicians.[54]

Rochlitz also narrates the tale of the Berlin job. The Prussian king offered Mozart a fat salary when he visited that capital in 1789.

> 'Shall I abandon my good Emperor?', said Mozart. But his friends in Vienna prevailed upon him, and he petitioned for his release. Joseph II replied 'Dear Mozart – you know what I think

[51] *MDB*, 462; Schlichtegroll, 30
[52] Niemtschek, 39–41
[53] *AMZ*, i (1798–9), 81–4 (7 November 1798)
[54] *AMZ*, i (1798–9), 146 (5 December 1798),

of the Italian musicians: and yet you want to abandon me?'
Mozart looked into his sad face, was moved, and stuttered out
that he would stay. 'But Mozart', one of his friends said afterwards, 'why did you not use the opportunity at least to request
a fixed salary?' 'Who the devil would think of such a thing at
such a moment?', replied Mozart.[55]

This story is suspicious. Mozart had in fact been receiving an
imperial salary from 1787. His letters home from Berlin make
no mention of an offer of a post, for which Rochlitz is the
original source. The accusation against Schikaneder may also
be unjust. It is documented that Mozart before his death and
Constanze after it were asking 100 ducats (450 gulden) for
copies of the score of *Die Zauberflöte*. A Leipzig newspaper
insisted in 1840 that Schikaneder had paid Mozart 100 ducats
for composing the opera.[56] But Rochlitz's stories are absorbed into Nissen's book, which adds a few more about
Mozart's gullibility in money matters.

Sophie Haibl told Nissen that when Mozart was in funds he
was all too ready to share them with others. But his choice of
friends, invited to join him at his table, was unfortunate. His
wife suffered in silence and suppressed her misgivings. He
was most abominably cheated by the clarinettist Anton
Stadler. He stole a pawnticket from Mozart's desk. When
Mozart received a payment of 50 ducats from the emperor,
Stadler asked to borrow it. Mozart needed the money himself,
so instead he lent Stadler two heavy repeating watches to
take to the pawnbroker, but when the day came to redeem
them, Stadler did not have the necessary cash. Mozart therefore gave him the 50 ducats after all, plus the pawnbroker's
interest. Stadler pocketed the money. Mozart merely told him
off, remained his friend and continued to entertain him.[57]

Remembering that Niemetschek as well as Nissen obtained
information from Constanze, it seems likely that one source

[55] *AMZ*, i (1798–9), 23 (10 October 1798)
[56] *NMD*, no.117; *Neue Zeitschrift für Musik*, xii (1840), no.45, 180
[57] Nissen, 674, 683

of the charge that Mozart was hopeless with money was the widow herself. Jahn surmised that she carried into her widowhood the rankling sense that her husband, for all his genius, had let her down badly in this respect.[58] The testimony of Constanze, the person most in a position to know, might be thought decisive; but the following assessment is not implausible. We are easily blinded by our preoccupations: Constanze's was money, for she had to run the household. Whenever money was concerned, she became an unreliable witness. Her tangled skein of deceptions about the Requiem has already been considered. She allowed Nissen to print the astonishing falsehood that she made no money out of Mozart's scores. She repeated the dubious story of the Berlin offer to the Novellos, including the misinformation that Mozart was receiving no salary whatever from Joseph II – 'it is to be hoped this generous sacrifice will not go unrewarded to his family by the Austrian court'.[59]

> Yet here I am still, and have gone through all this suffering . . . Mozart not only died poor, but left some debts, when the youngest son was 13 he took a benefit concert and the receipts went among the creditors – how few but the widow and child of a professional man would, after such a lapse of time, have dedicated the money to such a purpose, for it must be recollected they had nothing, except a trifling pension allowed by the Emperor of Austria – all Mozart's operas were either given, or stolen, the remainder of his music was sold for a mere trifle.[60]

The younger son will have been 13 in 1804; but already in 1798 Niemetschek said that the debts had been paid.[61] Indeed, in 1797, a few days after a benefit concert in Prague at which little Wolfgang performed, Constanze lent 3500

[58] Jahn, ii, 265n
[59] Novello, 81–2
[60] Novello, 98
[61] Niemtschek, 40

gulden to the Duscheks.[62] In 1792 the King of Prussia purchased eight scores from the widow for the amazingly generous sum of 3600 gulden.[63] After selling many scores to
Breitkopf & Härtel, she sold the remainder to André in 1799
for 3150 gulden.[64] It is not surprising that Niemetschek
wrote to Breitkopf & Härtel advising them not to believe
everything that Frau Mozart said.[65]

Of course Mozart had debts, and not only in the lean years
1788–90. In 1785 his father came to stay with him in Vienna
and was impressed by the size of the income he generated in
a whirl of activity, giving concerts and selling compositions.
'If my son *has no debts to pay*, I think that he can now lodge
2000 gulden in the bank'. Yet by the end of that year he was
seeking a loan from Hoffmeister, the music-publisher.[66]
Nevertheless an unprejudiced reading of the correspondence
turns up evidence suggesting that Mozart was not wholly a
gullible idiot in money matters. His own statement gives the
lie to the story of him turning down the Prussian offer
because he would not abandon his good emperor:

> Besides the Emperor is a niggard. If he wants me, he must pay
> for me, for the honour alone of serving him is not enough.
> Indeed, if he were to offer me 1000 gulden and some Count
> 2000, I should decline the former proposal with thanks and go
> to the Count – that is, of course, if it were a permanent
> arrangement.

His correspondence with his sister and brother-in-law about
the disposal of his father's estate gives a distinct impression of
a man with a sharp eye for the main chance.[67] He failed,
however, to join the Tonkünstler-Sozietät, which would have
given his wife a pension. His application was not processed

---

[62] *MDB*, 484–5
[63] *MDB*, 440–1
[64] *MDB*, 490
[65] Favier, 69
[66] *LMF*, 889n, 894
[67] *LMF*, 799–800, 827–8, 909–10

because he did not produce his baptismal certificate.[68] Presumably he never intended to die young.

The mainstream of Mozart biography has insisted upon his foolish extravagance. Certainly he adopted a high standard of living in Vienna. His passion for fine clothes and his costly wardrobe have already been mentioned. In 1783 the young couple gave a ball in their rooms. In 1785 he moved into a magnificent apartment at a rent of 500 gulden a year, more than his annual salary at Salzburg had been. The inventory at the time of his death reveals an expensively furnished apartment, with a billiard room and billiard table. He kept a horse, and in 1790 travelled to the coronation in Frankfurt in his own carriage, pawning his silver in order to finance the expedition.

According to the memoirs of the composer and Kapellmeister Destouches, recorded in 1815,

> Mozart bought six small Polish ponies which caused much comment; it was seemly only for princes, they said, to drive out with six horses. 'Yes', he said, 'if they *were* indeed horses; but these are only ponies, and there is no regulation about them'.

This is scarcely believable; from the same source comes the following:

> He was a passionate player of billiards, and played badly. Whenever a famous billiard-player arrived in Vienna, it was of more interest to him than the arrival of a famous musician. The latter, he opined, would come to him all right, the former he looked up himself; he played for high stakes, whole nights long.[69]

This is no more than the after-dinner gossip furnished by a guest to repay his host. There is no other contemporary or near-contemporary evidence that Mozart gambled away his

[68] H. C. Robbins Landon, *Mozart: The Golden Years* (London, 1989), 124
[69] *MDB*, 515–6

substance. Given all the malicious gossip about him, if he had done so we would surely know. Yet Schurig, who had been told by Wyzewa that there were notes in Mozart's handwriting containing long rows of 'Amben und Ternen' (twos and threes? doubles and triples?) argued that Mozart was a keen gambler.[70] More recently it has been argued that Mozart earned a vast income – 10,000 gulden a year or more – and gambled it away on cards.[71] Any sober historian cannot but be astonished at the presentation of so extravagant a hypothesis with no better evidence than the gossiping of Destouches. The estimate of Mozart's income is absurdly inflated. Kraemer thinks that his theory makes sense of Mozart's agonized begging letters to his fellow-mason and friend, the Viennese merchant Puchberg. He was afraid of the consequences of failing to pay his debts of honour. But this does not square with Mozart's plea to Puchberg: 'You certainly cannot doubt my integrity, for you know me too well for that. Nor can you distrust my assurances, my behaviour or my mode of life, as you are well acquainted with my manner of living and my conduct'.[72]

It has been surmised that Mozart's extravagance and debts flowed from a vain attempt to emulate the lifestyle of his Viennese friends, wealthy merchants and actors and opera singers who enjoyed higher salaries than he received or could expect.[73] A balance sheet of Mozart's finances will have to wait until a later chapter. For the time being, the thought should be entertained that Mozart's high spending was not folly, but part of a rational strategy. He wished to establish himself, not as a musician-servant like his father, but as a high-status professional, mixing with aristocrats and

---

[70] Schurig, ii, 396; Kreitmeier, *Characterzeichnung*, 175
[71] Uwe Kraemer, 'Wer hat Mozart verhungern lassen?', *Musica*, xxx (1976), 203–11
[72] *LMF*, 931–2
[73] Andrew Steptoe, 'Mozart and poverty: a Re-examination of the evidence', *Musical Times*, cxxv (1984), 199; Rudloph Angermüller, *"Auf Ehre und Credit": Die Finanzen des W. A. Mozart* (Salzburg, 1983), 5

courtiers, paid accordingly. In order to achieve this, he had to keep up appearances, dressing well, living in a handsome apartment, travelling in his own carriage, giving and lending his money open-handedly. Perhaps it made sense to get into debt in order to keep this up. Such behaviour is recorded among artists of the Italian Renaissance, who were also trying to establish a new status for themselves.[74] What was rational for a nineteenth-century shopkeeper may not have been rational for an eighteenth-century courtier. Extravagance and debts did not have the same social and personal meaning in 1791 as in 1891, or 1991.

Mozart has been accused of irregularity and unreliability in his work. When he left Salzburg service, his post as organist was given to Michael Haydn, with the additional stipulation 'that he show more diligence, instruct the chapel boys, and compose more often for our Cathedral and chamber music'. This looks more like a criticism of Mozart's diligence than of Haydn's. According to Schlichtegroll, he composed from six or seven o'clock in the morning until ten, usually in bed, but not during the main part of the day unless he had a deadline to meet. Stendhal repeats this, commenting, or rather adding, that his manner of working was very unequal.[75]

Many stories tell of him getting works ready at the very last minute. The most celebrated of these concerns the overture to *Don Giovanni*. There are a number of slightly differing versions; the exact truth will never be known. Niemetschek says that it was composed during the night before the first performance, and copied just in time: the orchestra played it without rehearsal. Rochlitz tells two versions, the first agreeing with Niemetschek. His second version relates that the

---

[74] P. Burke, *Tradition and Innovation in Renaissance Italy* (London, 1974), 83–96
[75] *NMD*, no.49; Schlichtegroll, 32; Stendhal, 291

overture was composed not one but two nights before the première, but after the dress rehearsal.

Nissen says the night before; the opera was due to begin at 7 but the parts, full of blotting-sand, did not arrive until 7.45. The orchestra sight-read the first performance. 'During the introduction Mozart said to some who were standing near him: "True, a lot of notes fell under the music-stands, but for all that the overture went off really well".'[76] Finally, Genast related that the overture was composed on the night before the dress rehearsal.

Rochlitz tells the story of his dilatoriness in writing a piano and violin sonata, which he was to perform before Joseph II with the violinist Strinasacchi. He wrote out her part at the last moment but did not have time for his own; the Emperor observed through his opera-glasses that Mozart was playing with blank music-paper before him.[77]

Nissen relates that a certain nobleman had asked Mozart to compose a dance for a ball; Mozart agreed, but no dance came. As the time drew near, the nobleman resolved on a strategy. He invited Mozart to dinner, but gave him a time one hour before the other guests were due to arrive. When Mozart came, he was shut in a room with paper and ink; by dinner time he had produced not one dance but four.[78]

There is a story that he was late with the overture to *La clemenza di Tito*. The story of his composing *Die Zauberflöte* while shut in a summerhouse is another example of his alleged reluctance to work. If these stories are meant to indicate that he was lazy, this cannot be believed, even though his father accuses him of laziness on one occasion.[79] The size and quality of his output refute the charge. But it cannot be doubted that he put off until the last possible moment and beyond it. Concerning *Figaro*, Leopold wrote to

[76] Nissen, 520–1
[77] *AMZ*, i (1798–9), 290 (6 February 1799)
[78] Nissen, 561
[79] *LMF*, 490

Nannerl: 'And no doubt according to his charming habit he has kept on postponing matters and has let the time slip by'.[80] *Don Giovanni* was not ready on time, and *Figaro* had to be performed instead. Mozart blamed the singers and the management.[81] The first performance of *Idomeneo* also was postponed. Mozart wrote to his father:

> It is true that during the last few days I had to compose the greater and most difficult part of my opera; yet this was not from laziness or negligence – but because I had spent a fortnight without writing a note, simply because I found it *impossible to do so*. Of course I had written it, but not in a clean copy. I admit that I lost a great deal of time in this way.[82]

Mozart did not work like Trollope, who sat down each day to write a set quota of words. It is possible that he worked best under pressure. He composed in his head while doing other things – according to Constanze, while travelling, while playing billiards or skittles – but put off the tedious, mechanical work of getting the notes on paper.[83] However he was not always unmethodical. He preserved his scores in good order through all his house-moves, and kept his thematic catalogue with meticulous care.[84]

Jahn argued that Mozart was unreliable as a teacher:

> Mozart was never a fashionable and well-paid music-master in Vienna, such as Steffan, Kozeluch or Righini. This may excite surprise, since he was so distinguished a pianist, but he was wanting in the patience and pliability necessary, and perhaps also in steadiness and regularity.
>
> Mozart's musical instruction was sure to be desultory. Freystädler relates that he generally received Mozart's directions and corrections of his musical exercises sitting at a side-

[80] *LMF*, 893
[81] *LMF*, 911–12
[82] *LMF*, 737
[83] Nissen, 559–61, 646–8; Novello, 95
[84] Alec Hyatt King, *Mozart: a Biography with a Survey of Books, Editions and Recordings* (London, 1970), 51

table, while a game of bowls was going on. Attwood also tells us that Mozart sometimes persuaded him to join in a game of billiards instead of taking a lesson.[85]

This also must be taken with a pinch of salt. Mozart's teaching 'was sure to be desultory' in the eyes of those having a fixed idea about his general negligence. A large exercise book of over 280 pages reveals the pains he lavished on Attwood, his composition pupil; there is a similar one for Stadler's niece.[86]

✻

After the accusation of perpetual childishness, the most serious charge against Mozart is that he was so incompetent at human relationships that he ruined his professional career. Hence the poverty, overwork and untimely end. He lacked the strong elbows necessary to clear a path through life. Outside his music he was wanting in energy and determination. Instead of asserting himself and dominating events he was passive and fatalistic.[87] When Mozart was in Paris, Baron Grimm wrote to Leopold:

> He is too trusting, too inactive, too easy to catch, too little intent on the means that lead to fortune. To make an impression here one has to be artful, enterprising, daring. To make his fortune I wish he had but half his talent and twice as much shrewdness.[88]

Leopold echoed this judgment a month later.[89] Without doubt the most damaging documented contemporary criticisms of Mozart the man come from his own father. Leopold

[85] Jahn, ii, 278–81
[86] King, 38; K. Kramer, 'Strittige Fragen in der Mozart-Biographie', Acta mozartiana, xxiii (1976), 79–81
[87] Kreitmeier, 192; Schiedermair, 160
[88] MDB, 177
[89] LMF, 605

thought that his son exhibited a dangerous combination of pride and naivete:

> You have a little too much *pride and self-love*; and secondly, you immediately make yourself too *familiar* and open your heart to everyone; in short! wishing to be unconstrained and natural, you fall into being all too unreserved . . . Your pride and self-love . . . are only touched when you do not at once get the appreciation you deserve. You think that even those who do not know you, ought to see by your face that you are a man of genius! But when it comes to flatterers who, in order to bend you to their selfish purposes, praise you to the skies, you open your heart with the greatest ease and believe them as you do the Bible.[90]

Mozart was also accused of having a sharp and tactless tongue, which made him many enemies. There are plenty of hints to this effect in Niemetschek: he was unworldly and incapable of currying favour; he was guileless; he was open and candid, often offended the *amour-propre* of others and thereby made many an enemy.[91] Niemetschek and Rochlitz independently tell stories of his causing offence by making his feelings known to an audience which was not listening with sufficient quiet and attention.[92] Rochlitz is the original source of the well-known story that Mozart liked to entertain the company by performing satirical impressions of other composers, virtuosos and singers. Sometimes this went beyond a joke.[93] His pupil Hummel later confirmed that 'in the circle of his good friends he could grow quite merry, lively, witty, even at times and on certain subjects satirical!'[94]

The substance of this charge can easily be believed. Mozart's letters are full of the most devastating remarks about

[90] *LMF*, 492–3; see also 815–6
[91] Niemtschek, 30, 60–2
[92] Niemtschek, 57; *AMZ*, i (1798–9), 50–51 (24 October 1798)
[93] *AMZ*, iii (1800–01), 591 (27 May 1801)
[94] *MDB*, 527

his contemporaries, sometimes witty, but often disturbingly uncharitable. The Bohemian composer Mysliveček was a longstanding friend of the Mozarts: Mozart had recently met him dying in the Duke Clemens hospital, Munich, of syphilis, his face partly eaten away. Mozart wrote to a friend about the search for a new Kapellmeister for Salzburg:

> It will not do to allow order, peace and co-operation to gain the upper hand in the orchestra, or the mischief will spread still further and in the long run become irremediable. Are there really no ancient periwigs with asses' ears, no lousy heads available, who could restore the concern to its former disabled condition? I shall certainly do my best in the matter. Tomorrow I intend to hire a carriage for the day and drive round all the hospitals and infirmaries and see if I can't dredge up someone for them. Why were they so careless as to let Mysliveček give them the slip? – and he was so near too! He would have been a fat morsel for them. It would not be easy to get someone like him and someone moreover who had just left the Duke Clemens Conservatorio! He would have been the man to terrify the whole court orchestra by his presence.[95]

Einstein comments upon the 'spitefulness that is a stain upon his letters' with reference to his remark 'that godless arch-rascal Voltaire has pegged out like a dog, like a beast! That is his reward'.

> One is continually astonished and often distressed to encounter in the letters . . . the most merciless reports about musical contemporaries. Praise for musicians, even for those to whom Mozart owed much . . . is scanty . . . His wicked tongue was not unknown. In 1791 Joseph Haydn heard in London that Mozart had made uncomplimentary remarks about him. 'I forgive him',

---

[95] *LMF*, 594–5

he said. Although the rumour was surely not true, it is distressing that Haydn could assume that it was.[96]

Taking these judgments of his character as a guide, it is easy to weave a story of self-destruction. Biographers have built such a story above all around the first occasion when Mozart was let out more or less on his own – his expedition with his mother to Paris in quest of an appointment. The long and detailed correspondence puts this episode under a brilliant spotlight. We see the young man in Munich, blurting out an embarrassed petition to the elector, who brushes him off. In Augsburg he is humiliated by the sons of wealthy burgesses. In Mannheim, a musical Mecca, he is drawn into the gossiping against Vogler, the Kapellmeister and royal favourite, allowing his sharp tongue to run away with him. He makes an exhibition of himself when playing the organ at mass before the royal household. No job is offered to him. He is flattered by the deferential friendship of the Weber family, spends his time coaching Aloysia, and dreams of a virtuoso tour with her.

In Paris people take advantage of him. The Comte de Guines does not pay him in full for lessons to his daughter. He supplies the ballet-master Noverre with compositions for which he receives neither payment nor public acknowledgement. He neglects to follow up a possibility of appointment as organist at Versailles, perhaps because he cannot bear the thought of being separated from Aloysia. He writes a sinfonia concertante which is not performed because (and this is his own explanation) he made an enemy of the composer Cambini.

Many have thought that his breach with Colloredo further revealed his unworldliness and immaturity. Colloredo was not a satanic tyrant, but a progressive, Josephinian ruler.

---

[96] Einstein, 45, 97. There is perhaps a slight excuse for Mozart with respect to the remark about Voltaire. Voltaire did in fact die a sordid, neglected, painful death, and Mozart probably knew: see Kramer, 'Strittige Fragen', 81

Mozart could have been more tactful and complaisant; instead he revealed himself as insolent and insubordinate, a bad employee. He wrote defending his conduct to his father: 'You are altogether mistaken if you think that I shall get a bad name with the Emperor and the nobility, for the Archbishop is detested here – and most of all by the Emperor'.[97] This seems to demonstrate a remarkable lack of judgment. To suppose that, just because they disliked Colloredo, the Imperial family and the nobility would be favourably inclined towards a musician, a servant, who had rebelled against his master, is surely naïve.

Mozart did not become more diplomatic once he had settled in Vienna. Soon his father heard rumours that 'the whole world declares that by my boasting and criticizing I have made enemies of the professors of music and of many others'.[98] A tournament of virtuosity before the Emperor was arranged between Mozart and Clementi, perhaps Mozart's equal as a pianist.[99] Clementi spoke generously about Mozart, but Mozart did not reciprocate: 'He is an excellent cembalo-player, but that is all. He has great facility with his right hand. His star passages are thirds. Apart from this, he has not a farthing's worth of taste or feeling; he is a mere mechanicus'.[100]

According to Rochlitz, when he was in Leipzig visiting the Thomaskantor, Johann Friedrich Doles, he criticized a mass (possibly by Doles's friend Johann Georg Naumann)[101] which Doles admired, making fun of it by persuading the company to sing it to risible words.[102] Rochlitz also relates

[97] *LMF*, 729
[98] *LMF*, 811
[99] Arthur Hutchings, *Mozart: the Man: the Musician* (London, 1976), 66–7
[100] *LMF*, 793
[101] Otto Keller, *Wolfgang Amadeus Mozart: sein Lebensgang nach den neuesten Quellen geschildert* (Berlin, 1926), 156, claims that the mass was by Naumann.
[102] *AMZ*, iii (1800–01), 493–4 (15 April 1801)

that Mozart told Frederick William II of Prussia that his orchestra would do better if the players played together.[103]

Mozart's incompetence at human relationships even caused an irreparable breach with his father, the father who had sacrificed so much to launch the career of the son he worshipped. Einstein remarks that in his latter years, Leopold in his letters to Nannerl could not bring himself to refer to Mozart as 'my son', or even 'Wolfgang'; instead, he put 'your brother', as if disclaiming any relationship. According to Schurig, he was gauche, rather petty bourgeois, a poor devil. Boschot judges him to have been out of his depth in polite society, fantastic, maladroit, brusque, giving an impression of arrogance.[104] Strangers sometimes took him for a lackey or an artisan. Consequently he gravitated increasingly to low company – Schikaneder, Leutgeb the cheesemonger and horn player, the Baden choirmaster Stoll, Süßmayr, Stadler the clarinettist, his brother-in-law Hofer the violinist. Here his naïvety, tactlessness and coarse humour would not be out of place.

The tale of Mozart's ineptitude in human relations is a vital ingredient in the thesis of self-destruction. But others have told an opposite, or nearly opposite story. The nineteenth-century novels of Mörike and Rau depict him as a sociable, lovable man, mixing on equal terms with the Viennese aristocracy and indeed lionized. Not only romantic novelists have thought this. One twentieth-century biographer, while admitting that a genius inevitably makes enemies because he is incapable of praising rubbish and pretending to enjoy inferior music, insists that Mozart was

> the rarest of all human beings, a saint who is not a bore; a nature so sound, sweet and passionate that I, personally, have for many years felt that among all the great artists of history

[103] *AMZ*, i (1798–9), 22 (10 October 1798)
[104] Schurig, ii, 380, 391, 397; Boschot, 98

Mozart and Shakespeare were the only ones whose moral superiority strikes to the core of one's being.[105]

He never failed in compassion and his sympathy was universal. Others have said that he had the ability to mix at all levels of society and that far from gravitating to low company (what a snobbish charge anyway!) he continued to move in aristocratic circles.[106]

Many have commented on the tactfulness with which he communicated the news of his mother's death to his father and sister. It is questionable whether his relations with his father were bad in later years. He warmly invited his father to visit him in Vienna, and Leopold's letters to Nannerl suggest he had a very good holiday, overstaying his leave of absence. It is true that Leopold often refers to Mozart in his letters to Nannerl as 'your brother' but nothing should be read into this. In his letters to Mozart he also refers to Nannerl as 'your sister' and in two letters he writes of 'my son'.[107]

Early biographies do not give a straightforward picture of a tactless fool. According to Niemetschek and Rochlitz, the enemies, if such there were, are the converse of the good friends, both procured by Mozart's warm and open nature. Stories abound of Mozart's kindness and modesty. Abbé Stadler spoke to the Novellos of Mozart as a pleasant friend. Kelly's well-known reminiscences depict him as delightful company. 'Mozart was very liberal in giving praise to those who deserved it; but felt a thorough contempt for insolent mediocrity.'[108] Lyser, who claimed that he had diligently collected Viennese memories, reported that Mozart was no *Salonmensch* but could move with ease in the highest circles.[109] All of these posthumous reports are more or less suspect, for various reasons; and it is impossible to ignore the

[105] W. J. Turner, *Mozart: the Man and his Works* (London, 1938), 123, 267–8
[106] Paumgartner, *Mozart*, 30, 261; Braunbehrens, 169
[107] *LMF*, 883, 884
[108] Novello, 166; *MDB*, 531
[109] Kayser, 6

copper-bottomed evidence in the letters of Mozart's capacity for uncharitable sharpness. Nevertheless an open-minded survey of the sources suggests a complex verdict about a complex man, who could be at once kind and cruel, frank and deceitful, tactful and tactless.

Mozart never managed to land a highly paid post; but this hardly proves unworldliness and incompetence. He got 800 florins as Imperial composer: Gluck, his predecessor, had received 2000. But Gluck did not get his big salary until he was sixty years old and a European celebrity; at Mozart's age he had struggled to earn a living. Much has been made of the failure of the trip to Paris, when Mozart was let out without Leopold for the first time. But when in previous years he went on tour with his father, seeking appointments in Milan, Florence, Vienna and Munich, the story was also one of failure. When in 1771 Archduke Ferdinand of Milan thought of employing Mozart, his mother, the Empress Maria Theresa advised him not to hire useless people who go about the world like beggars.[110] In the light of this it is difficult to sustain a contrast between bold, sensible, enterprising and worldly Leopold and irresolute, tactless and ineffectual Wolfgang. Leopold himself failed to obtain the Salzburg Kapellmeistership three times.

> It now depends solely on your good sense and your way of life whether you die as an ordinary musician, utterly forgotten by the world, or as a famous Kapellmeister, of whom posterity will read – whether, captured by some woman, you die bedded on straw in an attic full of starving children, or whether, after a Christian life spent in contentment, honour and renown, you leave the world with your family well provided for and your name respected by all.[111]

This was Leopold's advice: but perhaps Mozart consciously and clear-sightedly rejected his father's plan for his life and

[110] *MDB*, 138,
[111] *LMF*, 475

death, preferring the difficult but forward-looking career of a freelance and independent artist. Maybe he did not wish to become 'a super-Leopold, a monumental, a colossal petit-bourgeois', and maybe he was right.[112]

A major ingredient of the story of Mozart, beast and angel concerns his relations with women. The next chapter will consider this, and then attempt to sum up this story as a whole.

---

[112] Jean and Brigitte Massin, *Wolfgang Amadeus Mozart* (Paris, 1959), 223

Chapter V

Eve's part in his downfall

There are two stories about Mozart and women. One, part of the image of him as sensuous and dissipated, is the story of Mozart the philanderer. The other is the story of a weak man who tragically fell victim to women's wiles. These stories are not as opposite as they seem, for they mirror one of the oldest archetypes. Woman as Eve the temptress deprived man of his immortality. The myth binds together sex and death.

Instead of tracing the legend of Mozart's love-life forward from the earliest hints, let us reverse the procedure and hunt it back.

> [Constanze] attested after his death that his friendship with fair pupils or fair singers sometimes led to infidelities which he at once confessed to her and which she freely forgave.[1]

Apparently he also seduced the servants:

> Some of the less slatternly ones may have been sent about their business by Constanze in little fiery fits of jealousy, more or less justified. For oddly enough – and yet understandably in a way – the young man who before his marriage had prided himself on his fastidiousness, now began to play with paltry temptations to extra-marital diversions, some of them none too dainty. How far his little infidelities went we do not know at all definitely, but we hear that before long Constanze had to listen, half dismayed and half amused, to lighthearted and loose-tongued confessions from a husband who was so entertainingly frank

[1] John Naglee Burk, *Mozart and his Music* (New York, 1959), 189

and at the same time so sincerely repentant that she could never refuse him an impulsively affectionate forgiveness.[2]

These narrations, from 1959 and 1935 respectively, might convince an unwary reader. The second is so specific, and both convey the impression that they rely upon the testimony of the widow herself, who could scarcely have had a motive to lie about this. But where does the information come from? Paumgartner, writing in 1927, reported that Constanze was willing to forgive affairs with servant girls – 'Stubenmädeleien', she called them – but not with artistic or educated women who might be a challenge to herself.[3] The same information is to be found in Abert's standard biography of 1919 and Schurig's of 1913. Belmonte's study of Mozart and women of 1905 recounts the 'Stubenmädeleien' story, adding that Constanze did not always forgive him readily; according to her sister there were furious rows.[4]

Somewhere about here, part of the trail goes to ground. I can find no earlier reference to seducing the servants. Where did Belmonte get it from? At one point he refers to 'Salzburg tradition', and informs us that he has gleaned family traditions from the granddaughter of Joseph Lange, who married Aloysia Weber, Mozart's sister-in-law. But what possible value can be attached to stray oral traditions, recorded over a century after the alleged events? The other part of the trail, the violent rows about Mozart's affairs, can however be traced back further – to no less an authority than the classic scholarly biography of Otto Jahn of 1856:

> 'He was so good, it was impossible to be angry with him; one was obliged to forgive him.' Her sister, however, betrays that Constanze was not always so patient, and that there were occasional violent outbreaks.[5]

[2] Eric Blom, *Mozart* (1935) (London, 1962), 120
[3] Paumgartner, *Mozart*, 273
[4] Carola Belmonte, *Die Frauen im Leben Mozarts* (Augsburg, 1905), 102
[5] Jahn, *Life of Mozart*, ii, 269

Many details of Mozart's alleged amorous entanglements are preserved in Jahn, and a good many stories were published in the 1840s, to which we must return in a moment. But for the time being let us stick to the trail of his confessions to Constanze. Yet another part of it has now come to a dead end. I can find no earlier reference to the violent rows. Jahn had collected oral traditions in Vienna and Salzburg, so perhaps his uncited source lies there. But if the sister in question was Sophie, it is strange that the sources which record Sophie's reminiscences – Nissen, Holmes and Lyser – make no mention of it.

We are still hot on the trail of Constanze's forgiveness, and two passages from Nissen lead us to think that we have cornered our quarry. One of them tells that he loved his wife truly, and told her everything, even his little sins, which she forgave. According to the other, he indulged in many gallantries outside marriage which his good wife willingly overlooked.[6] But this passage is simply plagiarized from Arnold's little book of 1803:

> At the same time he was a married man, fathered four children, loved his wife dearly and also outside the marriage bed indulged in many gallantries with pretty actresses and such fine maidens and married women, which his good wife gladly overlooked.[7]

As was argued in the first chapter, the fact that material from other writers was scissors-and-pasted into Nissen cannot be taken to prove that Nissen and Constanze endorsed that material, much less that it told the truth. This is one of the few scraps of information in Arnold not plagiarized from Niemetschek – and Arnold gets the number of children wrong. In fact it may be nothing more than an imaginative expansion of Niemetschek: 'He loved her truly, confided everything to her, even his petty sins – and she rewarded him

---

[6] Nissen, *Biographie*, 690, 569
[7] Arnold, *Mozarts Geist*, 65

1. The best-known portrait of Mozart, as we would like to see him, sensitive and serious. By his brother-in-law, Joseph Lange, probably painted c.1789–90. An idealization?

2. A beautiful portrait of Constanze as Frau Mozart. But has Joseph Lange prettified her?

3. *Spitzer's miniature of Constanze of 1826, three years before the Novellos visited her. It hides her age (early 60s) but suggests her strength.*

4. *A less idealized picture, by Doris Stock, of Mozart during his expedition from Berlin, 1789.*

5. *Anonymous painting of Mozart's lodge, c.1790. Some have optimistically persuaded themselves that the figure in the bottom right-hand corner is the composer.*

6. *The rehearsal of the Requiem on Mozart's last day – a senti-mental nineteenth-century vision of the death-bed. But it cannot have been like this. The story is highly dubious, and Mozart would not have been able to sit and conduct.*

REQUIEM

7.   *The legend of his death in an odour of sanctity. Frontispiece of the first edition of the Requiem, Breitkopf & Härtel, 1802. Is the weeping woman meant to be Constanze? In fact she did not attempt to visit his tomb until 1808 or 9. She did not find it; it had never been marked with a cross or stone.*

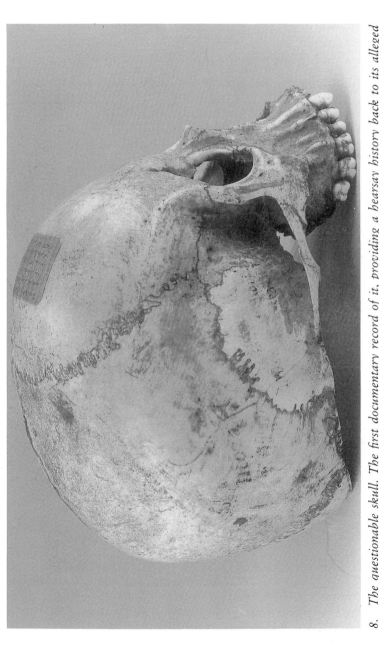

8. *The questionable skull. The first documentary record of it, providing a hearsay history back to its alleged recovery from the earth in 1801, dates from 1875. The results of a major new inquiry are expected in this*

9. *Probably the last notes Mozart wrote, in the 'Lacrymosa' of the Requiem.*

10. The house in the Raubensteingasse where Mozart died, probably in the first-storey corner room on the left.

with tenderness and true care'.[8] This is the source also of
the first passage in Nissen mentioned above. Here at last, it
may be surmised, is Constanze's own testimony, given to and
recorded by Niemetschek; here is the seed out of which it all
grows. But it does not prove that Mozart was a philanderer.
'Petty sins' is unspecific. The sowing of wild oats is a possible
meaning; but, if Constanze really did feel aggrieved about
money, it might mean that instead.

Apart from this tradition stemming from Niemetschek, a
wealth of stories and speculations gradually appeared in
print, most of them half a century or more after Mozart's
death. No doubt some of them were based on the gossip of
his contemporaries; but none of them can be securely
anchored in the testimony of a witness who was in a position
to know.

Suard's 'Anecdotes sur Mozart' of 1804 not only claim that
he indulged in extra-marital affairs. Suard also relates and
disputes a rumour that Mozart was persuaded to write *Die
Zauberflöte* by a woman of the theatre who gave him her
favours in return and a fatal illness in the process.[9] This
story was amplified in an anonymous article of 1857 which
named Barbara Gerl, the first Papagena.[10] But the 'Joseph
Deiner' memoirs point the finger at the first Pamina, Anna
Gottlieb, still living in 1856 at the age of 88, as does Lyser in
the *Mozart-Album* of that year.[11] The fanciful may imagine
for themselves what went on in Schikaneder's wooden summerhouse, where Mozart is said to have composed the opera.

In 1827 Zelter remarked to Goethe in a letter that Mozart
had destroyed his health by womanizing.[12] In 1829 the
banker Henickstein, whose sister had been one of Mozart's

---

[8] Niemtschek, 64
[9] *MDB*, 498
[10] Chailley, *The Magic Flute*, 303–4
[11] *MDB*, 654; Kayser, *Mozart-Album*, 85. Lyser claims to have obtained his
information from the first Pamina herself, but refers to her as Mme Uhlich.
[12] Schurig, *Konstanze Mozart*, 146

piano pupils, told the Novellos that Mozart was always in love with his pupils and that he would not take pains with any he did not love. According to Stendhal, the first Don Giovanni, Luigi Bassi, told him in 1813 that Mozart 'was very popular with the ladies, in spite of his small size; but he had a most unusual face, and he could cast a spell on any woman with his eyes'.[13]

The most damaging scandal associated with Mozart's name was the Hofdemel affair. Hofdemel, a government official and lodge-brother of Mozart's, had lent the composer money. His wife was Mozart's piano pupil. The day after Mozart's death he attacked his wife, who was pregnant, with a knife, severely wounding her about the face and neck. Then he cut his own throat. A short story published in 1841, 'Mozart and his lady friend', is obviously based on this incident although it does not name the Hofdemels.[14] According to the story, the Baron is jealous of his wife's (Platonic) adoration for the dying Mozart; he is also a miser. He asks his wife to lend him 3000 florins. She has to confess that she has already lent the money to Mozart; part indeed she has paid for the Requiem, which she has secretly commissioned in order to help him out. The Baron is furious but consoled by the doctor's statement that Mozart will not die. The doctor meant that Mozart's fame will be immortal, but the Baron has understood him literally. Friends burst in to announce Mozart's death: the Baron realizes that the money is gone for ever. Left alone, they quarrel. The wife admits she has kissed Mozart's hand and forehead, and her husband insults her. She throws her wine at him, and he lunges with a table-knife, wounding her. She faints and he cuts his throat.

The author insists that the story is a true one, already leaked in the press. But it contains details that are patently

[13] Novello, 144, 150; *NMD*, entry for 1787
[14] L. Schefer, 'Mozart und seine Freundin', *Orpheus*, ii (1841), 273–339. The earlier press reports claimed by Schefer have not been found. When John questioned Schefer, by then an old man, he could not remember his sources.

false, such as the attribution of the commissioning of the Requiem to Frau Hofdemel instead of to Count Walsegg. It seems likely however that rumours had been around, perhaps since the suicide. According to Jahn, Beethoven once refused to play before the widow Hofdemel because she had been Mozart's mistress.[15] Jahn and most subsequent scholars have not credited the story.

An unusually rich vein of gossip appeared concerning the Prague connection and the première of *Don Giovanni*. According to Lyser in the *Mozart-Album* of 1856, Mozart was Josepha Duschek's 'Anbeter' or 'Cicisbeo' – recognized admirer (platonic, Lyser unconvincingly adds). He had a passion for Teresa Saporiti, the first Donna Anna. She remarked on one occasion on his unprepossessing appearance. Caterina Bondini, the first Zerlina, reported this to him, so as to transfer his attentions to herself: he had an especially long relationship with her.[16]

According to Rochlitz, when Mozart arrived in Berlin in 1789 *Die Entführung* was being performed. He entered the theatre unannounced, drew attention to himself by his travelling garb and interjections when he did not like the performance, and finally brought the whole thing to a halt by shouting out: 'Damn it – why won't you play D natural!'. The part of Blonde was being sung by Madame Baranius, a very attractive actress (who had been the king's mistress). She was reluctant to sing in front of the composer. 'Madame', he said to her, 'what nonsense is this? You have sung gloriously, really gloriously: and – so that you can be even better in the future, I will go through the part with you myself!'[17] Perhaps

[15] Otto Jahn, *Gesammelte Aufsätze über Musik* (Leipzig, 1866), 230–5. Jahn first heard of the affair in 1852 from Karl Czerny, Beethoven's piano pupil. Czerny's father had known Frau Hofdemel well. No testimony other than this and Schefer's story links Mozart to the Hofdemel tragedy. No testimony suggests that Hofdemel murdered Mozart, as Francis Carr claims, in his *Mozart and Constance* (London, 1983)
[16] Kayser, 18–19, 24–5, 85
[17] *AMZ*, i (179809), 21–2 (10 October 1798)

at this point Rochlitz withheld part of the gossip, perhaps others embroidered his story. Jahn says that, 'according to old tradition in Berlin', Mozart became deeply involved with her, and it cost his friends much trouble to extricate him. Apparently this tradition, which Jahn doubts, did not get into print until 1856.[18]

Some of this gossip has a suspiciously predictable look to it: he had an affair with Henriette Baranius, who was singing the role of the pert Blondchen in an opera about a harem, another with Barbara Gerl, who was playing Papagena, always portrayed as sexy; and when he went to Prague to mount the first performance of *Don Giovanni* he behaved like his hero.

The list of women with whom Mozart is alleged to have had an affair has continued to grow since 1856. The first Susanna was Nancy Storace, a very beautiful singer, separated from her brutal husband; she lived unmarried with Francesco Benucci, the original Figaro in Mozart's opera, Lord Barnard and John Braham the singer, and may even have been a mistress of the Prince of Wales (the future Prince Regent). The tale of Mozart's love for her is based upon the aria with piano and orchestral accompaniment, '*Ch'io mi scordi di te*' K505 which he composed 'For Mselle Storace and myself' – a 'declaration of love in music' – and upon the allegation that she kept his letters for her own eyes only, destroying them before her death.[19] All this is circumstantial and speculative.

It has been said that he had an 'amitié amoureuse' with his pupil Frau von Trattner. There was perhaps a scandal and the affair broke up in the autumn of 1784. The evidence cited for this is the Piano Sonata in C minor and fantasia in that key, dedicated to her and published in autumn 1784 and spring

[18] Jahn, *Life of Mozart*, iii, 234
[19] Einstein, 85. Nancy Storace's relationship with the Prince is touched upon in Curtis Price, 'Italian Opera and Arson in Late Eighteenth-Century London', *Journal of the American Musicological Society*, xlii (1989), 66–7, 70, 72

1785 – 'tragic works impregnated with the most unmistake-able passion'. He sent her two letters about how they should be played which she refused to hand over to Constanze after Mozart's death and which are now lost.[20] This is the story: in fact, it was not Thérèse von Trattner who refused to hand over these letters but her heirs. They had not been kept secret: Niemetschek had seen one of them, and Constanze herself may have read them.[21]

It has been suggested that he had carnal knowledge of his cousin, on the basis of possible sexual innuendo in his letters to her and his remark 'A propos, since I left Augsburg, I have not taken off my trousers, except at night before going to bed'.[22] It is fitting to conclude with one final allegation that he deflowered an unmarried woman – Constanze herself. Schurig suggests that this is why he had to marry her. It has also been surmised, on the basis of no evidence whatsoever, that she fled to the home of Baroness Waldstätten because Mozart had made her pregnant and that the illness for which Mozart pledged the C minor Mass K427, should she recover, was a miscarriage.[23]

Where Mozart's sex life is concerned, the authorial imagin-ation has worked overtime. It would be wrong and indeed anachronistic to embrace the opposite extreme, reconstruct-ing him on a nineteenth-century petty bourgeois model of respectability and marital fidelity. Insofar as eighteenth-century court society permitted sexual freedom, no doubt Mozart made use of that freedom. But what hard facts on this topic can be gleaned from the letters? Two of them, both by Mozart himself and both from the beginning of his Vienna period, show that there was gossip about him during his life. Someone has said that Mozart only left Salzburg for the Viennese women, and Leopold has heard that his son danced

[20] Massin, *Wolfgang Amadeus Mozart*, 426, 976
[21] Niemtschek, 59; Schurig, *Konstanze Mozart*, 22
[22] *LMF*, 403; Wolfgang Hildesheimer, *Mozart* (1977) (London, 1983), 63
[23] Massin, 389; Schurig, *Wolfgang Amadé Mozart*, ii, 91

with a courtesan at a ball.[24] There is a letter, to Baroness Waldstätten, suggesting that Mozart affected a gallant and flirtatious approach to women:

> Since the night when I saw your ladyship at the ball with your hair so beautifully dressed – gone is my peace of mind!. . . . I should almost be prepared to wager that your Ladyship had the same experience *à proportion*! You smile! You blush! Ah, yes – I am indeed happy. My fortune is made! But alas! Who taps me on the shoulder? Who peeps into my letter? Alas! alas! alas! My wife![25]

The letters prove beyond reasonable doubt that Mozart was a lusty man. When he was proposing to marry Constanze, he wrote to his father: 'The voice of nature speaks as loud in me as in others, louder, perhaps, than in many a big strong lout of a fellow'. He continued that he would not seduce an innocent girl nor frequent whores:

> Besides, if such a thing had occurred, I should not have concealed it from you; for, after all, to err is natural enough in a man, and to err *once* would be mere weakness – although indeed I should not undertake to promise that if I had erred once in this way, I should stop short at one slip.[26]

Writing from Berlin in 1789, he not only threatened to take Constanze by the front curls, but also to give her a thorough spanking on her 'dear little kissable arse', and in the next letter he describes his mounting excitement at the thought of sleeping with her:

> Arrange your dear sweet nest very daintily, for my little fellow deserves it indeed, he has really behaved himself very well and is only longing to possess your sweetest . . . Just picture to yourself that rascal; as I write he crawls on to the table and

[24] *LMF*, 752, 743
[25] *LMF*, 824
[26] *LMF*, 783

looks at me questioningly. I, however, box his ears properly – but the rogue is simply . . . and now the knave burns only more fiercely and can hardly be restrained.[27]

The letters do not prove, however, that Mozart strayed beyond the marriage bed, though of course it is possible to 'read between the lines' and interpret them in that way. If the reader begins with the assumption that Mozart was Don Giovanni, his letter of good advice to his young friend Gottfried von Jacquin will be interpreted as cynical and rather sinister jesting:

> Surely you are becoming every day more convinced of the truth of the little lectures I used to inflict upon you? Surely the pleasure of a transient, capricious infatuation is as far removed as heaven from earth from the blessed happiness of a true and rational love? Surely in your heart of hearts you often feel grateful to me for my admonitions! You will end up by making me quite conceited. But, jesting apart, you do owe me some thanks after all, if you have become worthy of Fräulein N—, for I certainly played no insignificant part in your reform or conversion.[28]

But if the reader approaches the correspondence with 'innocent' eyes, unprejudiced by the legends, she is likely to be impressed with Mozart's devotion to his wife, a devotion which verges upon obsession. He begs her to write more often, worries about her health and that she might fall when getting into the baths at Baden. He also worries that she is flirting with other men. Before their marriage he was horrified to hear that in a game of forfeits she had allowed a gallant to measure her calves. Many years later he wrote that she had been too free and easy at Baden, with men who consequently became too familiar:

[27] *LMF*, 927, 929
[28] *LMF*, 913

127

Eve's part in his downfall

> A woman must always make herself respected, or else people
> will begin to talk about her. My love! Forgive me for being so
> frank, but my peace of mind demands it as well as our mutual
> happiness. Remember that you yourself once admitted to me
> that you were inclined to *comply too easily*. You know the
> consequences of that . . . Oh, God, do try, my love! Be merry
> and happy and charming to me. Do not torment yourself and
> me with unnecessary jealousy. Believe in my love, for surely
> you have proofs of it, and you will see how happy we shall be.
> Rest assured that it is only by her prudent behaviour that a wife
> can enchain her husband.[29]

Some have read this as proof that both husband and wife
were playing around, others as testimony to Mozart's obsession with his honour, and devotion to the romantic ideal of
the 'companionate marriage' as opposed to the laxity of court
society. It certainly testifies to a love which had not gone
cold; one is reminded of Kelly's remark that Mozart was
passionately fond of his wife. The argument recently proposed, that Constanze was having an affair at Baden with
Süßmayr, who was the real father of Franz Xaver Wolfgang,
collapses utterly under scrutiny: the *coup de grâce* is the fact
that both Mozart and his son had a hereditary deformity of
the left ear.[30]

The disapproving story of a man destroyed by lechery is an
archetype of great antiquity, set to music, indeed, by Mozart
himself. Only in archetypes does exuberant sexual activity
inevitably bring death. In Mozart's case any notoriety might
have made it difficult for him to get young female piano
pupils, and might also have earned the disfavour of Joseph II,
who was more than a little puritan. Whether philandering is
disapproved depends on the moral stance of the observer.

[29] *LMF*, 933
[30] Dieter Schickling, 'Einige ungeklärte Fragen zur Geschichte der
Requiem-Vollendung', *MJb 1976–7*, 265–76; answered by J. H. Eibl, 'Süßmayr
und Constanze', *MJb 1976–7*, 277–80

Some biographers have accepted the tales about Mozart and have obviously thought them to his credit:

> Also, in his disillusionment, and with an ill wife, he began to have intrigues. While he was in Berlin there is no doubt that he had a love affair with an actress called Henrietta Baranius, who was a mistress of the king's. It is futile to deny this, as does his biographer [Jahn]. . . . But no lover of Mozart can grudge him this last warming of his blood: for soon he was to lie cold in his grave.[31]

Especially in the heyday of Romanticism it was thought that artists behaved like that. How could an opera composer convincingly depict emotions he had not experienced? The novel by Heribert Rau accordingly invents a passionate adolescent affair with Giuditta Uslinghi, daughter of the house where Mozart and his father lodged in Rome, just in time to prepare him psychologically for the composition of *Mitridate*. Rau has her renew the affair at the time of the composition of *Don Giovanni* in order to give him a booster dose. Schurig has a Nietszchean admiration for this opera in which he beholds the eternity of passion and a life driven by elemental powers; evidently he thinks that Mozart was no stranger to such drives. Schiedermair argues that Mozart must have experienced the appetites of the Don in order to understand and depict the type. Abert insists that the role of love in Mozart's life is not to be understood in the gossipy way of philistines. The creative genius experiences love in a different way from ordinary men, passion being central to his nature. Mozart describes love in all its forms in his operas, and experienced it in all its forms in his life.[32]

* * *

[31] Sacheverell Sitwell, *Mozart* (Edinburgh, 1932), 127–8
[32] Schurig, *Wolfgang Amadé Mozart*, ii, 208–10: Schiedermair, *Mozart*, 359; Hermann Abert, *W. A. Mozart* (1919–21) (Leipzig, 1985), ii, 12–13

According to the second story of Mozart destroyed by women, he was no Don Giovanni, not masterful and successful with women at all. On the contrary, he was small, unprepossessing, and lacking in charisma. But he was susceptible and uxorious. It was his misfortune to be pulled into the orbit of the Weber family.[33] He first met them in Mannheim in 1777 or 1778. The father, Fridolin, had had a minor post as an official but had thrown it up in 1765 to live poor and insecure at Mannheim, as a singer, copyist and prompter. This unwise move, perhaps instigated by the mother, Maria Cäcilia, herself from Mannheim and doubtless longing to return from provincial obscurity to the bright lights, typifies the bohemian, gypsy-like, 'Weberisch' nature. Maria Cäcilia was the driving force and she was to become Mozart's bad fairy.

The second daughter Aloysia, a beauty and a fine singer, used all her coquetry to entrap the young man. Besotted with her, he dallied in Mannheim where he had no prospects instead of journeying on to Paris. When he eventually arrived in Paris he could not settle there because of the thought of her; indeed he turned down the promising offer of the post of organist at Versailles. But when he returned to her in Munich, where she had been hired as a singer with a good salary, it became clear that she, and the family, had merely been using him. He had trained her voice, and had seemed a source of useful contacts, but now she no longer needed a poor musician with no prospects. She dropped him.

Mozart renewed his acquaintance with the Webers in 1781, when he went freelance in Vienna. In the meantime father Fridolin had died, leaving nothing but debts. The mother now rented an apartment in a house called 'Zum Auge Gottes', heading a lax and disorderly household. She

---

[33] My account of Mozart, Eve's victim, is assembled from the following: Belmonte, *Die Frauen im Leben Mozarts*; Schurig, *Wolfgang Amadé Mozart* and *Konstanze Mozart*; Blümml, *Aus Mozarts Freundes- und Familien kreis*; Boschot, *Mozart*; and Einstein, *Mozart*.

drank too much and the daughters gave their attention to dress rather than housework. Thrift was beyond them: they kept a maid even though they could not afford it. Mozart took lodgings with them, and the mother determined to offload the third daughter, Constanze, on to him. There was a bad precedent, had Mozart known about it. Aloysia had meanwhile married the actor Lange, and in return for her hand the mother had extorted a contract in which he agreed to pay the mother a lump sum of 900 gulden, plus an annual income of 700 gulden for life. Of course Mozart was not told about this; instead he was fed the lie that Aloysia had abandoned her destitute family without resource.

Soon Mozart was caught in her web. Constanze lacked all talent, was uneducated and not pretty; but the Papageno in Mozart was drawn to this primitive, sensual being. His father understood the Webers well enough and was horrified; he launched alarmed, angry letters from Salzburg. Maria Cäcilia now brought Constanze's guardian, Johann von Thorwart, into action. He compelled Mozart to sign a contract agreeing to marry Constanze within three years, or pay her 300 gulden per annum for life. Constanze artfully entangled him further by tearing the contract up before his eyes, declaring that she did not doubt his love. The mother tried a new tactic; she forbade Mozart to see her daughter. Mozart now arranged for Constanze to take refuge with Baroness Waldstätten (novelists later delighted to call her flight the 'Entführung aus dem Auge Gottes' – *Die Entführung* was being premièred at this time). Maria Cäcilia threatened to have her brought back by the police; this brought matters to a head and the couple married, before Mozart had received his father's consent and blessing.

This was the catastrophe of his life; now his martyrdom began. If he was to succeed in Viennese society, he had to shake off all traces of provincial vulgarity; his marriage made this impossible, for Constanze was in no way superior to his Augsburg cousin, and she constantly pulled him down to her own level. When he took her to Salzburg Leopold and Nannerl were ashamed of her; relations between father and son never properly recovered. She should have levelled his path, for his own energies were totally absorbed in his creative life. But because she was incompetent as a housewife she failed to provide him with the secure, stable, comfortable home background he needed. Her extravagance and mismanagement led to the cycle of debt and overwork. She did not even feed him properly. She indulged her hypochondria and love of pleasure in expensive holidays in Baden while he was left to fend for himself like a young bachelor. His health was not up to it.

Her flirting destroyed his peace of mind. For she did not give him the warmth and love he needed. It is to be doubted whether she actually loved him; she had no respect for the man who played the silly ass with her, and failed to establish himself in the world. Only after his death, when his scores began to fetch high prices, did she realize that she had been living with a genius. She was too uncultured and unmusical to be his soul-mate. None of the works composed specifically for her was ever finished; one can imagine him giving them up in despair when her boredom became apparent. She was insignificance personified, an insipid doll. Mozart was defeated and destroyed by his marriage.

Her disservices to him continued after his death. She did not attend his funeral, nor visit his grave, nor have it marked with a monument; hence his grave was lost. She destroyed letters which reflected ill upon herself, and broke his death-mask when dusting it, throwing the remains into the bin. Her trivial chatter entered and contaminated the biographical record; she delighted to pose as the long-suffering wife who forgave her husband's dissipation. By contrast she admired her second husband, the dull and worthy Nissen, who gave her a respectable position in the world. When he died she erected a monument to him in Salzburg and carefully tended it.

* * *

That is the story: can we believe it? The alarms and excursions of his courtship are narrated in Mozart's own letters, and in one of them he surveys the Weber family:

> The eldest is a lazy, coarse perfidious woman, and as cunning as a fox. Mme Lange is a false, malicious person and a coquette. The youngest – is still too young to be anything in particular – she is just a good-natured, but feather-headed creature! May God protect her from seduction! But the middle one, my good, dear Constanze, is the martyr of the family and, probably for that reason, is the kindest-hearted, the cleverest and, in short, the best of them all. She makes herself responsible for the whole household and yet in their opinion she does nothing right. Oh, my most beloved father, I could fill whole sheets with descriptions of all the scenes that have troubled us both in that house. . . . [Constanze] is not ugly, but at the same time far from beautiful. Her whole beauty consists in two little black eyes and a pretty figure. She has no wit, but she has enough common sense to enable her to fulfil her duties as a wife and mother. She is not inclined to be extravagant, that is absolutely false. . . . most things that a woman needs she is able to make for herself; and she dresses her own hair every day. Moreover she understands housekeeping and has the kindest heart in the world.[34]

Mozart is evidently trying to arouse his father's sympathy; the story he is telling Leopold, and perhaps himself, is of the need to rescue the poor, deserving girl. He had a gift for sharp judgments; these were to be manna for later biographers, but they do not show that the Weber household was bohemian and slovenly. Mozart himself had insisted that he was comfortable and well looked after there.[35]

The anonymous postscript in Nannerl's letter to Schlichtegroll contained the remark: 'He married a girl quite unsuited to him, and against the will of his father, and thus

[34] *LMF*, 784
[35] *LMF*, 756, 763

the great domestic chaos at and after his death'. Schlichtegroll did not use this, putting instead 'In Vienna he married Constanza Weber and found in her a good mother of the two children of their union, and a worthy wife who, moreover, sought to restrain him from many foolishnesses and excesses'.[36] Schlichtegroll's revised version was accepted by most nineteenth-century authors,[37] but the postscript ticked away in the archive like a time-bomb. Another mine waiting to explode was the question of Mozart's grave. Johann Andreas Streicher the pianoforte maker criticized Constanze to the Novellos. According to Vincent Novello, 'Mozart's monument a sore subject with Streicher as well as with Gyrowetz and every other person of good taste and feeling I have yet met with'.[38] The suspect 'Joseph Deiner' memoirs of 1856 told that at the time of the funeral Constanze had blithely assumed that memorial crosses were erected on graves by the authorities. Nissen's biography reported that she did not visit the cemetery to find the grave until 1808, when all traces of it had been lost.[39] The graves were regularly cleared and re-used and the grave-digger who interred Mozart was dead. Nissen also remarked that at first she had been 'perhaps more attracted by his talents than by his person'.[40]

Every scrap of evidence that could be used against her was marshalled, interpreted and over-interpreted when the anti-Constanze story took final shape in the first decades of the twentieth century. It is difficult to avoid the conclusion that this was part of the anti-feminist backlash at a time of growing women's emancipation. But the story of man destroyed by woman is an immemorial archetype.

[36] *MDB*, 462, 469
[37] Jahn thought she lacked the ability and culture to appreciate and influence him, that she blamed him for their money difficulties and that she was better pleased with Nissen as a husband; *Life of Mozart*, ii, 266
[38] Novello, 187, 191
[39] *MDB*, 565; Nissen, 576
[40] Nissen, 415

The essentials of the story are to be found in Belmonte's book of 1905. It is the source of the story of Constanze destroying the death mask, which he attributes to 'Salzburg tradition'. Furthermore,

> She, who had called perhaps the noblest man of his time her own, thought herself, as Madam Privy Councillor von Nissen, sufficiently distinguished to throw a letter of Mozart's, which had been brought to her for authentication, *contemptuously to the ground*, when she came across the expression of the 'Hagenauer Mensch' (a common word at that time for servant girls) in it.[41]

Too much weight should not be placed upon such 'traditions'.

The classic version of the anti-Constanze story is Schurig's. It also displays the most striking anti-feminism. The Countess in *Figaro*, with her bourgeois view of sexual morality, deserves what she gets; the faithful Ottavio is a weakling beside the strong seducer Giovanni. *La clemenza di Tito* is about the mad jealousy of an insignificant woman. Yet he has a distaste for *Così fan tutte*, which depicts 'Venus vulgivaga, who gives herself to whoever pleases her at the moment'. Evidently, sexual freedom is right for men but not for women. Schurig exhibits a distaste for female sexuality. Constanze was a primitive, sensuous being and 'now the marriage robbed his artistic productivity of its intensity'.[42] So if Mozart had had less sex, there would be more symphonies.

Schurig was a good Mozart scholar, and he later brought out a valuable book on Constanze herself. In it he claims to have revised his opinion in her favour. He now thought that Constanze was not primarily responsible for the domestic disorder and debts. She was a woman who took on the character of those she lived with. Hence when she married

---

[41] Belmonte, 71, 84
[42] Schurig, *Wolfgange Amadé Mozart*, ii, 131, 249, 296, 315–6

Nissen she became dull and respectable, a good housewife and mother. When she lived with Mozart, she adapted herself easily to his bohemian way of life; the fault then was primarily his. This is surely to damn with faint praise, and the anti-feminism is still in evidence; for instance, Nannerl was an embittered woman because she had not found herself a man.

The most extended indictment of the Weber family is by Blümml, who makes a great deal out of very little evidence. He reads Cäcilia Weber's character (unfavourably) from her silhouette, claims that she was responsible for Fridolin's giving up his safe official position and that the girls devoted themselves to dress rather than housework – for all this there is no evidence. He insinuates that their keeping a servant was extravagant, which is surely anachronistic. To have a servant played an important part in the maintenance of status, and maids were very cheap. The part played by the mother in Aloysia's and Constanze's marriage negotiations is susceptible of a less black interpretation. Blümml depicts her playing a clever game of cat-and-mouse in order to entrap the suitors, Lange and Mozart. But her behaviour could have been the result of indecision rather than cunning and policy, of reluctance to let her daughters go rather than determination to get rid of them. The financial settlement with Lange, unreasonable from a twentieth-century point of view, may have seemed entirely reasonable in the eighteenth. There is no evidence that Lange, a well-paid actor about to marry a well-paid singer, entered the arrangement reluctantly. The lump sum of 900 gulden was to pay off a loan, an advance on Aloysia's salary from the theatre which employed her, given to tide the family over when they settled in Vienna. Mozart himself was not dragged kicking and screaming into marriage. When the tiff occurred over the episode of the measuring of Constanze's calves, she gave him the opportunity to break the relationship off, as his letter makes clear.[43]

[43] *LMF*, 802–3

The sources will support a much more favourable assessment both of the Weber family and of Constanze.[44] In spite of his sharp remarks before his marriage, Mozart appears later to have enjoyed friendly relations with the mother and all the daughters: Blümml himself provides the evidence for this. When Leopold visited his son in Vienna, he had lunch with Frau Weber: 'I must tell you that the meal, which was neither too lavish nor too stingy, was cooked to perfection. The roast was a fine plump pheasant; and everything was excellently well prepared'.[45]

Leopold also wrote about his son's domestic arrangements: 'So far as eating and drinking is concerned, the housekeeping is economical in the highest degree'.[46] Nothing about extravagance here; but perhaps a hint at meanness? Almost a year earlier Mozart wrote that he had opened a letter by his maid, Liserl Schwemmer, to her mother:

> Then she complains about the food and that too in the most impertinent fashion. She says she has to starve and that the four of us, that is, my wife, myself, the cook and she do not get as much to eat as she and her mother used to have between the two of them.[47]

This incidentally is a black mark on Mozart's own record; he opened the maid's letter and then decided to get rid of her because of what he read in it.

Apart from the anonymous postscript in Nannerl's letter to Schlichtegroll, there is absolutely no evidence that Constanze was a bad manager – and that postscript probably comes from a Salzburg source. An unprejudiced reading of the evidence suggests the contrary. Mozart's own letter, in which he insisted on her good sense and thriftiness as a house-

[44] Constanze has recently been defended by Braunbehrens, *Mozart in Wien*, and Robbins Landon, *Mozart's Last Year*.
[45] *LMF*, 887
[46] *LMF*, 889
[47] *LMF*, 878

keeper, has already been quoted. It appears that he had sufficient confidence in her practicality to leave the arranging of a loan of 2000 gulden in her hands.[48] As a widow she strode purposefully through life, establishing security for herself and her sons. Doubtless she was aided by good friends, but she is the connecting thread. The completion of the Requiem was organized, and she obtained a pension from the emperor even though she was not officially entitled to one. She began to raise money on the scores. From 1795–7 she mounted a series of benefit concerts in Vienna, Prague, Berlin, Leipzig, Dresden, Graz and Weimar. At the end of this period she was able to lend 3500 florins to the Duscheks. This, moreover, was before she made the acquaintance of Nissen, so Schurig's claim that her later good qualities owed much to his influence must be rejected. The later letters to publishers in her name were written by Nissen. They reveal a tenacious determination to drive a good bargain. Is the determination Nissen's, or hers? When she died her estate had the considerable net value of 27,192 gulden – worth more than Haydn's, and two-and-a-half times Beethoven's. Less than a third of this came from the estate of her second husband Nissen. The rest, therefore, derived from her exploitation of Mozart's legacy of fame and unpublished scores.[49]

The tale that Constanze was completely unsuitable as a companion for Mozart, indeed not particularly musical, must also be doubted. Mozart wrote to Leopold that Constanze liked fugues, particularly those of Handel and Bach, and had encouraged him to write some.[50] Naturally the anti-Constanze biographers dismiss this as a lie, told by the son to his father to reconcile him to his bride-to-be. But Mozart composed things for her to perform, including soprano solos

[48] *LMF*, 942–3
[49] Julia Moore, 'Mozart in the Market-Place', *Journal of the Royal Musical Association*, cxiv (1989), 42
[50] *LMF*, 801

in the C minor Mass, which she sang when Mozart directed it in Salzburg.[51] She played and sang his compositions with him when he wanted to try them out.[52] She sang in some of her benefit concerts as a widow.

Constanze is elusive; constantly in the picture, rarely in focus. We have Mozart's letters to her but not hers to him. Her testimony lies behind the biographical information of Niemetschek and Nissen, but we can never be sure that it is her voice we hear. Nissen wrote her letters for her. By far the best eye-witness account of her, admittedly by observers strongly biased in her favour, is in the diaries of the Novellos, who met her as an old woman. She told them that Mozart liked to hear her sing 'Se il padre perdei' from *Idomeneo*, and that they had sung the quartet 'Andrò ramingo' when they visited his family in Salzburg. She knew the operas by heart, but could not bear to hear the Requiem or *Idomeneo* performed; the last time she heard *Don Giovanni* she was not calm for a fortnight. When the Novellos' daughter Clara sang 'Non più di fiori' from *La clemenza di Tito* to her she was moved to tears.[53] From a friend's letter we hear of her reading through the score of a mass by Keller which had caught her eye.[54]

When they met the pianoforte-maker J.A. Streicher in Vienna they found he had a low opinion of Constanze: their own impressions were quite different. She was a 'well-bred lady, whose conversation is particularly attractive', 'Her voice is low and gentle, her manners well-bred and prepossessing, unconstrained like a person who has lived much in society and seen a good deal of the world'.[55] The inhabitants of Salzburg showed her great respect. Her son was very proud

[51] This is stated in Nissen and confirmed by Nannerl's diary; *MBA*, iii, 290
[52] Schurig, *Konstanze Mozart*, 28; Novello, 94, 126
[53] Novello, 94, 102, 115, 216
[54] Robert Münster, 'Nissen's "Biographie W. A. Mozarts"', *Acta mozartiana*, ix (1962), 6
[55] Novello, 218, 82

of his mother, and Aloysia Lange thought that her sister's understanding was very superior.[56]

If the real Mozart is hidden by layers of myth, then the real Constanze is obscured by anti-feminist stereotypes. Some cluster around the archetype of the petty and scheming woman, who fails to support, indeed acts as a drag on the greatness of her man. Others revolve around the archetype of the woman who fails to fulfil her duties as wife, mother and household manager; she flirted with other men, did not love Mozart, neglected her children, was slovenly and bohemian. Most or all of this is myth and injustice.

*

> Oh, I could say a great deal more in reply to your last letter and make many remonstrances, but my maxim is: what does not affect me I do not consider it worth while to discuss. I cannot help it – such is my nature. I am really shy of defending myself, when I am falsely accused. I always think that the truth will come out some day.[57]

Mozart wrote this to his father in 1782. In this instance at least he was naive. The truth has *not* come out; instead there are legends, often contradictory.

Mozart was not a perfect human being, if such a thing is possible. His letters prove that he could be waspish, snobbish, uncharitable and a liar. The anti-feminist story about Constanze must be recognized for what it is. But if Constanze was a perfect wife, it would follow that Mozart was less than a perfect husband. Many of the discreditable tales about him, especially where money is concerned, appear to stem from

[56] Novello, 102, 150
[57] *LMF*, 791

her. So either he was imprudent, or she was not a reliable witness.

When one contemplates all the legends about Mozart's extravagance, unreliability, tactlessness, drinking and womanizing it is tempting to conclude that there is no smoke without fire. No doubt there was exaggeration, but a grain or two of truth must be at bottom of it all. But such a verdict is by no means secure. This chapter and the preceding one have traced the history of some of these legends, showing how they grew. Very often a cloud of witnesses evaporates when it becomes plain that they have all plagiarized and embroidered upon a single original source, itself of doubtful validity. The legends are like inverted pyramids, vast superstructures resting on vanishing points. But if the legends are so fishy, why did they grow and cluster about Mozart?

Niemetschek says that 'Mozart's enemies and detractors became so vicious, so outspoken, especially towards his end, and after his death . . . this gossiping and lying was so shameless, so scandalous'. This phenomenon has to be understood in the context of court society, which is quite unlike our own. We live in a world of elections, public examinations, formal selection procedures, rational bureaucracies and impersonal market forces. Hence we have a reduced sense of the importance of individual decision and personal influence. But in court society, patronage comes immediately from the man (or woman) at the top, or mediately from those who surround him and enjoy his favour. If our vast and impersonal society generates paperwork, in forest-endangering quantities, court society, small and face-to-face, is a hotbed of intrigue, flattery and gossip. Flattery is a means of personal advancement, gossip a way of eliminating a rival.

It is possible also that the gossip about Mozart was an attempt to discredit someone who was a freemason.[58] In the aftermath of the French Revolution freemasonry came to be

---

[58] Massin, 580

associated in many minds with jacobinism. Frightened conservatives spread rumours of gluttony, gambling and debauchery behind the closed doors of the lodges. Mozart was a mason: the possibility that he was unconventional and bohemian in his lifestyle, therefore an easy target for such rumours, is tempting and plausible. Rochlitz refers to his 'liberal life, his all too open character, his scorn for all the gossip about himself'.[59]

The legend of his eternal childhood was encouraged by the pattern of survival of the evidence. Reliable information is rich for his early years and young manhood, comparatively poor for the years of his maturity. Almost inevitably this has produced a distorted picture. Schlichtegroll's influential obituary devotes twenty-five pages to his childhood and adolescence and a mere six to his adult life, the period when his masterpieces were composed.

The story of Mozart, beast and angel is so strange that one is driven to reflect on the motives of those who have constructed it. Does it stem from a German-Austrian inability to bear the guilt of (allegedly) having allowed a Mozart to die poor and neglected? Certainly the story, which puts the blame on Mozart himself, came to full flower in the heyday of German nationalism.[60] Or is it a manifestation of a dualist frame of mind? Human existence is imperfect through and through; good and evil, happiness and unhappiness come inextricably mixed. It is uncomfortable to recognize this, difficult to accept it. Dualism, or manicheism, is a perennially attractive mode of thought because it enables the dualist to avoid the discomfort. It does this by drawing an impassable line between black and white, Satan and God, evil and good. All the good is specialized, concentrated, pure on one side; on the other we have the unmitigated essence of evil. It is psychologically satisfying to think in this way. And, after a fashion, this is what some admirers of Mozart have done.

[59] *AMZ*, i (1798–9), 17 (10 October 1798)
[60] Keller, *Wolfgang Amadeus Mozart*, 4

They love his music so much that they find it difficult to cope with evidence that he did not always live up to their own idealized and time-bound image of what a man should be; and so they split him in two, isolating and insulating his artistic life from his life in general, which is then depicted in the blackest colours so as to confirm and underline the separation.

The next chapter, on genius, will throw further light on the genesis of this legend. For the time being we may say that the story of Mozart, beast and angel, has not absolutely been disproved. But examination of the growth of the legend and of the sources on which it is based have considerably undermined it.

Chapter VI

Genius and misfit

There are two types of 'psychological' story which explain Mozart's death in the context of his personality. The first is the 'beast and angel' story of the previous chapters. The second, the subject of this chapter, is less disapproving. It too sees Mozart as unfitted for worldly success, destroyed by professional failure; but it maintains that the very characteristics which so unfitted him were necessarily, ineluctably connected with his genius. Hence the catastrophe of his last years and death was not his own fault but the fault of his contemporaries, who could not understand and cope with him. As Shaw put it, geniuses are seldom liked until they are dead. Hildesheimer's biography of 1977 is the fullest working-out of the story of the lonely genius, lonely because of his greatness and destroyed by that loneliness.[1] Accordingly this chapter will begin with a narrative along Hildesheimer's lines.

* * *

Mozart was not merely one genius among others, but outstanding even by that elevated standard: 'Thus died Mozart, perhaps the greatest genius in recorded human history'.[2] Mozart's brain was uniquely, marvellously powerful. This is revealed primarily of course by the brilliance and originality

---

[1] W. Hildesheimer, *Mozart* (Frankfurt, 1977)/(London, 1983)
[2] Hildesheimer, 366

of his compositions. But it is also demonstrated by his astonishing precocity, and his ability to do what seems impossible. The most celebrated example of the latter is the story of the Allegri *Miserere*. This polyphonic masterpiece, which is in four and five parts with a final nine-part chorus, was the exclusive property of the Sistine chapel choir, which allowed no copy to be made. Mozart heard it in Rome and afterwards wrote the whole out from memory. His method of composition illustrated the same ability. He worked out an elaborate composition entirely in his head, and then, perhaps later, sat down to write it straight off; and the writing was so much a mechanical process that he could engage in a game of skittles, or a conversation, at the same time.

Mozart's genius went hand in hand with a near total absorption in the subject of it, which rendered him unfit for everyday life. He had an overmastering compulsion to compose, and there was no deflecting his will; he would not compromise his primary mission for the sake of worldly considerations. His absorption in music made him a narrow man, with no interest in other aspects of cultural and intellectual life. It tended to cut him off, not only from others but also from materiality itself; his humour is in part an attempt to get back in touch with everyday things, and because the life of his musical mind was so abstract and elevated, the more concrete and earthy that humour the better. Some of his critics have thought that his letters could be not only childishly obscene, but also very silly:

> Write without delay, for it is cold today and keep your promise too or else forsooth I'll spue. Adieu, mon Dieu, I send you a great dollop of kisses, slap bang wollop!
>
> Ma trés chère cousine,
> Were you never in Berlin?
> Your cousin of virtues rare
> In weather foul or fair
> W. A. MOZART,

Who shits without a fart.[3]

But Hildesheimer maintains that the apparent silliness of the humour is another manifestation of the working of an utterly out-of-the-ordinary mind:

> Mozart's musical genius shines out in his words as well, when he manipulates them like musical associations . . . His compulsive delight and ease in association are capable not only of producing euphony and rhythm with disparate and seemingly arbitrary combinations of sound but also of keeping the connotations always in mind. In writing he yields himself up to the flow of words, going far beyond the comprehensible, reveling in, intoxicated by the sounds and the continually changing meanings they suggest. In this intoxication the inhibitions of convention and bourgeois taste fall by the wayside.[4]

Mozart's mind was so unlike that of other mortals that no-one could really understand him; indeed Hildesheimer thinks that he could not understand himself. Because those he knew were so different from him, they could not function as a mirror in which he could observe from a detached standpoint psychological workings analogous to his own. Conversely, his own inner experience provided no key to the understanding of others; hence he did not realize the effect which his words and behaviour had upon them. His letters home from Paris prove this; he wants to demonstrate that he is behaving in a responsible fashion, making his best efforts to secure his future, to persuade his father to go along with his plans. But it is obvious to the reader that the letters will have the opposite effect, proving to Leopold that his son is all too easily deflected and lacking in judgment. Leopold's replies, with their unease mounting to anger, confirm this. Hildesheimer goes so far as to say that Mozart was semi-

---

[3] Hildesheimer, 404; this is a free translation which nevertheless preserves the spirit.
[4] Hildesheimer, 119

autistic: 'He does not seek self-knowledge, gives no account of himself, neglects and consumes himself. He burns up, but does not defy the burning; rather, he ignores it. He doesn't see himself in relation to the world. He doesn't see himself at all.'[5]

Mozart relates to others through *topoi*, conventions which he has learnt. He adopts them and discards them as one puts on and takes off clothes; they never express his true inner self. They are masks; except in his music, he always advances wearing a mask. The begging letters to Puchberg which commentators have found so distressing may not mean that Mozart really felt desolated by his debts; they are to be regarded as tragic arias from *opera seria* transmuted into epistolary prose. And the last letter to his father about death is not a statement of personal philosophy, a uniquely profound self-revelation; it is a close paraphrase of a passage from Moses Mendelssohn.[6] This gives insight into the buffoonery and coarse humour. It too is a mask, behind which the genius hides from others who, he subconsciously feels, are unworthy to be admitted to his inner sanctum; it is also a vehicle for relaxed and friendly relationships without the mutual self-revelation which he neither wants nor can attain. What he says to others is as it were always quotations; for apart from music Mozart does not have speech of his own. He is desperate for human contact, terrified of loneliness. Hence he incessantly seeks company, even when he should be working, and so his work has to be done during the night. But he never escapes from isolation, not even with Constanze; always he is an outsider. His failure to achieve any real involvement with another human being is illustrated by his remarkable composure at the time of his mother's death and by his ability to speak ill of his closest 'friends', such as Haydn or Nancy Storace.

[5] Hildesheimer, 57
[6] Hildesheimer, 190

Genius and misfit

Mozart's genius had its own laws and necessities. It drove him to explore and develop musical form and expression, composing according to criteria other than those of popularity and accessibility. Until his mid-twenties he made some attempt to please, to give his patrons what they wanted; but after that he increasingly gave himself up to his genius. This, coupled with his semi-autism, coupled with the eccentricity which his genius produced, made him virtually unemployable; hence the impoverishment of the last years. For he was a very strange and difficult man. His isolation meant that he lacked tact, and so he accumulated enemies; ultimately he had few friends in the casual sense of that word, and no real friends at all. By the end, he did not even want the company of Constanze, who was constantly sent off to Baden. His abstraction produced strange and irritating behaviour and mannerisms. His sister-in-law remembered in 1828:

> He was always in a good-humour, but even in his best mood very pensive, at the same time looking one straight in the eye, giving a deliberate answer to any question, whether it be cheerful or sad, and yet he seemed at the same time to be working away deep in thought at something quite different. Even when he washed his hands in the early morning, he walked up and down the room at the same time, never standing still, at the same time tapped one heel against the other and was always thoughtful. At table he often took a corner of his napkin, crumpled it up tightly, rubbed it round below his nose, and appeared in his thoughtfulness to be unaware of what he was doing, and often he would grimace with his mouth at the same time . . . Also, he was always moving his hands and feet, always playing with something, *e.g.* with his hat, pockets, watch-ribbon, tables, chairs, as if they were a clavier.[7]

Karoline Pichler, who as a girl had known Mozart, wrote as follows in 1843. Mozart had been playing beautifully at the clavier: 'But then he suddenly tired of it, jumped up, and in

[7] Nissen, 627–8

148

the mad mood which so often came over him, he began to leap over tables and chairs, miaow like a cat, and turn somersaults like an unruly boy.'[8] Hildesheimer remarks:

> It would be nice to know how much Mozart's appearance betrayed the out-and-out eccentric or what impression he gave away from the piano, when he was listening, or fell silent, or spoke, or moved abruptly . . . We should ask ourselves if we would have felt comfortable in his company. Would his extremely, indeed often violently disorderly behaviour have helped us to relax with him, or hindered us? . . . the mercurial, restless little man capable of driving us mad.[9]

All of this goes to explain why Mozart, by far the greatest living composer, was a professional failure in his last years. He was not one of the musicians invited to attend the coronation of Emperor Leopold at Frankfurt. He *was* invited to compose the coronation opera at Prague, but only because Salieri had turned the commission down because of other engagements and perhaps because of the ridiculously short time allowed for composing the work.[10] Mozart, desperate for employment and money took on the job of composing *La clemenza di Tito* and drove himself to exhaustion in order to be ready on time. The composition of *Die Zauberflöte* is a sign of how low he had sunk; he contracted to produce a popular entertainment to an absurd libretto for a suburban theatre. In his last year he was driven to take commissions to compose for mechanical organ and glass harmonica. And would a successful composer have agreed to write a Requiem for a patron who would then pass it off as his own? All this was the result of his eccentricity; it is impossible to envisage him in royal service as a Kapellmeister, organizing and directing the musical life of the court.

---

[8] *MDB*, 556
[9] Hildesheimer, 94, 281, 270
[10] *NMD*, entry for 8 July 1791

Around 1790, Vienna had temporarily abandoned Mozart; it seemed to be waiting until this unpleasant and ultimately asocial character, uncomfortable and potentially rebellious, had transformed himself by his death into a great man . . . After his death, the process reversed itself.[11]

Mozart could not fail to recognize his professional failure; but the tragedy of his last years was that finally he recognized his social failure also. He realized that he was, and always had been, cut off from others. This knowledge destroyed him, extinguishing his will to live. His state of mind is revealed in one of his last letters, written on 7 July 1791 to Constanze. It is not a series of *topoi*, of quotations. Mozart's inner self is before us in a flash of revelation:

I can't describe what I have been feeling – a kind of emptiness, which hurts me dreadfully – a kind of longing, which is never satisfied, which never ceases, and which persists, nay rather increases daily.[12]

In his desperation, with Constanze away at Baden, he embarked upon an orgy of self-destruction, burning the candle at both ends in the disreputable company of Schikaneder and his troupe.

Our picture of the Mozart of the final Viennese years is of a man trying, unceasingly, to communicate with a world ever more indifferent to him. Frustrated, his own voice weakens and the world no longer takes any notice of him at all. He disappears from it and his circle grows smaller. Finally, there remain only the few men with whom, according to tradition, he rehearses on his death bed the *Lacrymosa* from his Requiem.[13]

In all likelihood, the caesura of his death did not even disturb Mozart's most intimate circle, and no one suspected, on 6 December 1791, when the fragile, burned-out body was

[11] Hildesheimer, 184
[12] *LMF*, 963
[13] Hildesheimer, 27

lowered into a shabby grave, that the mortal remains of an inconceivably great mind were being laid to rest – an unearned gift to humanity, nature's unique, unmatched, and probably unmatchable work of art.[14]

* * *

If this story is true, it is appallingly moving and distressing. If it is true, it is also of the utmost importance, for it has a lesson to teach us. We need to ponder on Mozart's tragedy in the hope that, should a comparable genius be vouchsafed in the future to undeserving humanity, in the field of music, or physics, or anything else, we will be able to recognize that genius and provide him or her with conditions for work and fulfilment, if not for happiness. But *is* this story true?

No one will dispute that Mozart's mind was remarkable and unusual, if not unique. There is no good reason to doubt that he could compose whole works in his head, and then write them out mechanically. Niemetschek states this, and Rochlitz on the strength of his own observation gives an example of Mozart producing a complex contrapuntal exercise in this way – though this anecdote appeared after he had read Niemetschek's biography.[15] Nissen, presumably drawing upon Constanze, backs this up and there is even confirmation from Mozart's own letters.[16] 'Everything has been composed, but not yet written down.' 'I composed in one day Adamberger's aria in A, Cavalieri's in B flat and the trio, and copied them out in a day and a half.' 'But I composed the fugue first and wrote it down while I was thinking out the prelude.'[17] The letters also testify to his absorption in composition and absent-mindedness: 'You know that I am, so to

[14] Hildesheimer, 366
[15] Niemtschek, *Leben*, 54; *AMZ*, iii (1800–01), 451 (25 March 1801)
[16] Nissen, *Biographie*, 568–9
[17] *LMF*, 702, 771, 800

speak, soaked in music, that I am immersed in it all day long and that I love to plan works, study and meditate.'[18]

None of this proves that he was always abstracted, and so unlike others that he could not understand them. The greatest difficulty for Hildesheimer's story is the commonly accepted opinion that Mozart in his operas showed outstanding insight into character and motivation.[19] Hildesheimer of course recognizes this difficulty, and attempts to remove it. He suggests that Mozart could not create a character out of his own resources; he needed a suitable singer of the role before him to serve as a model.[20] But this will not do; if Mozart used real people as the models for his fictional characters, this surely implies that he understood those models. According to Hildesheimer, Mozart conceived his characters at a subconscious level and expressed them in music, without at any stage attaining a conscious knowledge of humanity. He was, as it were, a medium through which truth and insight passed to his audience, himself ignorant of and unaffected by that truth.[21] It is difficult to make any sense of this. If Mozart apprehended character not consciously but intuitively, surely this would have expressed itself in an intuitive tact in human relations.

As for the letter of 7 July 1791 which speaks of emptiness and longing, why should we not take it at face value as an expression of longing for Constanze? To see it as a unique revelation of despair and utter loneliness is a strained interpretation, an interpretation which makes sense only in the context of the traditional prejudice against Constanze as a suitable wife for Mozart. It is not proven that he was a lonely man; his letters tell a different story. The Cannabichs (Christian Cannabich was director of instrumental music at the Mannheim court) and the Webers wept when he left

[18] *LMF*, 587; see also 305, 425, 468
[19] Robert B. Moberley, *Three Mozart Operas* (London, 1967), 20, 28, 30
[20] Hildesheimer, 126–7
[21] Hildesheimer, 241

Mannheim.[22] On the journey back from Paris he made a new
friend:

> We constantly shed tears when we think that we shall have to
> part. He is not a learned man, but a man of experience; and we
> live together like children. When he thinks of his wife and
> children, whom he has left in Paris, I try to console him; and
> when I think of my own people, he endeavours to comfort
> me.[23]

From the Vienna years, his letters suggest that he found good
friends in the Jacquin household, in the family of Count
Cobenzl, and in the family of Count Thun, who did him many
a service.

It is of course possible that all of this is an illusion: that
Mozart was deceiving his father and himself. Certainly in a
letter from Strassburg he seems to protest too much: 'Strassburg is loth to let me go! You cannot think how much they
esteem and love me here. They say that everything about me
is so distinguished – that I am so composed – and polite – and
have such excellent manners.' But this is evidently tongue-in-
cheek, for he goes on to refer to Kapellmeister Richter, who
'now lives very economically, for instead of forty bottles of
wine a day he only swills about twenty'.[24] According to
Niemetschek, Mozart was good company and well-liked: 'His
friends in Prague think with pleasure of the happy hours they
spent in his company; they cannot praise his guileless kind
heart enough; in his company one entirely forgot that one
was with Mozart, the admired artist.'[25] Perhaps this is senti-
mental falsehood, rosy posthumous hagiography. But if
Hildesheimer's interpretation is to be accepted, we shall have
to convict Mozart and many of those who met him of deception or self-deception. Maybe neither he nor they could

22 *LMF*, 414, 518, 641
23 *LMF*, 628
24 *LMF*, 629
25 Niemtschek, 60

distinguish between loneliness-in-company and true friend-ship; are *we* sure that we can? Does the hypothesis of Mozart's loneliness rest upon an exaggerated romantic conception of the union of two souls?

So what is the evidence to show that Mozart was eccentric in his behaviour? Hildesheimer rests his judgment especially upon three witnesses, two of whom – Sophie Haibl and Karoline Pichler – were quoted earlier. The third is Joseph Lange, husband of Aloysia, Mozart's onetime love and Constanze's sister; Lange, who painted the famous unfinished portrait of Mozart.

> Never was Mozart less recognizably a great man in his conversation and actions, than when he was busied with an important work. At such times he not only spoke confusedly and disconnectedly, but occasionally made jests of a nature which one did not expect of him, indeed he even deliberately forgot himself in his behaviour. But he did not appear to be brooding and thinking about anything. Either he intentionally concealed his inner tension behind superficial frivolity, for reasons which could not be fathomed, or he took delight in throwing into sharp contrast the divine ideas of his music and these sudden outbursts of vulgar platitudes, and in giving himself pleasure by seeming to make fun of himself. I can understand that so exalted an artist can, out of a deep veneration for his Art, belittle and as it were expose to ridicule his own personality.[26]

Hildesheimer is surely right to regard this as one of the most valuable descriptions we have of the mature Mozart. In addition to Hildesheimer's three witnesses, one more may be added and three passages from the correspondence. Luigi Bassi, Mozart's first Don Giovanni in Prague, is said to have told Stendhal that 'Mr Mozart was an extremely eccentric and absent-minded young man'. In 1778 Leopold Mozart wrote to his son: 'When you were at Wallerstein you caused the company great amusement, you took up a violin, and danced

[26] *MDB*, 503

about and played, so that people described you to absent friends as a merry, high-spirited and brainless fellow.' A year earlier, Mozart himself confessed to his father that 'in the presence and company of the said Cannabich, his wife and daughter, the Treasurer, Ramm and Lange I did frequently, without any difficulty, but quite easily, perpetrate – rhymes, the same being, moreover, sheer garbage, that is, on such subjects as muck, shitting, and arse-licking'. He confessed to playing the fool again in the company of the Cannabichs just before leaving Salzburg service to settle in Vienna.[27]

'There's a damn queer little man!' the Elector Palatine's court painter remarked of him;[28] it cannot be doubted that on occasion his behaviour was odd and wild. Odd by every-day standards, not necessarily odd for artists. Some Renaissance painters and sculptors cultivated eccentricity in order to mark themselves out as special persons, deserving high social esteem. Such behaviour may be a standard strategy when artists are attempting to claim more status.[29] Where Mozart is concerned, none of the sources says that he was eccentric to the point where others shunned his company. Karoline Pichler did not single Mozart out as an oddity; she thought the same of Haydn and Schubert.

There is an interesting parallel between Sophie Haibl's description of Mozart's behaviour and Schindler's (1840) of Beethoven: 'Beethoven, in a fit of abstraction, would pour several jugs of water on his hands, "humming and roaring". After wetting his clothes through, he would pace up and down the room with a vacant expression of countenance, and eyes frightfully distended.'[30] This parallel prompts the question whether Mozart's, and indeed Beethoven's, eccentricity

---

[27] *NMD*, entry for 1787; *LMF*, 476, 373, 736–7
[28] Erich Schenk, *W.A.Mozart: eine Biographie* (1955), Eng. trans., *Mozart and his Times* (London, 1960), 253
[29] Burke, *Tradition and Innovation*, 92–6
[30] The parallel is noticed by Holmes, *Life of Mozart*, 240

was emphasized simply because such behaviour had come to be expected of 'the genius'. Lange wrote in 1808, Sophie Haibl in 1828 and Karoline Pichler in 1843; they had had plenty of time to organize their memories into an appropriate image. Is theirs a mythical Mozart? Myths need not be pure fictions; they may have a basis in fact, but fact that has been selected, heightened and coloured. Can we observe in the literature the gradual emergence of an image of Mozart the genius? To approach the sources with this question in mind is not in any way to question Mozart's outstanding abilities. If the word 'genius' is to be used at all, it must be applied to him. But so complex a word is not a simple label, like 'red', or 'chair'; it comes loaded with theories and expectations. When a nineteenth-century writer applies this term to Mozart that is already, to an extent, a commitment to a certain interpretation of him. This interpretation may tell some part of the truth about Mozart, but by its emphasis and selectivity it runs the risk of exaggeration. It may ignore or hide other aspects of his personality.

*   *   *

The word 'genius' itself is of great antiquity, going back to classical Latin. During the eighteenth century, first in England and afterwards in Germany, it came to occupy a key position in aesthetic theory – for example of the *Sturm und Drang* movement and of Romanticism. The evolved conception of genius is many-sided, but all its aspects emphasize the separateness of the genius from 'normal' men and women and from society.

Genius is contrasted with skill or craft, which anyone can learn. Genius has nothing to do with universal rules or norms; it is unique to its possessor and cannot be acquired. Its origin is sometimes thought to be external to the individual, but this origin is not an everyday or social one. This is indeed one of the older usages of 'genius', meaning a spirit which possesses, inspires and speaks through the specially gifted, often without their conscious intervention or control. Genius understood in this way is supernatural. It puts the person it possesses in touch with a mysterious and hidden realm lying beneath or behind commonplace surface appearances. Romanticism has a dark side, reflected in its interest in the 'gothic', the unearthly and even the satanic; a dark view of genius sees it as a daemonic force which speaks through the artist.[31] The daemonic power of the genius is not always conceived as supernatural. It is sometimes thought of as a primitive subconscious drive, passionate, destructive and irrational. The gift of genius is therefore a blessing and a curse; it confers insight and makes possible artistic greatness, but at the same time it sets the genius at odds with the tame, reasonable, orderly everyday world.

The idea of genius as inspiration directed attention to the myth of Prometheus. Prometheus was a Titan who rebelled against Jove, stealing fire in order to give it to humanity: rebel against God, benefactor of humankind. For Romantic writers he symbolized romantic rebellion; the fire he brought to earth represented the divine spark of genius.[32]

Perhaps the central characteristic of romantic aesthetic theory is subjectivism. That is to say, the work of art is considered as orientated primarily, not towards the universe it depicts or the audience it affects, but towards the artist's self.[33] It expresses the inner being or impulses of the artist, which well up irresistibly, taking shape in the work of art. This self-unfolding and self-revelation is thought of as an organic and spontaneous happening, like the growth of a plant. It is natural, instinctive or intuitive, not artificial or

[31] R. Taylor, *The Romantic Tradition in Germany* (London, 1970), 53–7
[32] R. Trousson, *Le thème de Prométhée dans la littérature Européenne* (Geneva, 1964). On genius, see P. Murray, ed., *Genius: the History of an Idea* (Oxford, 1989).
[33] M. H. Abrams, *The Mirror and the Lamp: Romantic Theory and the Critical Tradition* (New York, 1958)

rational. Accordingly Schiller describes the naïve genius, who creates unselfconsciously, the genius who is always childlike.[34] And Hegel argues that artistic creation is not an activity of the reason, but of sense and intuition.

The late eighteenth and early nineteenth century conception of genius provides the key to the emergence of the story of Mozart as beast and angel set out in the previous chapters. For it proposes that the genius is divorced from the ordinary world, passionate, sensual, rebellious, disruptive, childlike. It makes possible the image of a strangely divided being, an insignificant mortal who is merely the medium through which inspiration speaks.

Mozart was not a typical Romantic genius; but nineteenth-century writers constructed an image of him as one. The beginnings of it can be found in Schlichtegroll. As explained in chapter one, Schlichtegroll used information supplied by Schachtner, by Mozart's sister and apparently, for the Vienna years, by some other unknown witness. Schachtner recorded of the infant: 'He was of a fiery disposition, no object held his attention by more than a thread.'[35] According to the sister, 'As soon as he sat down at the clavier he was absolutely the master . . . He was irritated by the slightest sound during a piece of music. In short, as long as the piece of music lasted, he was all music himself; as soon as it was over, one saw the child again.' (It is not clear whether the last remark is a reference to Mozart when he was a child, or to the continuing childishness of the man asserted in the anonymous postscript.) 'He was never forced to compose nor to play, on the contrary he always needed to be restrained, he would otherwise have remained sitting over his clavier or his compositions day and night.'[36] Schlichtegroll, probably drawing upon his third source, works these hints into his picture of the passionate, irregular, absent-minded genius:

[34] F. Schiller, *Über naive und sentimentalische Dichtung* (1795)
[35] *MDB*, 452
[36] *MDB*, 462

His body was in constant movement; he always had to have
something for his hands or feet to play with. He loved billiards
passionately . . . Even his expression did not stay constant, but
always betrayed the outer state of his soul . . . for his own spirit
was constantly preoccupied with a mass of other ideas, and
hence for the most part devoid of any inclination for other
serious considerations . . . But this very man, always absent-
minded, always trifling, appeared to become quite different,
appeared to become a higher being when he sat down at the
clavier. Then his spirit became concentrated and his undivided
attention was directed at the pure object for which was born,
namely the harmony of sounds . . . Music was the main business
of his life and also his favourite recreation. Never, not even in
his earliest youth, was it necessary to make him play music; it
was much more necessary to try to restrain him, lest he should
forget himself and damage his health. From childhood on he
liked best to play by night.[37]

Schlichtegroll accepts the stereotype of genius as associated
with sense and emotion, rather than with the faculty of
reason.[38] Hence his sketch of Mozart as a sensual man,
lacking in all capacity for order and proportion, incompetent
in everyday affairs. This character sketch exercised a powerful influence over subsequent writers. Niemetschek has some
reservations about Schlichtegroll's account, but the idea of
genius is the organizing principle of his biography. He emphasizes Mozart's astonishing musical memory and is the first
to describe his ability to compose whole works in his head.
Genius for him is not derived from outside influences, nor
does it relate its possessor in a conventional and secure
manner to the outside world. It is a power which unfolds and
expresses its nature in accordance with an inner compulsion.
Therefore the child learnt about music with amazing speed;
learning was like an awakening of what he already knew.
From this stemmed also his gift for free improvisation:

[37] Schlichtegroll, *Mozarts Leben*, 29–32
[38] Favier, *Vie de Mozart*, 103

It has already been said above, that even in his adulthood he spent half the night at the clavier, truly these were the hours of creation of his heavenly songs! In the quiet repose of the night, when no obstacle hindered his soul, the power of his imagination became incandescent with the most animated activity, and unfolded all the wealth of tone which nature had placed in his spirit . . . Only the person who heard Mozart at such times knows the depth and the whole range of his musical genius: free and independent of all concern his spirit could soar in daring flight to the highest regions of art.[39]

'Independent of all concern' – that is the leitmotif. Absorbed in his art, Mozart wrote as his genius dictated, without regard to the preferences of the stalls. He would play to connoisseurs who appreciated music, but could not be bothered to entertain the merely rich and powerful. His unworldly nature was incapable of currying favour, and he would not take the trouble to outwit those who cheated him. Self-forgetful, absorbed in music, he neglected his health; even his small build resulted from the overtaxing of his brain. At one point only does Niemetschek confront and challenge the conception of the genius. He is aware of the opinion, shared by Schlichtegroll, that artistic genius is the work of the non-intellectual faculties; but he questions the view, reported in a Berlin musical journal and often repeated in subsequent decades, that Mozart lacked general intellectual culture. He cites Mozart's liking for arithmetic, his knowledge of French, English, Italian and some Latin, and concludes that he 'had at least as much historical knowledge as was necessary for an educated man . . . Mozart had seen the world, he knew the authors of the most cultivated nations'.[40] To this we might add that Mozart was brought up by an educated and cultured father, and that he had in effect done the Grand Tour, that climax of eighteenth-century education. He was an indefatigable theatregoer, and his own letters demonstrate a critical

[39] Niemtschek, 55
[40] Niemtschek, 59

understanding of drama and poetry. One of his letters tells of him carrying a book in his pocket to read in spare moments.[41]

Rochlitz, for the most part independent of Niemetschek but like him following Schlichtegroll, gives a similar account of the composer as genius. There is the same emphasis upon the memory and upon the speed of composition. He also insists upon Mozart's indifference to the opinion of great personages and his unconcernedness when cheated by publishers and others. Most relevant of all is Rochlitz's penultimate anecdote.[42] It tells of an evening at the house of Friedrich Doles, the Leipzig Cantor. Mozart had been merry, had spoken in rhyme, and suddenly became withdrawn and pensive, going to the window where he played on the windowsill as if it were a clavier. This little detail confirms Schlichtegroll's and Sophie Haibl's testimony, of which Hildesheimer has made so much, that Mozart in his absorption was restless and odd. It *may* be that Rochlitz and Haibl are simply embroidering Schlichtegroll, but the detailed differences argue for an independent authentic memory.

Rochlitz goes on to relate that Mozart became melancholy and nostalgic, recalling the naïve and comforting piety of his childhood, concluding with the story of how

> Empress Maria Theresa had commissioned him, then a fourteen year old boy, to compose a *Te Deum* for the consecration of a great hospital or some other such foundation – I cannot remember the details – and to conduct it himself at the head of the whole imperial orchestra. What a time that was for me! – What a time that was for me! – he repeated. But it will never return. One drifts into the empty routine of everyday life, he concluded, became bitter, drank a lot of strong wine and did not speak another sensible word.

[41] *LMF*, 429. For a defence of Mozart as a cultured man, see Kramer, 'Strittige Fragen', 76; also King, *Mozart: a Biography*, 10; and Massin, *Wolfgang Amadeus Mozart*, 113, 577
[42] *AMZ*, iii (1800–01), 494–7 (15 April 1801)

According to Rochlitz, this story illuminates his character. Like all highly imaginative and sensuous artists, he longed for the ideal, but despaired of ever finding it. Having no assurance of attaining it in the future, he located it in the past. But the pleasures of nostalgia could not satisfy him. This longing and despair was an intrinsic part of his artistic greatness, but it also caused him to seek to forget himself, and to behave in common, disorderly and foolish ways. 'Mozart never really attained the place which was fitted for him; and precisely when he had perhaps attained it, harsh fate cut the thread of his life.'

This is a perfect sketch of the genius, alienated by his genius from the world. Too perfect, perhaps? It is artfully done, especially the half-remembered reference to the youth's triumph before the whole court, which can be confirmed from the letters. The story is in Schlichtegroll, but Rochlitz has not copied him. According to Rochlitz Mozart conducted a *Te Deum*, according to Schlichtegroll an Offertorium and a trumpet concerto. In fact, he conducted a Mass (the 'Waisenhaus Mass, κ139), an Offertorium (κ47*b*) and a trumpet concerto (lost) for the consecration of an orphanage. Schlichtegroll gives Mozart's correct age of twelve, while Rochlitz says fourteen. If his anecdote is authentic, it is fascinating and revealing; but is it a complete fabrication?

Mozart's alleged letter to the Baron von P., published by Rochlitz in the *Allgemeine musikalische Zeitung* in 1815, is a forgery. It is a letter which, from the point of view of the Romantic student of the genius, he ought to have written. For he describes how his compositions teem out, produced by the working of an inscrutable inner inspiration:

> I can really say no more on this subject than the following; for I myself know no more about it, and cannot account for it. When I am, as it were, completely myself, entirely alone . . . my ideas flow best and most abundantly. *Whence* and *how* they come, I

know not; nor can I force them . . . All this fires my soul . . . All this inventing, this producing, takes place in a pleasing lively dream.[43]

The letter is quoted from Holmes's biography. Holmes also tells the story that Constanze 'had been counselled by the Baron van Swieten as to the most prudent course for the management of a genius, whose life had become public property'.[44] Did Van Swieten really see Mozart in this way before the posthumous growth of the composer's reputation?

Other biographers followed this pattern. Chapter 2 of Arnold's derivative book is entitled 'On artistic talent or genius'; it paints more purple over Niemetschek's purple prose. Stendhal was equally interested in the genius phenomenon, and even more derivative. He argues that if the vital forces are highly specialized in one direction as Mozart's were, then in all other respects they will be weak; hence the feeble growth of his body, his lack of control over his bodily movements, his perpetual childishness, his eventual self-destruction through overwork.

Arnold wrote gothic romances, and Stendhal is best known for his great novels; they were not the only writers of fiction to romanticize Mozart's character. E.T.A. Hoffmann's novel *Don Giovanni* of 1812 proposes a 'daemonic' composer, in touch with supernatural powers. Kierkegaard's discussion of the same opera in his *Either/Or* of 1843 depicts the genius as one driven by sub-rational sensuous and erotic forces. Mörike's little novel *Mozart auf der Reise nach Prag* of 1855 maintains that Mozart's weaknesses of character were the other, and necessary side of his artistic greatness, 'the inevitable complement to the very qualities we most admire in Mozart'.[45] All of these propose that genius is an other-worldly, uncontainable or disruptive force which unfits its

[43] Holmes, 255–6
[44] Holmes, 203
[45] Eduard Mörike, *Mozart auf die Reise nach Prag* (1855), Eng. trans. (London, 1957), 20

possessor for ordinary life. And so we return to the testimony of Karoline Pichler, one of the pillars of Hildesheimer's case, herself a novelist. She had an extravagant conception of artistic inspiration, which she regarded as something miraculous, operating independent of all other intellectual aptitudes, independent, almost, of the artist's conscious participation.[46] A Mozart who was inspired where music was concerned, but otherwise incompetent, accorded perfectly with her prejudices about genius.

This description of Mozart's character, once established, influenced memory. Michael Kelly, who took the parts of Basilio and Don Curzio at the première of *Figaro* was perhaps under its spell when he wrote his reminiscences in 1826:

> All the original performers had the advantage of the instruction of the composer, who transfused into their minds his inspired meaning. I shall never forget his little animated countenance, when lighted up with the glowing rays of genius; – it is as impossible to describe it, as it would be to paint sunbeams.[47]

This memory sounds so right, it accords with our expectations; and yet other sources insist that Mozart had a large head and a dull expression.

Jahn's great mid-nineteenth-century biography stands apart from the tradition described so far. Jahn saw Mozart as a Classical composer, not a Romantic one. He was not unique in this. In the first decades after Mozart's death, the mainstream of criticism assimilated Mozart to Romanticism, judging his music to be expressive and passionate. But by mid-century, a different picture of Mozart had emerged as a result of contrasting him with Beethoven. Beethoven was thought to epitomize Romantic rebelliousness and sublimity, Mozart Classical beauty and formal perfection. Hoffmann, Kierkegaard and Mörike, who persisted in seeing him as daemonically inspired, were exceptions, swimming against

[46] Blümml, *Aus Mozarts Freundes- und Familien kreis*, 105–11
[47] *MDB*, 533

the tide.[48] The pendulum did not swing back again until the beginning of the twentieth century. The crucial turning-point was Heuss's article on 'The daemonic element in Mozart's works'.[49] Heuss thought that to depict Mozart as a sweet and gracious composer was to diminish him. It was necessary to recognize the explosive, wild, pessimistic undercurrents in his music, the darkness constantly waiting to break out. The influential German biographies of the first half of the twentieth century – Schurig, Abert, Paumgartner – followed Heuss.

Schurig maintains that Mozart was an astonishingly one-sided man who understood nothing but his music. The other arts were closed kingdoms to him and he was utterly lacking in general education. For the genius, so remarkable in his special sphere, is in other respects like a child. He is a strangely divided being, living a double life. The higher life of his creativity cuts him off from others, indeed he is impelled to hide behind an assumed mask. At the same time he has a compensating need for the company of cheerful, lively, almost primitive beings. Hence his self-presentation as a naive, coarse, natural man. Schurig's hypothesis of the divided self is rooted in nineteenth-century German metaphysics. Dialectical thinking, from Hegel to Nietzsche, argues that each thing exists in a necessary relationship with its opposite; hence Mozart's unearthly genius requires an earthy instinctive self as its counterpart.[50]

According to Schurig, genius is produced by very special circumstances. Just as diamonds are formed by nature under great pressure, so genius comes forth from early pain and agony of soul. Mozart did not have a normal childhood; excessive demands were made upon him in his early years.

---

[48] Martin Staehelin, 'Zum Verhältnis von Mozart- und Beethoven-Bild im 19. Jahrhundert', *MJb 1980–3*, 17–22
[49] Alfred Heuss, 'Das dämonische Element in Mozarts Werken', *Zeitschrift der Internationalen Musikgesellschaft*, vii (1905–6), 175–86
[50] Schurig, *Wolfgang Amadé Mozart*, ii, 407–10, 384; i, 29; ii, 88, 387, 351

This turned him into a great artist, but at enormous cost. His head, too large for his body, reveals how his musical brain sucked up all too much of his strength. Just as the genius results from abnormal circumstances, so is he not to be measured by normal rules of bourgeois morality. He cannot fulfil his high mission, if he tries to conform to the world. When Mozart strove to please his contemporaries, in his first years in Vienna, he was a worldly success; but his inner compulsions could not be resisted for long. *Figaro* was an attempt to meet the taste of the crowd, but after that, his higher self gained the ascendancy, and he slipped from favour.[51]

All of this strikingly anticipates Hildesheimer, and is itself anticipated in earlier biographies. Schurig is distinctive in the weight he places on Mozart's divided nature, and in a somewhat Nietzschean conception of Mozart's 'daemonic power'. Even this is anticipated to some extent in Kierkegaard's discussion of *Don Giovanni*. For Schurig, Giovanni, who expresses a part of Mozart's own essence, embodies indestructible elemental powers and a triumphant sensuality which is nobler than everyday morality and justice. The legend itself, he suggests, may have originated in the immemorial struggle of the Spanish grandees, defending the life-loving spirit of antiquity against the invading *Weltanschauung* of the Nazarene, corrupted as it had been by Phrygian eunuchs and mad monks. Such a daemonic individuality inevitably comes into conflict with the surrounding world, which eventually destroys him.[52] Here Giovanni is intensified into the *Übermensch*, the Nietzschean superman who dares to give free rein to the life forces within him, defying convention and timid moderation.

Abert, who reworked Jahn's standard biography, dissents from Schurig at certain points but is nevertheless deeply indebted to him. He takes over lock, stock and barrel the

[51] Schurig, ii, 372; i, 152; ii, 393, 131, 261
[52] Schurig, ii, 207–16

notion of a divided personality, daemonically possessed and driven by his genius, torn between a desire to satisfy the public and the inner compulsions of his art. His *Dämon* was responsible for his greatness but also for his dark end. Mozart's genius was not like Beethoven's; it did not manifest itself in a Promethean struggle against the world. Abert's denial of a titanic aspect to Mozart's genius implies further that he was not a social or political rebel. His genius was naive and spontaneous, unfolding the inner forces of its many-sided nature, oblivious of its surroundings. But it did experience crises, when a particular circle of spiritual experience was exhausted or when his inner powers reorganized themselves. Two such crises occurred in his latter years: between *Figaro* and *Don Giovanni* and before *Die Zauberflöte*. These were explosive reorientations, crises of his being verging on destruction, manifested outwardly in dark, pessimistic, passionate tendencies; they dragged his body down. Mozart fell ill after *Giovanni* and never completely recovered.[53]

French interpretations of Mozart, man and artist, have differed from German. There is a distinct French catholic version of his genius, without the darkness and instinctual passion; the daemon becomes an angel:

> And genius in his case, more than in any other, was a *gift*, a *grace* and a *charisma* coming from 'elsewhere' – like ecstasy or sanctity. And just as a man of prayer annihilates himself as it were to receive God, it seems as though nature had in advance annihilated in Mozart as far as possible everything in body, heart and mind that might have impeded the free passage of the gift.
>
> His angel in the Christian sense. His demon in the Socratic sense. And that is no mere figure of speech; I believe in Mozart's angel.[54]

[53] H. Abert, *W. A. Mozart*, i, pp.xiv, xvi, xix-xx; ii, 2, 14, 15–17, 27
[54] Ghéon, *In Search of Mozart*, 340–1

The Mozart of Wyzewa and Saint Foix is yet further removed from the German daemonic genius tradition. Their account of him explains his artistic development in terms of the context, the musical traditions, the work of other composers which he absorbed and assimilated. Their Mozart is formed from the outside, by the society and culture in which he moves: it is an environmentalist account of him. Environmentalism has been a powerful current in French thought since Montesquieu. The Mozart of German scholarship, more precisely of that tradition running from Schlichtegroll through Abert to Hildesheimer, embracing most of the notable German biographies apart from Jahn's, has been dominated by a Romantic conception of the artist. This chimes with that powerful neo-Kantian turn in German thought, according to which the self is not to be understood as the mere product of its environment. Rather the self grows from within, unfolding, projecting, expressing itself.

This account of Mozart's being, an account shaped by the presuppositions of German thought still influences our image of him. It is still common to draw a sharp distinction between those works Mozart composed for the crowd and those he composed to satisfy his inner compulsions. No such distinction is conclusively supported by the sources. Schurig thought that *Figaro* was a 'popular' work, *Don Giovanni* a work of genius. A recent study of the Da Ponte operas argues that Mozart and his librettist knew that the story of the stone guest was outmoded; they chose it because they could quickly rework an existing libretto and pass it off on the less sophisticated public of Prague.[55] It may have appealed to Mozart but there is no reliable evidence that he preferred it to *Figaro*.

Schurig's theory of him as a split personality is fundamental to Einstein's well-known biography. And the conception of

---

[55] Andrew Steptoe, *The Mozart-Da Ponte Operas* (Oxford, 1988), 117

genius as something miraculous, mysterious and other-worldly continues to cast its shadow. Hence Sitwell thought that he created effortlessly, and Blom thought that his dae-mon worked at an unconscious level.[56] According to Einstein, 'Mozart was by the very fact of his towering genius unsuited for this life'. He was sacrificed, as every great artist must be, to his art. His creative activity 'remains, of course, essentially an impenetrable and eternal mystery'.[57] And finally, according to Levey, writing in 1971, 'Far from strug-gling to create, he had to struggle to remain calm amid perpetual creative fever . . . What has often been described as the childlike quality which he retained into adulthood was in fact a retention of energy: pure, unhindered and of almost explosive force'.[58] Hildesheimer's interpretation is simply a heightened and particular version of this enduring tradition.

*

No belittling of Mozart's greatness is implied by asking whether it is revealing or distorting to construct him as a genius, in accordance with Romantic aesthetic ideas. A com-mitment to seeing him in this way leads to a selective reading of the evidence, one which picks out everything suggestive of his unworldliness, absorption and difference from others. It almost renders obligatory an interpretation of him as a div-ided personality, in order to cope with all the evidence telling the other way. For another selection from the evi-dence would reveal him as an everyman, who enjoyed gossip and was interested in the doings of the family pet, who worried about money and the education of his son, who liked a game of billiards or shooting at targets and who longed for the warmth of the matrimonial bed when away from home.

[56] Sitwell, *Mozart*, 119; Blom, *Mozart*, 292–3
[57] Einstein, *Mozart*, 36, 103, 148
[58] Michael Levey, *The Life and Death of Mozart* (London, 1971), 23

Genius and misfit

A good deal of myth-making has gone on, even about his activity as a composer. Niemetschek said that as a child he already seemed to know everything his father wished to teach him. Most biographers have taken it for granted that he rapidly outstripped Leopold Mozart, who gave up composing in order to devote himself to the showcasing of his son's talent. Yet Wolfgang Plath's studies of the handwriting of the autograph scores have revealed the extent of the father's involvement in the early works. A considerable proportion of those written up to the age of twelve are partly or wholly in Leopold's hand, and the father continued to give this help until the son was fifteen or sixteen. Nor was the father merely an amanuensis: this is proved by the fact that some works in Wolfgang's hand have corrections in Leopold's.[59] Like other mortals, Mozart had to learn his craft.

Leopold Mozart himself helped to construct the myth, occasionally understating his small son's age. He prepared the way for later biographers, making much of the feat of writing out the Allegri *Miserere* after a single hearing. A feat it was, but not a miracle. It is not an elaborate contrapuntal work, and it repeats the same material five times; there were in fact copies of it to be found.[60] Leopold also boasted about his fourteen-year old son's triumph at the entrance examination for the Accademia Filarmonica of Bologna, brilliantly completing the set task in half-an-hour. The autographs survive, and they reveal that his first attempt was not very good; Padre Martini, the distinguished music-scholar and teacher of that city, then wrote out an impeccable model, which Mozart copied and submitted. The records of the academy state that 'At the end of less than an hour Signor Mozart brought his essay, and in view of the special circumstances it was adjudged sufficient'.[61] After this, one is almost tempted to believe the story of the composer Grétry:

[59] Ivor Keys, *Mozart: his Music in his Life* (St Albans, 1980), 244–5
[60] Keys, 66–7
[61] Keys, 69; Einstein, 158

Once in Geneva I met a child who could play everything at sight. His father said to me before the assembled company: so that no doubt shall remain as to my son's talent, write for him, for tomorrow, a very difficult Sonata movement. I wrote him an Allegro in E flat; difficult, but unpretentious; he played it, and everyone, except myself, believed that it was a miracle. The boy had not stopped; but following the modulations, he had substituted a quantity of passages for those which I had written.[62]

Mozart's methods of composition may not have been as astounding and unique as has been supposed. Handel too could compose rapidly, often in his head, and write the final version very fast (for example, *Messiah* in three weeks). Like Mozart he was gifted at improvisation. Yet no one suggests that Handel's gifts made him a social misfit.[63] Michael Tippett could write out an entire composition from memory. From the publication of Nissen's biography, in 1828, evidence has been available to show that Mozart did not always compose final versions quickly in his head. Typically, Nissen is self-contradictory. He records the story of fluent, easy composition, lifted without acknowledgment from Niemetschek. But he also takes from Rochlitz the story that Mozart made jottings, which he collected in a notebook. He relates that composition was effortful for him, and that he frequently made corrections and improvements.[64] Jahn was well aware of the Romantic bias in accounts of his rapid productivity, and he draws attention to surviving sketches and alterations, insisting that many more will not have survived. He denies the story that Mozart composed entirely in his head, without working things out at the clavier: 'Karajan tells me that his barber used to relate in after-years how difficult it was to dress his hair, since he never would sit still;

---

[62] *MDB*, 477
[63] Winton Dean, *Handel* (London, 1980), 79
[64] Nissen, 648–9; Rochlitz, *Für Freunde der Tonkunst*, ii (Leipzig, 1825), 281–8

every moment an idea would occur to him, and he would run to the clavier, the barber after him, hair-ribbon in hand'.[65]

On the basis of Mozart's own account it is plain that he sometimes found composition laborious and difficult – the 'Haydn' and 'Prussian' quartets are the best-known examples. Tyson's studies of the autograph scores have confirmed this. The Haydn quartets were composed over two-and-a-half years, with second thoughts and corrections. Apparently Mozart sometimes got stuck, laid a work aside, and returned to it later. This was also the case with some of the concertos. In 1800 Constanze Mozart provided Breitkopf & Härtel with a list of 98 fragments, only 58 of which survive today. All but four are from the Viennese years, so there must once have been many more than 98. Some are rejected first thoughts. Others are starts, to which no doubt Mozart intended to return later. All of this throws doubt on the myth.[66]

Surely the myth does Mozart a disservice; for it underestimates the amount of effort and devotion he put into his art. To see him as a facile composer is only one step away from judging his compositions as facile, churned out to order. It de-emphasizes the care and craftsmanship. Our own post-romantic age is increasingly impressed with this. We admire the mastery of form in the piano concertos, and the careful tonal planning of the opera finales, indeed of the operas as wholes. A recent book identifies the portions of the Requiem to be attributed to Mozart himself by the superior mastery of counterpoint evident in them. He is recognized for his skill in writing for difficult combinations of instruments – for example, the quintet for piano, oboe, clarinet, bassoon and horn K452 of which he remarked in April 1784, 'I myself consider it to be the best I have ever composed'. Whereas genius as understood by the Romantics is a purely personal

---

[65] Jahn, *Life of Mozart*, ii, 420, 433
[66] Tyson, *Mozart: Studies of the Autograph Scores*, 30ff, 94, 105, 126–7, 136, 150–1

possession, a divine afflatus, an inner power in no way dependent upon social context, craftsmanship by contrast is traditional and social. It comes from outside, is acquired from teachers and models, is embodied in rules and conventions which are not private but shared. Like language, it connects its possessor with the world, especially with other craftsmen, the 'Kenner' or experts to whom Mozart refers and whom he wished to please. Genius is a concept which does not admit of degree; a very few are gifted with it, the great mass have none at all. Craftsmanship by contrast is graded; the supreme craftsman is not utterly different, but rather some steps ahead of lesser artists. Mozart thought of as a craftsman cannot easily be thought of as semi-autistic.

For the sake of completeness, brief reference should be made to one other way of arguing that qualities which may have made Mozart a great composer also contributed to his tragedy. This is the psychoanalytic story, according to which Mozart suffered from a psychological complex or disorder. The well-documented and close relationship with the father is a wellspring of inspiration to those who like this kind of story. Brigid Brophy argues that *Don Giovanni* expresses sexual revolt against the father-figure (symbolized by the Commendatore) and also guilt because of a repressed longing for his death (Leopold had just died, and the Commendatore is killed at the beginning of the opera).[67] Ehrenwald finds that Mozart conforms to 'the classic psychoanalytic concept of an inverse oedipal conflict propelling Wolfgang into a compliant, passive-submissive – if not altogether feminine – attitude towards his father'. The Pa-pa-pa-Papageno aria in *Die Zauberflöte* is 'glorified baby talk raised to the heights of an eternally childlike genius'; Mozart's dependence on his father is symbolized by the fact that he hummed the aria as he lay semi-conscious on his

[67] Brigid Brophy, *Mozart the Dramatist* (1964) (London, 1988), 251

death bed.[68] Davies argues that Mozart, like many gifted children, was emotionally retarded because his emotional maturation could not keep pace with his intellectual development. This made him emotionally insecure and dependent. His dependency trait affected him powerfully all through his life. It caused him to seek security in the fellowship of freemasonry, and by trusting in God. It making him vulnerable to exploitation by Mme Weber, Stadler and Schikaneder, binding him in loyalty to Joseph II in spite of the failure of the court adequately to recompense him, above all tying him to his father, whose death set him on a path of depression and decline. Early acclaim had given him a hyperinflated self-image, which he never lost; but when the world failed to value him at his own estimation, he could not cope. Hence he developed manic-depressive tendencies. These account for his feverish, elated productivity and phenomenal hard work, also for his reactions into lassitude and despair. His mood-swings are reflected in his music, giving it much of its character and power. His manic-depressive tendencies were responsible for his excessive exuberance, hypersexuality, liking for drink, lavatory humour and domestic disorder.[69] They made him odd and difficult to live with.

What are such explanations worth? They appear to have scientific credentials, but in fact they are the epitome of the interpretative narrative, which weaves a pattern into the accepted data in the light of a speculative theory. They pick and select the data which accord with their preconceptions. No doubt such narratives on occasion brilliantly reveal a hidden truth; the difficulty is how to test and validate them. 'Freudian' analyses of hidden complexes are debatable even when a trained analyst confronts a living patient; how much more debatable are they when the patient is long dead,

[68] J. Ehrenwald, *Neurosis in the Family and Patterns of Psychosocial Defence: a Study of Psychiatric Epidemiology* (New York, 1963), 104–7
[69] Davies, 'Mozart's Manic-Depressive Tendencies', *Musical Times*, cxxvii (1987), 123–6; Part II, cxxvii (1987), 191–6

unable to answer for himself and to endorse or deny the truth of the interpretation. Such explanations are inherently ahistorical; they asume a timeless norm of healthy emotional life and behaviour. But Mozart's apparent submissiveness towards his father may simply reflect contemporary standards, and the lavatory humour was perhaps common in his circle. Norms are intolerant; if someone works hard and intensively, then relaxes in exuberant high spirits, must we judge that person abnormal to the point of illness?

In their search for confirmation, such explanations all too often treat the evidence uncritically. It is not proven that Mozart was exploited by Mme Weber or by Schikaneder, nor that he had a drink dependency, nor that he was oversexed. There is absolutely no evidence that he hummed the Papageno aria on his deathbed. His depression after his father's death is susceptible to other explanations – the death of his children, the illness of his wife, money problems – as is the disorder of his domestic life, if disorder there was. If joining the masons, and loving God, are signs of instability, then there is a great deal of mental illness in the world. Many have commented on the emotional complexity of Mozart's music, the way in which happiness is constantly shadowed by melancholy. But why should a liking for expressive complexity be taken as evidence for manic-depressive tendencies? Only Romantic aesthetics take it for granted that a work of art expresses the artist's own feelings. If a particular mode of aesthetic expression is effective, then that in itself may be a sufficient reason for adopting it. There is no need in addition to seek a psychological cause.

*

In conclusion, then, is there any plausibility in the story of Mozart, genius and misfit? Many will find the view of him as transcendent genius more convincing than that of him as outstanding musical craftsman. But it is essential to bear in mind the weight of historically specific cultural baggage carried by that term, vital to remember the way it has shaped the biographical tradition. The concept predisposed biographers to look for evidence of Mozart's strangeness and alienation from society. The power of the concept has made that alienation a commonplace, even though the evidence for it is very poor. In this century, the Romantic idea of genius has gradually lost its centrality in Western culture. But the story of Mozart the misfit which it produced has not retreated as rapidly. Biographers have therefore found it necessary to fill the gap left by the decline of the genius-concept, producing other narratives to explain his supposed status as outsider. One of the most important of these narratives is the subject of the next chapter: the story of the social rebel.

Chapter VII

The rebel

According to this story, the tragedy of Mozart's life and death resulted from his involvement in the social conflicts of his time. He was in revolt against a hierarchical society based upon patronage and deference, and was aligned with middle-class circles increasingly impatient of aristocratic dominance. Accordingly he had drunk deep at the well of enlightenment egalitarianism and humanism. This is an appealing story: Mozart depicted as rebel is Mozart as hero and standard-bearer of the forces of progress. There is also a German nationalist dimension.

The two thousand little courts and territories of Germany furnished legendary examples of arrogance and extravagance and of slavish imitation of Versailles.[1] Even Frederick the Great said that German was a language to use when addressing animals, and preferred nobles to bourgeois as officers in his army.[2] Mozart's career marked the difficult transition in status for a musician from servant to artist. When J.S. Bach asked permission to leave the service of the Duke of Weimar, the latter clapped him in gaol; and Haydn's contract of employment with Prince Esterházy of 1761 specified that he should wear livery, appear in the antechamber for instructions each morning, and consider his compositions the property of his employer. But when Mozart came to maturity, the idea of genius was already in the air, and he knew his own worth. Why should he defer to very ordinary beings, simply

[1] A. Fauchier-Magnan, *The Small German Courts of the Eighteenth Century* (London, 1958) is a vivid account, though the reader must guard against the author's liking for a good story.
[2] Fauchier-Magnan, 31, 52

because they were born with wealth and title? Beethoven was later to adopt this attitude, and get away with it. When Prince Lichnowsky, at whose house he was staying, threatened to arrest him because he refused to play in front of enemy officers, the composer simply reminded him that a Beethoven was worth more than a prince.[3] But Beethoven lived in a period more receptive to such attitudes, and in any case Mozart had opened the way for him. Mozart's own rebellion was too costly, in career and psychological terms; it brought upon him neglect and poverty. To compensate for the poverty he destroyed his health by overwork. Worry and despair took their toll, and the combined result was his early death. His was the tragedy of a defeated rebel.

This story, which I will first outline and then discuss, has been told many times. Elements or variants of it can be found, for example, in the books by Hildesheimer, Schenk, Ottaway, Thomson, Wangermann, Brophy and Braunbehrens.[4] Its origins can be traced back to Schlichtegroll, Niemetschek and Rochlitz. The most thoroughgoing narration of his career along these lines is a French study, learned, thoughtful and detailed, by the Massins.

* * *

Mozart's struggle against the *ancien régime* in Germany had its origin in his father's temperament and the early travels. Musicians in mid-eighteenth century Germany were largely employed in courts or households, and they were merely servants. A man might be hired as a valet and violinist. Leopold Mozart entered service at Salzburg, as a musician in the court of the archbishop who ruled that tiny state; but he

---

[3] Massin, *Wolfgang Amadeus Mozart*, 133–4, 142, 173
[4] E. Schenk, *Mozart and his Times* (London, 1960); Hugh Ottaway, *Mozart* (London, 1979); Katharine Thomson, *The Masonic Thread in Mozart* (London, 1977); Ernst Wangermann, *The Austrian Achievement 1700–1800* (London, 1973)

had ideas above his station. With his university education he was a cultivated man, who wrote an influential treatise on violin playing. Probably he saw the brilliance of his only son as a heaven-sent opportunity to emancipate himself from lowly status. The tours of the courts of Europe began, and Leopold took great care to assert a position above that of mere servant. He and his family dressed well, and stayed in the best inns. They carried letters of introduction to members of the aristocracy. As strangers and foreigners from outside the indigenous status systems of the countries they were visiting they were often well received; Leopold was delighted when George III acknowledged them in St James's Park.

The Mozarts, back in Salzburg, felt superior to their fellow-musicians in the court; they did not hesitate to show it and they resented the failure of their employers to recognize them as special people. Leopold was determined to assert the rights of his genius son. He himself, despite his abilities as composer and performer, was repeatedly passed over for the post of Kapellmeister at Salzburg. Leopold was socially aspiring, but no revolutionary; he wished to succeed, and he wished his son to succeed, within the established framework, attaining a Kapellmeistership. Mozart himself wanted such a post, but would have been restive under the restrictions and dependency it entailed. For his social unease was greater, and his experiences progressively radicalized him. Success on society's terms was not his goal. He had been made a knight of the golden spur by the Pope, an honour also conferred upon Gluck. Gluck always referred to himself as 'Ritter von Gluck', and Leopold wanted his son to make use of the decoration and the title; but Mozart disdained to do so.

Given his democratic feelings, it was inevitable that Mozart would find his position suffocating as he came to adulthood. From spring 1775 until autumn 1777 he remained in Salzburg; he mingled with the nobility of that provincial court, and composed the *galant* music they liked. But increasingly he felt wasted upon such trivialities, and galled by the condescension of his social superiors. His employer, Archbishop Colloredo, did not even bother to be polite. He suggested that Mozart ought to go to Italy to learn how to compose – a breathtaking insult to one who had three times visited that land in triumph, who had twice been commissioned to compose the carnival opera for Milan, and who had been honoured with membership of the musical academies of Bologna and Verona. Colloredo hated Mozart, and was filled with an almost sadistic desire to bring an insubordinate underling to heel.[5] The hatred was reciprocated; 'Mufti H. C. [Hieronymus Colloredo] is a prick', Mozart later wrote to his father.

In 1777, after some unpleasantness, Mozart, now aged 21, quit Salzburg service and set out on his travels, seeking a more congenial post. He went via the courts of Munich and Mannheim to Paris. His expedition, a complete failure, probably confirmed his resentment of the *ancien régime*. He sought employment with the Munich elector, for whom he had composed *La finta giardiniera*, premièred in 1775; but the elector told Prince Zeill that it was too soon, and Mozart himself that there was no vacancy.[6] He was not going to take on a rebellious servant who had left his former employer, a neighbouring prince, under a cloud. Mozart was no more successful at the court of Mannheim, with its brilliant orchestra and music-loving prince. There he fell in love with Aloysia Weber, and the fact that her father had suffered at the hands of a former noble employer may have added to her attraction in the eyes of the idealistic young man. Hitherto in Mannheim Mozart had spent much time in the company of the Wendlings, an established musical family including two excellent sopranos and a daughter who had been the elector's mistress. Writing to his father, he presented the transference of his allegiance from the Wendlings

[5] Massin, 151
[6] *LMF*, 283, 285–6

to the Webers as a reaction away from the immorality of the court towards a simple, virtuous, oppressed family.[7]

Mozart's love for Aloysia drove him to an outburst against the aristocratic arranged marriage:

> People of noble birth must never marry from inclination or love, but only from interest and all kinds of secondary considerations . . . But we poor humble people can not only choose a wife whom we love and who loves us, but we may, can and do take such a one, because we are neither noble, nor highly born, nor aristocratic, nor rich, but, on the contrary, lowly born, humble, and poor; so we do not need a wealthy wife, for our riches, being in our brains, die with us – and these no man can take from us unless he chops off our heads.[8]

Leopold had no sympathy with his son's desire to marry Aloysia and go off freelancing with her to Italy, she to be a *prima donna* and he a composer of operas for her to sing. He ordered his son to set out for Paris forthwith. Mozart was now faced with the key decision of his life; should he follow his father's plan for him, seeking a position at court, or should he make a bid for personal and creative freedom?[9] For the time being, he obeyed his father; but the rebellious fires within him had not been quenched. He would never crawl to get a job; from Munich he had written 'and let there be no cringing, for I cannot bear that'.[10]

Leopold, remembering their warm reception in Paris when his son was eight years old, wrote 'From Paris the name and fame of a man of great talent resounds throughout the whole world. There the nobility treat men of genius with the greatest deference, esteem and courtesy'.[11] But Paris had

[7] *LMF*, 459–62; Massin, 209–10
[8] *LMF*, 467
[9] Massin, 223
[10] *LMF*, 415
[11] *LMF*, 478

changed. France was now touched by that aristocratic reaction which prepared the way for revolution.[12] Here is Mozart's own report of his visit to the Duchesse de Chabot:

> I had to wait for half an hour in a large ice-cold, unheated room, which hadn't even a fireplace. At last the Duchesse de Chabot appeared. She was very polite and asked me to make the best of the clavier in the room, as none of her own were in good condition. Would I perhaps try it? I said that I would be delighted to play something, but that it was impossible at the moment, as my fingers were numb with cold; and I asked her to have me taken at least to a room where there was a fire. 'Oh oui, Monsieur, vous avés raison', was all the reply I got. She then sat down and began to draw and continued to do so for a whole hour, having as company some gentlemen, who all sat in a circle round a big table, while I had the honour to wait. The windows and doors were open and not only my hands but my whole body and my feet were frozen and my head began to ache . . . At last, to cut my story short, I played on that miserable, wretched pianoforte. But what vexed me most of all was that Madame and all her gentlemen never interrupted their drawing for a moment, but went on intently, so that I had to play to the chairs, tables and walls.[13]

His stay in Paris brought him neither a permanent post nor a profit. He became very unhappy there, and wrote to the family friend Abbé Bullinger 'You know well that the best and truest of all friends are the poor. The wealthy do not know what friendship means, especially those who are born to riches'.[14] He had to return, defeated, to Salzburg in 1779, where his father had contrived for him a rather better post with his former employer. But this return simply prepared the way for Mozart's most dramatic confrontation with the social order.

[12] Massin, 237
[13] *LMF*, 531
[14] *LMF*, 593

The crisis came when Mozart's employer, Archbishop Colloredo, went to Vienna in 1781, taking his musicians with him. Mozart was not allowed to live out, but was accommodated in the household. He wrote to his father:

> We lunch about twelve o'clock . . . Our party consists of the two valets. . .the controleur, Herr Zetti, the confectioner, the two cooks, Ceccarelli, Brunetti and – my insignificant self! By the way, the two valets sit at the top of the table, but at least I have the honour of being placed above the cooks.[15]

Mozart would not behave as a servant should, waiting outside until summoned. On one occasion Colloredo took his musicians to the house of Prince Galitzin, the Russian ambassador:

> When we are summoned to a house where there is a concert, Herr Angebauer has to watch outside until the Salzburg gentlemen arrive, when he sends a lackey to show them the way in . . . I thought to myself, 'Just wait till I come along!' . . . When I got upstairs, I found Angebauer standing there to direct the lackey to show me in. But I took no notice, either of the valet or the lackey, but walked straight on through the rooms into the music room, for all the doors were open, – and went straight up to the Prince, paid him my respects and stood there talking to him.[16]

No doubt in retaliation, the archbishop prevented Mozart from making money on the side, by performing for a fee; on one occasion Mozart lost 50 ducats as a result, a sum equivalent to half his annual salary. Mozart abused the archbishop in his letters home, disdaining to write in the family code, knowing that the letters might be opened and read by Colloredo's agents. Finally, his employer instructed him to leave for Salzburg immediately, carrying an important package. But this would have meant that Mozart could not collect monies due to him in Vienna, and so he declined to go,

[15] *LMF*, 713–4
[16] *LMF*, 717

making an excuse. Here is Mozart's account of the show-down; the archbishop addressed him as *er* (*he*), a mode of address contemptuously reserved for underlings:

> Then it all burst out – I was the most dissolute fellow he knew – no one served him so badly as I did – I had better leave today or else he would write home and have my salary stopped. I couldn't get a word in edgeways, for he blazed away like a fire. I listened to it all very calmly . . . He called me a scoundrel, a rascal, a vagabond . . . At last my blood began to boil, I could no longer contain myself and I said, 'So Your Grace is not satisfied with me?' 'What, he dares to threaten me – the scoundrel, O the scoundrel! There is the door! Look out, for I will have nothing more to do with such a miserable wretch' . . . I hate the archbishop to madness.[17]

But he was not allowed to go just yet; he had to petition for his dismissal, and it was another month before he was re-leased in the most humiliating way, with a kick on the arse from Count Arco, a senior member of the household. Mozart wrote to his father:

> It is the heart that ennobles a man; and though I am no count, yet I have probably more honour in me than many a count. Whether a man be count or valet, the moment he insults me, he is a scoundrel.[18]

This was a landmark, not only in the life of Mozart, but in musical history, for it marked the first open rebellion of a musician against feudal society.[19]

After 1781 Mozart was based in Vienna; he did not again seek employment at a noble or princely court. He wanted an imperial appointment however, being happy to serve the progressive Joseph II, the emperor who dispensed with eti-quette, who walked among his subjects in the parks of Vienna

[17] *LMF*, 727–9
[18] *LMF*, 747
[19] Thomson, 51

and who took a hand at the plough when travelling in the countryside. It was because of his progressive social views that Mozart turned down a lucrative post at the Prussian court, preferring to stay with his good emperor.[20] This was the reason for his special rapport with Prague, a radical city, the centre of Bohemian nationalism, with a strong anti-feudal bourgeoisie.[21] Significantly, the Prague Symphony omits the aristocratic minuet.[22]

Mozart obtained the imperial appointment he desired, but not until 1787; and the salary, of 800 florins per annum, did not suffice to keep him and his family. How was a musician, at odds with the aristocratic patronage system, to live? From 1777, when he first left Salzburg service and sought his fortune on route to Paris, we find Mozart in quest of a wider paying audience. The Concert des Amateurs in Paris, a series of concerts aimed at a wide audience, showed him the way. When finally he settled in Vienna, he enjoyed a spell of prosperity after 1782, based to a considerable extent on a series of public concerts or academies, beginning with those in the Augarten.[23]

Mozart's bid for an existence based upon a wider public failed, plunging him into debt and despair. Aristocratic patronage was still essential; for Austria, backward in trade and industry, lacked a substantial urban bourgeoisie.[24] In 1788–9 his subscription concerts collapsed, as the aristocracy increasingly turned against him.[25]

Johann Georg Naumann, composer and Kapellmeister to the court of Dresden, is said to have referred to Mozart as 'a musical sans-culotte'.[26] Aristocratic listeners would have

[20] J. S. Curl, 'Mozart Considered as a Jacobin', *Music Review*, xxxv (1974), 136
[21] Ottaway, 128; Thomson, 99
[22] Thomson, 111
[23] Massin, 386
[24] P. G. M. Dickson, *Finance and Government under Maria-Theresa 1740–1780* (Oxford, 1987), i, 51–2
[25] Massin, 508
[26] Ottaway, 97

been offended by a rebelliousness in Mozart's music. The German *Sturm und Drang* movement, which affected music in the 1770s and literature in the 1780s, was a movement of revolt. In the first place it was a revolt against classical moderation and reason – an outburst of wildness and passion. Secondly, it was a rebellion against French cultural hegemony and standards of taste. But thirdly, it was a repudiation of aristocratic rococo, superficiality and frivolity. Instead of providing light entertainment for courtiers, the *Sturm und Drang* artist expresses himself, and especially the boiling turmoil of passion within him. It is a liberty-affirming assertion of the individual against a suffocating social order, a rebellion which is constrained to take a cultural rather than political form, because of the economic backwardness of Germany.

In the creative output of Haydn and Mozart, the so-called *Sturm und Drang* compositions mark only a brief and passing phase. The rebellious élan of the early 1770s broke against the demand of princely employers for *galant* music. Musicians were as yet slaves, and had to submit their necks to the yoke again. But while Haydn conformed, Mozart did not, and this is the measure of his courage and grandeur as an artist.[27] He worked within the characteristic forms of the *galant* style, namely the concerto and the *opera buffa*, he maintained the appearance of providing courtly entertainment music: but by filling them with expressive, passionate content, he subverted the spirit of those forms. This was one of the most important revolutions in the history of music, far more important than Haydn's formal innovations. His aristocratic audiences in Vienna became increasingly uneasy, sensing that he was not playing the game according to the rules; they progressively withdrew their support. The centrality of the piano concerto in his output of these years is significant, for the debate between soloist and orchestra symbolizes the

[27] Massin, 689

growing alienation of the non-aristocratic individual from the society of the *ancien régime*.[28]

There was a further shift in Mozart's style, of political significance, in his last years. This is the development of his so-called 'humanist' style. The sentimentalism of the literature of the third quarter of the century, and the *Sturm und Drang*, concern themselves with individual feeling and passion, with romantic love and longing, with compassion for dying lambs and frost-bitten shepherds. During the last quarter, this mood develops into something grand, serious and universal - into an enthusiasm for the love which binds, or should bind, a nation, or indeed the whole of humanity. This is a central aspect of the aesthetic tendency known as neoclassicism; it culminates in the last movement of Beethoven's Ninth Symphony, the 'Ode to Joy', really to freedom, with its vision of universal brotherhood: words by Schiller, music by Beethoven, both archetypical artistic and social rebels. But Mozart anticipates this mood, in his masonic music, in *La clemenza di Tito* and in *Die Zauberflöte*.[29]

A major part in the story of Mozart as social rebel is played by the operas of his maturity. Or maybe the story starts even earlier, with *Bastien und Bastienne*, composed in 1768 when Mozart was twelve to a story by Rousseau. Ignoring juvenilia, where opera is concerned Mozart's radicalism is revealed in his attitude to genre. Opera was an Italian invention, and Italian opera had an enduring prestige. Italy supplied a treasure house of librettos, and a succession of celebrated composers and singers. Italian opera was paramount in Mozart's Germany. Yet he was enthusiastic for the German Singspiel, a genre of opera in the German language with spoken dialogue, composing *Die Entführung* and *Die Zauberflöte* and founding the tradition of German opera in the process.

[28] Massin, 891, 958, 1027
[29] Thomson, 45; Wangermann, 148

> I do not believe that Italian opera will keep going for very long, and besides, I hold with the Germans. I prefer German opera, even though it means more trouble for me. Every nation has its own opera – why shouldn't we Germans have ours? . . . Were there but one good patriot in charge – things would take a different turn. But then, perhaps, the German national theatre which is sprouting so vigorously would actually begin to flower; and of course that would be an everlasting blot on Germany, if we Germans were seriously to begin to think German, to act German, to speak German and even to sing German!![30]

For Mozart's democratic humanism aligned him with German nationalism and put him at odds with Frenchified and Italianate court society. His enthusiasm for German singspiel stemmed from his determination, already noted, to find a wider, non-aristocratic audience.

Die Entführung is a progressive enlightenment opera.[31] Pasha Selim is a noble Turk, after the pattern of Lessing's Sultan Saladin or Goethe's King Thoas, his rational tolerance providing at once a contrast with European religious fanaticism and a complement to the enlightenment of Emperor Joseph II. Hence a central theme of the opera was the overcoming of national hatreds, and the ideal of human reconciliation. Alongside this was placed the sub-plot, comic, but with a serious message: the conflict between the servants, Blonde and Osmin, a conflict between the spirit of liberty and bloodthirsty despotism. For Blonde, as she insists, is 'an Englishwoman, and born to freedom'. We are reminded of Mozart's remark in a letter to his father three months after the première: 'Indeed I have heard about England's victories and am greatly delighted too, for you know that I am an out-and-out Englishman'.[32]

[30] *LMF*, 839, 891
[31] Wangermann, 152; Massin, 900–1
[32] *LMF*, 828

When the attempt to establish German opera failed, Mozart had to turn back to Italian. In this context, Mozart's enlightened humanitarianism is revealed in his preference for *opera buffa* over *opera seria*. Traditionally, serious opera had the higher prestige. Like the historical paintings on the walls of Baroque palaces, it depicted the tragic and heroic actions of gods, kings and warriors. The appropriate lofty and dignified style was captured in the admired librettos of Metastasio, often taking their themes from Greek and Roman history and mythology. It was a genre adapted to the celebration of an idealized monarchy and aristocracy, but the stage action could be all too conventionalized and stiff, with a repetitive rhythm of recitative followed by exit aria. Gluck was the instigator of a reform, designed to make this genre less wooden and more dramatic. When he had no choice but to compose *opera seria*, Mozart followed Gluck. The heroes of his mature operas in this form – Idomeneus and Titus – take on something of the enlightened benevolence of Sarastro and Pasha Selim.[33] Hence the dislike of the assembled court for *La clemenza di Tito* – dismissed by the new Empress, according to legend, as 'German swinishness'.[34]

Opera buffa, comic opera, was looser in structure, faster and more dramatic, concerned with the modern world, with ordinary people and servants as well as aristocrats. It offered the opportunity for the depiction of character and real-life emotion. The social and political meaning of *opera buffa* for Mozart is evident above all in *Le nozze di Figaro*. As everybody knows, the libretto, written by Lorenzo da Ponte, was closely based on the play by Beaumarchais. His *Le mariage de Figaro* was highly critical of the *ancien régime*. It was meant to be subversive and was a *succès de scandale* in Paris. Though the play was banned in Austria, Mozart himself chose it as the subject for his opera. Da Ponte insisted in his memoirs that he got it past the censor by appealing direct to

[33] Levey, *Life and Death of Mozart*, 133; Ottaway, 176
[34] Schenk, 439

Joseph II, promising to leave out the offending portions. For all that, the opera remains a tale of conflict between a lascivious count, reluctant to forego the feudal *ius primae noctis*, and his servants who outwit and humiliate him at every turn. Admittedly the debunking and hoodwinking of the high and mighty by their servants was an established part of the *opera buffa* convention; this *genre* is a form of charivari, of licensed impertinence. But the difference with *Le nozze di Figaro* is that licensed impertinence continually topples over into rebellious insolence, because of the passion and seriousness of the music. 'Figaro was to be the beginning of his ruin. The upper classes, used to seeing themselves as characters in *opera seria*, glorified in everlasting kindness and sovereignty, . . . didn't much like it'.[35] So *Figaro* never achieved in Vienna the success it deserved.

Figaro is the most obviously subversive of the Da Ponte operas; but *Don Giovanni* could be regarded as a satire on the dissolute manners of the aristocracy, and it was at first banned in Munich. In recent times Joseph Losey found no difficulty in turning the opera into a film with a marxist message. In the catalogue aria, we witness the spectacle of a valet putting down an aristocratic lady, rather sadistically. Masetto's aria is an explicit protest against aristocratic privilege; he is 'a peasant ready for armed revolt'.[36]

Così fan tutte looks like a pulling back from radicalism, a bit of frivolous rococo intended to please aristocratic circles. The languid Count Zinzendorf, whose Vienna diaries are often quoted, for once found the work charming, his only recorded complimentary remark about a Mozart opera. But even here Mozart's progressive social stance can be discerned. Despina is contrasted with her mistresses, the social parasites she serves; she is 'the element of penetrating intelligence among the vapid lovers'. Alternatively, the opera as a whole has been interpreted as a commentary on the conflict

[35] Hildesheimer, *Mozart*, 182
[36] Massin, 1055

between love and the arranged marriage, ending with under-
tones of tragedy when the arranged marriages of the *ancien
régime* are reasserted.[37]

Brigid Brophy argues that the rebellion expressed in the
Da Ponte operas is sexual, generational and feminist as well as
social. The enlightenment in her view is a revolt on behalf of
the pleasure principle, against taboo and against Christianity.
It is therefore a revolt also against the father, who upholds
the taboos in order to restrain the sexuality of the children,
and against society, which incarnates the father in its class
system. Mozart was a rebel in all these ways. His scatalogical
humour was a manifestation of his repudiation of taboo, and
he was a frankly sensual man, enjoying a fulfilled erotic
relationship with his Constanze. He turned from Christianity
to freemasonry, and freed himself from bondage to his father
and to his Christian-princely patron at the same moment. His
rebellion was also on behalf of women. Opera lent itself to
this; it gave a central role to the soprano, female voice and it
also fostered female stars celebrated for their musical and
sexual glamour. All of this is expressed in his operas. In
Figaro we witness an alliance of all the oppressed classes, of
servants, women and the young.

Mozart's social and cultural radicalism is revealed above all
in his enthusiasm for freemasonry and his masonic compositions, especially *Die Zauberflöte*. He joined the Viennese
lodge *Zur Wohltätigkeit* ('Benevolence') on 14 December
1784. When the lodges were reorganized by Imperial edict in
1785, Mozart's became part of the *Neugekrönte Hoffnung*
('New Crowned Hope' – the 'New' was later dropped from
the title).[38] His contact with freemasonry and the enlightened culture which influenced it was of longer standing. His
father had many enlightened attitudes, and under Archbishop
Colloredo, Salzburg came to have a reputation as a city where

---

[37] Curl, 136; Massin, 1105ff
[38] For the established facts of Mozart's masonry, as opposed to fable and
speculation, see Deutsch, *Mozart und die Wiener Logen*

ideas could be exchanged freely and advanced publications purchased.[39] The Mozarts had several close friends among Salzburg and Munich masons; some were also Illuminati.[40] This organization, which began in Bavaria, was distinct from freemasonry; but it adopted a policy of entering masonic lodges with a view to taking them over. Its ideas were those of the radical enlightenment.

A number of Mozart's friends and patrons in Vienna have been cited as Illuminati, the most important being Van Swieten and Ignaz von Born. Born was a distinguished chemist, and Grand Master for a time of the elite Viennese lodge, *Zur wahren Eintracht* ('True Concord'). Mozart often visited this lodge, and his cantata *Die Maurerfreude* was composed and performed in honour of Born. It has been argued that he was greatly attracted to and influenced by Born, that Born suggested some of the ideas of the libretto of *Die Zauberflöte* and that Born was the model for Sarastro.[41]

Where ideas are concerned, actual membership of the Illuminati is not crucial. Many masons shared with the Illuminati the humanitarianism and egalitarianism of the progressive enlightenment. These attitudes take on significance in the contexts of Mozart's career and music. For example, an Illuminatist publication advised: 'Aim at preventing servile respect of princes . . . Flattery corrupts men – speak to them as equals, so that they may learn that they are men like other men, masters only by convention'.[42] Lessing wrote in his *Masonic Dialogues*:

> By the exercise of Brotherly love we are taught to regard the
> whole human species as one family, the high and the low, the

---

[39] Heinz Schuler, 'Freimaurer und Illuminaten aus Alt-Bayern und Salzburg und ihre Beziehungen zu den Mozarts', *Mitteilungen der Internationalen Stiftung Mozarteum*, xxv/1–4 (1987), 21
[40] Schuler, 14–19, 25–33, 35–7
[41] Thomson, 63; Chailley, *The Magic Flute*, 16–17
[42] Thomson, 52

rich and the poor, created by one Almighty Being, and sent into the world for the aid, support and protection of each other.[43]

And when Van Swieten heard in 1774 that general primary education was to be provided in the lands of the Habsburg monarchy, he declared: 'At last the time has come when the truth is emerging in new splendour from the dark clouds which have enveloped it, and is entering upon its rights'.[44] How reminiscent this is of Sarastro's majestic proclamation before the final chorus of *Die Zauberflöte*: 'The sun's radiance drives away the night, destroying the fraudulent power of the hypocrites'.

Whatever Mozart's relationship to the Illuminati may have been, there can be little doubt that he was an enthusiastic mason. Where records survive, we find him a regular attender at lodge meetings; he composed works for masonic festivities and for fellow-masons, he performed in masonic concerts. It may be that his warm reception in Prague was prepared and aided by the masons there.[45] His last completed composition was a masonic cantata; he directed the first performance of it at his lodge seventeen days before he died.

Mozart's masonic enthusiasm earned him the suspicion of the rich and powerful. For example it turned him into an outsider by weakening his orthodox Catholic faith. Perhaps this was why he was unable to complete the C minor Mass. He began work on the Credo, but had to stop halfway through.[46] The masonic historian Paul Nettl notes that references to religion in Mozart's letters become less frequent as time goes on; it is true that in a letter to his wife of June 1791 he announced that he would join the Corpus Christi procession on the following day carrying a candle, but he signed the announcement with his fool's name, 'Snai'.[47]

[43] Thomson, 13
[44] Wangermann, 148
[45] Favier, *Vie de Mozart*, 78; Nettl, *Mozart and Masonry*, 20
[46] Massin, 933
[47] Nettl, 115–6; *LMF*, 957

Did Mozart receive the last sacraments as he lay dying? According to Sophie Haibl's famous letter to Nissen of 1825, telling about Mozart's last days:

> My poor sister followed me to the door and begged me for Heaven's sake to go to the priests at St Peter's and implore one of then to come to Mozart – a chance call, as it were. I did so, but for a long time they refused to come and I had a great deal of trouble to persuade one of those clerical brutes to go to him.[48]

This gives the impression that a priest came in the end; but later Sophie told a different story to J. P. Lyser. According to him the priest said: 'This musician was always a bad Catholic. I'm not going to him!'[49] So Mozart did not receive communion, perhaps because he was a mason;[50] 'but another, more tolerant priest anointed his body'.

The texts of Mozart's masonic compositions probably seem bland, high-flown and generalized to most people today. They revolve around a number of abstractions: knowledge, wisdom, truth and light; nature; virtue; brotherhood, benevolence, union of hearts, and humanity. These are the themes of *Die Zauberflöte*, in which the empire of light and truth overcomes the darkness of ignorance, love triumphs over hatred and envy. To attuned contemporary minds, however, they would not have seemed bland. The ideal of universal brotherly love is not only cosmopolitan; it also calls into question the rigid, divisive hierarchy of the old regime. Hence there is salvation even for Papageno, the servant: 'But Tamino himself cannot be truly happy unless Papageno is happy also. Papageno's success is an integral part of Tamino's, for happiness must either be universal or a nullity. Such is the supreme moral of the *Flute*.'[51] This egalitarianism may

[48] *LMF*, 976
[49] Kayser, *Mozart-Album*, 64
[50] Massin, 573
[51] Massin, 1159; Wangermann, 153

embrace women also. Chailly thinks that one of the messages of *Die Zauberflöte* is criticism of the female Lodges of Adoption. Yet in spite of this Pamina leads Tamino through the initiatory trials of water and fire, and is received with him into the temple. Other commentators have unequivocally hailed the opera as a feminist work.[52] There can be little doubt that the opera, and the masonic compositions in general, would have struck contemporaries as scarcely veiled attacks upon intolerance and superstition. Their hymn to reason and truth advocates free inquiry and implicitly criticizes the catholic church. From a progressive point of view, *Die Zauberflöte* was 'the culmination of the Austrian achievement in the age of Enlightenment'.[53]

Mozart's strong, thought-out commitment to freemasonry damaged his worldly prospects and darkened his last years. For the tide turned decisively against the masons. The trouble really began in Bavaria in 1784, with a spate of sensational revelations about the activities of the Illuminati. Their founder, Adam Weishaupt, had built a secret organisation, modelled, it was said, upon the Jesuits, spreading its tentacles all over Germany and indeed Europe, exercising power behind the scenes, plotting to overthrow religion and the social order. Illuminism and masonry were not the same, but many masons were, or were thought to be, Illuminists, and so suspicion fell on the orthodox masons as well. In June 1784 the Bavarian elector published an edict forbidding his subjects to be members of secret associations; in March he explicitly condemned the Illuminati *and* the freemasons. Eventually the death penalty was decreed for anyone attempting to recruit to the order.

There had been greater official tolerance of freemasonry in the Habsburg lands, but in December 1785 Joseph II published an edict on the subject. The preamble criticized the

[52] Brophy, *Mozart the Dramatist*, 71, 299–300
[53] Wangermann, 155

masons for their secrecy and for corruptly favouring their own members. It also suggested that there was too much gambling and gluttony in the lodges. Joseph ordered a reduction of membership and a uniting of the eight Viennese lodges into three. Meetings were to be notified to the police and lists of members supplied. The golden age of Austrian masonry was over. The rising tide of anti-masonic publications was swelled by the French revolution of 1789; many maintained that the revolution was caused by a masonic conspiracy. Mozart, as an active and enthusiastic mason, fell under suspicion. This was a major cause of his fall from favour with the Viennese nobility and court. This is why he was not invited to the music-making at the coronation of Leopold II at Frankfurt, in spite of his high position in the court's musical establishment.[54] At this time the Viennese authorities were becoming increasingly concerned about the activities of the masons. In October 1791 a confidant wrote to Leopold about an Illuminatist conspiracy, implicating Mozart's patron Van Swieten. On the very day of Mozart's death, Swieten was dismissed from his official position. If Mozart had lived he would probably have been sacked too; *Die Zauberflöte* was a standing invitation to the police and there may well have been a file on him.[55] Some of his circle – friends, and fellow Viennese masons – were caught in the toils of the Jacobin trials of 1794. Von Taufferer was executed; von Urazowa's body was publicly hanged after he had committed suicide in prison; Prandstätter died in prison and Wolstein was banished.[56]

Immediately after Mozart's death, nasty rumours began to circulate about his alleged dissolute life. Was this an attempt to discredit a mason? Anti-masonic literature frequently employed this tactic, hinting at excesses and vices of all kinds

[54] Massin, 518–20,
[55] Robbins Landon, *Golden Years*, 225–9; Ottaway, 179
[56] Hans Wagner, 'Das Josephinische Wien und Mozart', *MJb 1978–9*, 8

in the lodges.[57] In response there was a concerted attempt, directed primarily by the widow, to clean up Mozart's image, purifying it of any suspicion of Jacobinism and infidelity. The keystone of the attempt to 'rehabilitate' Mozart was the Requiem, and this dishonest purpose is a major source of the legends and lies surrounding it. The aim was to depict Mozart dying in an odour of sanctity, moved to the core of his being by this work, desperately trying to complete it, his master-piece, his final testament. In truth it may be doubted whether it interested him very much. The correspondence of his last months bears testimony to his excitement about *Die Zauberflöte* but makes no mention of the Requiem. Constanze said that he broke off work on the Mass because she took away the score, concerned about his health. In all probability he worked on it only in odd moments, gladly turning to other projects such as the Clarinet Concerto, and finally taking up something which interested him much more, the masonic cantata *Laut verkünde unsre Freude*. This, not the Requiem, was his final testament.[58]

* * *

The story of Mozart the defeated rebel is undoubtedly im-pressive. It weaves a pattern into the known facts of his life and death, embracing and ordering a great many of them. Does this pattern have validity? Let us begin by considering the social, political and religious significance of Viennese freemasonry, both in general, and specifically for Mozart.

The first point to make is that the hostility of emperors Joseph II and Leopold II should not be overstated. Joseph was not himself a mason; but he began his independent reign regarding the masons as allies in the cause of enlightened reform. More than this, he hoped to use the organization to

[57] Massin, 580; J. M. Roberts, *The Mythology of the Secret Societies* (London, 1972), 60–61
[58] Massin, 559, 565, 568, 1162

The rebel

promote and propagandize his policies.[59] The élite Viennese lodge was the *Wahren Eintracht* ('True Concord'), with a membership including distinguished writers, artists, scientists and politicians; Joseph may have thought of it as an intellectual powerhouse of reform. Its Grand Master, Ignaz von Born, was an Imperial counsellor and was honoured by the emperor with the title of Imperial Knight in 1785. In the light of this, Joseph's edict of 1785 should perhaps be understood, not as an attack on the masons but as an attempt to control and use them more effectively.

Joseph's succesor, Leopold, was thought by many to be a mason. He combined his predecessor's enlightened reforming aims with a greater tact and realism. Inevitably he regarded the masons with some suspicion; his sister, Marie Antoinette, was in great trouble in France and there were those who blamed the French revolution upon the freemasons. But if some of his advisers were telling him about masonic plots, others were advising him that the masons were harmless.[60] Reaction did not set in in Austria until the reign of Leopold's successor, Francis II, who came to the throne after Leopold's sudden death in March 1792.

If Mozart's masonry did him no great harm in the eyes of reforming emperors, did it damage his reputation with the Viennese aristocracy, not all of whom sympathized with reform? Did it associate him in their eyes with a rising and potentially revolutionary bourgeoisie? In fact, eighteenth-century freemasonry took its colour, chameleon-like, from its surroundings. In economically advanced centres and commercial districts it was dominated by the new bourgeoisie; in

[59] This is the argument of H. Wagner, 'Die politische und kulturelle Bedeutung der Freimaurer im 18. Jahrhundert', *Beförderer der Aufklärung in Mittel- und Osteuropa: Freimaurer, Gesellschaften, Clubs*, ed. E. H. Balazs, L. Hammermayer, H. Wagner and J. Wojtowicz (Berlin, 1979); 'Die Freimaurer und die Reformen Kaiser Josephs II', *Quatuor Coronati Jahrbuch*, xiv (1977)
[60] Robbins Landon, *Golden Years*, 230–3; F. Bernhardt, 'Freemasonry in Austria', *Transactions of the Ars Quatuor Coronatorum* (1963), 76

198

ports by merchants; in garrison towns by officers; in provincial towns with little industry by the notables of the *ancien régime*; and in capital cities by courtiers, soldiers and government officials.[61]

Viennese masonry was no exception. A printed list survives of the members of Mozart's lodge for 1790.[62] There were 200 brothers plus twelve servants, 'serving brothers'. 45% of the non-serving brothers were noble, over half of these being counts or barons. The Grand Master was Count Johann Esterházy, and the Master of Ceremonies was Prince Nikolaus Esterházy, Haydn's employer. Over half of the attending brothers were soldiers or officials, easily outnumbering the combined total of teachers, doctors, artists, musicians, merchants, manufacturers and bankers. Mozart's lodge does not have the appearance of a socially subversive organization.

Throughout Europe, eighteenth-century freemasonry had no difficulty in accommodating the landed aristocracy. In theory, all masons were brothers; but in practice, some lodges were socially selective and many adopted the 'Scottish' rite which permitted the preservation of social hierarchy by a system of higher grades. The orthodox masons in Vienna, however, followed the 'English' rite with three grades only. The top grade of Master Mason was open to all, and in Mozart's lodge in 1790 half of the serving brothers were Master Masons. One wonders whether they addressed Prince Nikolaus as 'Brother'; even more interesting, whether *he* spoke to *them* in such familiar language. Some Viennese masons were later to side with political reaction;[63] but much goes to suggest that freemasonry in the Austrian capital was enlightened and progressive, and this must be regarded as

[61] French scholars have done excellent work on the sociology of freemasonry; see D. Ligou, ed., *Histoire des francs-maçons en France* (Toulouse, 1981), 97–116
[62] Published in Robbins Landon, *Golden Years*, and in his *Mozart and the Masons: New Light on the Lodge "Crowned Hope"* (London, 1982)
[63] Wagner, 'Das Josephinische Wien und Mozart', 8

prima facie evidence for Mozart's own stance. But it does not make him a revolutionary, or an outsider. There is absolutely no direct evidence that he was regarded as such, nor that he was affiliated to the Illuminati.

It cannot be inferred that, because a man was a mason in eighteenth-century Vienna, therefore he was anti-Christian or anti-Catholic. Seven priests belonged to Mozart's lodge, and the masonic funeral oration in his honour spoke of dying as a mason and a Christian. The German enlightenment, unlike the French, was markedly religious. It is difficult to believe that Mozart did not receive the last sacraments; Lyser's report should be regarded with suspicion. Shortly before his death, Mozart was appointed deputy-Kapellmeister at St Stephen's Cathedral, a post which would hardly have been given to a notorious bad Catholic. The Massins are probably right in saying that he did not spend much time working on the Requiem; but he certainly had not lost interest in church music. Tyson's work on paper-types and watermarks has shown that a number of transcriptions and fragments of religious music, hitherto attributed to the pre-Vienna period, in fact came from the last years of his life.[64]

A man might join the masons for other reasons than to affirm social and cultural radicalism. Mozart, it has been suggested, may have joined because masonic teaching and rituals helped him to come to terms with the terrors of death.[65] Membership had advantages for those whose business caused them to travel; as visitors they could enter a lodge in a strange town and have a ready-made social circle – hence the appeal of freemasonry to soldiers, sailors, merchants and travelling actors and musicians. Mozart almost certainly benefited in this way in Prague, and perhaps in other towns too. He borrowed money, probably on better

[64] Maunder, *Mozart's Requiem*, 10; Tyson, *Mozart: Studies of the Autograph Scores*, 26–7
[65] Brophy, *Mozart the Dramatist*, is good on this; see also Schiedermair, *Mozart*, 269

than market terms, from fellow-masons, Hofdemel and above all Puchberg. Finally, membership could appeal to the social climber rather than the social rebel; in the Viennese lodges a commoner could mix on easy terms with the highest aristocracy of the land.

Nothing conclusive can be inferred about Mozart's convictions from his masonic compositions. In spite of the attempt, by Chailly and others, to argue that Mozart played a major part in writing the libretto of *Die Zauberflöte*, it is perfectly possible that the title-page is correct, and that the libretto was entirely Schikaneder's work. His letter of application to join the masons in Regensburg demonstrates that he could write in the elevated style required.[66] None of the other masonic texts is by Mozart himself. Their sentiments are of such a general nature that no revolutionary passion would be required to set them effectively. Joy, benevolence, majesty, the dawning of light – Mozart would have been able to provide appropriate music to accompany these themes, even if he had never been a mason.

Did Mozart's operas really strike his audience as unusually subversive? Whatever the intended message of *Die Zauberflöte*, only freemasons would have grasped most of it. No contemporary document says that *Figaro* was thought politically suspect. It is true that there is a letter by Mozart himself, describing the opposition of a prominent lady in Prague to the mounting of the opera there in 1787 in honour of Archduchess Maria Theresa and her new husband. She found it

> very ridiculous, unsuitable, and Heaven knows what else that the Princess should be entertained with a performance of Figaro, the 'Crazy Day', as they like to call it. It never occurred to them that no opera in the world, unless it is written especially for it, can be exactly suitable for such an occasion.[67]

[66] Nettl, 61
[67] *LMF*, 911

It is by no means obvious that the unsuitability perceived by this 'high and mighty' lady was in fact political – perhaps she found it too frivolous, or licentious. She was overruled by Joseph II himself. If Mozart was seen as enlightened and progressive, perhaps he was considered one of the emperor's men. This may have gained him enemies among the opponents of Joseph's reforms: it would not have earned him general ostracism. It has recently been suggested that *Figaro* disappointed the Viennese because it was not *more* inflammatory; they were expecting a scandal and a sensation and they did not get it.[68] As Sacheverell Sitwell wrote in the 1930s,

> All political feeling, all the revolutionary moral, had been stripped from the play, and Mozart turned it, instead, into a mirror for all the finer feelings and fine manners of the old time. A person who wanted to see the old world of Europe at its best, before it was touched by industrialism, and by America, need only hear *The Marriage of Figaro*.[69]

An obvious reason why Mozart might have chosen the Beaumarchais play was that it was the sequel to *The Barber of Seville*, which had recently been turned into an opera by Paisiello with great success. Comparison of the scores of the two operas reveals that Mozart had Paisiello's setting in mind; there are echoes and even musical links.[70] The opera often appears to reflect and endorse the social hierarchy. Its arias have a marked class character: the Count's revenge aria is more dignified than Bartolo's; the Countess has an aristocratic charisma that Susanna does not possess.

The hypothesis that Mozart's socially progressive stance is revealed in his attitude to genre – preferring German Singspiel to Italian opera, and *opera buffa* to *opera seria* –

---

[68] Steptoe, *The Mozart-Da Ponte Operas*, 184
[69] Sitwell, *Mozart*, 42–3
[70] Daniel Heartz, 'Constructing *Le nozze di Figaro*', *Journal of the Royal Musical Association*, cxii (1987), 77–98

must also be rejected. His passion was to compose operas, and he was ready to write in whatever genre was required. Questions of genre paled beside his demand for a good, singable, dramatic libretto. There are letters in which he expresses a preference or argues for German opera. On another occasion he wrote 'Do not forget how much I desire to write operas. I envy anyone who is composing one. I could really weep for vexation when I hear or see an aria. But Italian, not German: seriosa, not buffa'.[71] The story that the Prague Symphony has only three movements because Mozart the radical was happy to please a radical city by omitting the courtly minuet is challenged by Tyson's suggestion that the three-movement form was the result of accident. Mozart planned to give the three-movement Paris Symphony, but with a new finale; then, realizing that the new movement sat ill with the first two, he replaced them as well.[72] In any case, the four-movement symphony was by no means established as a near-universal norm in 1786.[73] In the previous decade Mozart had been composing symphonies without minuets for the Salzburg court.

Mozart's social demeanour in his Vienna years remains a mystery. When with the nobility, was he assertive and surly, uneasy or at his ease, frank or mildly sycophantic? Hostility to the aristocracy is expressed in his correspondence during two limited periods of his life only: at the time of his unhappy expedition to Paris, and on the occasion of his final breach with Colloredo. He had plenty of aristocratic patrons – the subscription list for his Lent concerts in 1784 reads 'like a cross-section of those appearing in the *Almanach de Gotha*, including the cream of Viennese society'[74] – and a number of aristocratic friends. He boasted about his social success in

---

[71] *LMF*, 462, 839, 891
[72] Tyson, 21–2
[73] Neal Zaslaw, *Mozart's Symphonies* (Oxford, 1989), 415–9
[74] Robbins Landon, *Golden Years*, 107

his letters to his father.[75] Mörike, in his charming novelette *Mozart auf die Reise nach Prag* depicts his hero mixing on equal terms with the nobility and even lionized by them. Perhaps this is how it was.

Alternatively, Mozart may have exhibited all the unease of a social climber in a rigidly hierarchical society. Not to challenge that society, but to rise within it, may have been his goal. His father constantly advised him how to do this: '*You can always be perfectly natural* with people of high rank; but with everybody else please *behave like an Englishman*'.[76] Mozart had a nasty experience in Augsburg: some young urban patricians mocked his papal decoration, suggesting that it could be bought cheaply by anyone and that the star was made of copper. We never hear of him wearing it, or using the title, again. The jeers of these rich bourgeois made him long to leave Augsburg: 'I shall be honestly glad to go off again to a place where there is a court'.[77]

Perhaps, like many insecure social climbers, he was a bit of a snob.[78] His correspondence occasionally suggests this. He visited the portrait painter Madame Rosa and her 'boorish spouse' (Johann Baptist Hagenauer, formerly a Salzburg court sculptor) and was rude to them. He found his pupil Fräulein Auernhammer 'as fat as a farm wench'. He wrote to his sister

> The Fischers are living in the Tiefer Graben where I scarcely ever happen to go; but if my way does take me in that direction, I pay them a visit of a few minutes, since I really cannot endure for longer their tiny, overheated room and the wine on the table. I am well aware that people of their kind consider this to be the greatest possible compliment, but I am no lover of such compliments and still less of people of that type.

[75] *LMF*, 717–8, 754, 859
[76] *LMF*, 474; see also 465, 472
[77] *LMF*, 326
[78] This is the argument of Hutchings, in *Mozart: the Man: the Musician*.

In his very last letter he complained about the school his son Karl was attending: 'They can doubtless turn out a good peasant into the world'.[79]

The theme of Mozart refusing to defer to the nobility goes back to the very first biographical sources. According to Schlichtegroll,

> Even as a child, he took no pride in the praise of the great. Even in those years he would play nothing but trifles when obliged to perform for those who had no understanding of music. By contrast, he was all fire and attention when playing to knowledgeable persons.[80]

Nannerl sent this information to Schlichtegroll; she in her turn got it from Schachtner. But in a sense, Schlichtegroll had fished for it; one of his questions asked how Mozart behaved in the presence of the nobility. Would this information have been forthcoming without that question? From this seed a mighty oak grew. Niemetschek made much of it.[81] Rochlitz tells an elaborate story of Mozart's showing open contempt for an inattentive audience of notables, and then going off to play seriously to his landlord and some old musicians of the town until after midnight.[82] All of this passed into Nissen and became part of the orthodoxy. It had great appeal to many writers. For example Heribert Rau, in his mid-nineteenth century novel *Mozart: ein Kunstlerleben*, draws a vivid contrast between the natural, virtuous, middle-class Mozart family and the corrupt decadence of French and Austrian courtiers.

Great care must be taken not to carry back later attitudes into Mozart's own time. Close attention to the words of Schachtner, Niemetschek and Rochlitz does not reveal a modern egalitarian, or even nineteenth-century middle class,

---

[79] *LMF*, 747, 760, 786, 971; see also 802
[80] Schlichtegroll, 12
[81] Niemtschek, 6, 30; see also 57, 61
[82] *AMZ*, i (1798–9), 49–51 (24 October 1798)

opposition to aristocracy. Over and over again, the contrast being drawn is between *Kenner* and *Liebhaber*, experts in music versus mere amateurs. The status system of the old régime is being challenged by a rival one, but it has nothing to do with class conflict or democracy. What is at issue here is the professional pride of musicians, a large group in late-eighteenth century Germany, important enough to sustain a number of magazines devoted exclusively to music. Mozart himself uses this terminology and expresses this professional pride. It is of the utmost significance that he dedicated his six quartets, on which he had lavished so much labour, to Haydn, an esteemed fellow-musician who could not reward him, rather than to a wealthy amateur who could.

What must be the final verdict on the story of Mozart the defeated rebel, destroyed by that defeat? Are we to agree with Ghéon, that 'his bird's brain was impervious to ideas'? Or with the Massins who regard him as a thinking progressive, almost a Jacobin? The latter school of thought has developed a powerful case, based upon circumstantial evidence – but it is largely circumstantial, or open to interpretation. The Massins appeal in particular to the silences – to the missing letters, allegedly destroyed because of their subversive sentiments, to his enthusiasm for the French Revolution which he dare not speak out. There is absolutely no documented reference by Mozart to the French Revolution; and there is no direct contemporary or near contemporary testimony that he fell into poverty and despair because he was perceived as a dangerous radical. The most that can be said is that this story is a possible one; it is definitely not proven.

Chapter VIII

A Theodicy

The stories considered so far have occupied the domains of the psychological, the social and the political. The last two stories, utterly opposed to each other, have a metaphysical dimension. The second, to which the next chapter is devoted, is bleak. The first, the subject of this chapter, brings consolation. I will begin by telling it in its essentials.

* * *

Two hundred years on, we are distressed by Mozart's death, by the thought of all that was lost thereby; this story tells us not to grieve, for all was accomplished.[1] Mozart had done his work. To think that he died young, that he died early, is to misunderstand him and his life-history. He lived a short life but this was simply because he lived much faster than normal mortals. He belonged to that ardent race whose very breath devours them. A torch is made to burn and he burnt it at both ends.[2] The infant prodigy matured early – he was fully matured as an artist by the age of nine – and had come to full ripeness in his last years. It is difficult to see what more he could have achieved.[3] His musical output in his thirty-six years was greater than Beethoven's, and not much less than Bach's or Handel's. He was not spared the cup of suffering during his lifetime, but without that suffering the deeper

[1] Roland Tenschert, *Wolfgang Amadeus Mozart* (Salzburg, 1952), 121–2; Blom, *Mozart*, 165, 299
[2] Ghéon, *In Search of Mozart*, 254
[3] Wyzewa and Saint-Foix, *Mozart: sa vie musicale et son oeuvre*, i, 92; Blom, *Mozart*, 165

springs of his musical soul would not have broken forth. In fact he chose this suffering for the sake of his art, forsaking the broad path of popularity.[4] Goethe told Eckermann that Mozart was like Raphael and Byron. He had lived his creative life, spent his vital energy, fulfilled his mission as an artist.[5]

The style of his last works is a late style, corresponding as it were to Beethoven's 'third period' – recognizably a late style by virtue of increasing spareness, simplicity and purity. The exuberant luxury of maturity is pared away, to reveal the musical and expressive essence; at the age of thirty-five Mozart has achieved a style usually associated with aged artists.[6] As his body grew weaker, his creative forces intensified: like a candle, flaring up before extinction, he was transfigured in radiance.[7] This late unearthly concentration is audible in several works: especially the Requiem, but also *Die Zauberflöte* and the 'autumnal' Clarinet Concerto. And what about the last, 'death chilled' piano concerto, K595 in B flat, first performed in Mozart's last year, in which a dying fall can be heard:[8]

> The mood of resignation no longer expresses itself loudly or emphatically; every stirring of energy is rejected or suppressed; and this fact makes all the more uncanny the depths of sadness that are touched in the shadings and modulations of the harmony. The Larghetto is full of a religious, or, as Mr. Girdlestone calls it, a 'Franciscan' mildness; the Finale breathes a veiled joyfulness, as if blessed children were playing in the Elysian fields, joyful, but without hate and without love. Mozart used the theme of this Rondo a few days later for a song entitled *Longing for the Spring*. The theme has the resigned cheerfulness that comes from the knowledge that this is the last spring. But the most moving thing about it is that in it Mozart received the divine gift of being able to tell the fullness of his suffering

[4] Kreitmeier, *Charakterzeichnung*, 176, 184
[5] Burk, *Mozart and his Music*, p.viii
[6] Levey, *Life and Death of Mozart*, 243
[7] Henri de Curzon, *Mozart* (Paris, 1920), 260
[8] Sadie, *Mozart* (1965), 143

. . . It is so perfect . . . The very act of parting from life achieves immortality.[9]

Mozart was ready for death, he sensed its imminence and may even have longed for it. The beginnings of this mood can already be found in the last letter he wrote to his dying father, in April 1787:

As death, when we come to consider it closely, is the true goal of our existence, I have formed during the last few years such close relations with this best and truest friend of mankind, that his image is not only no longer terrifying to me, but is indeed very soothing and consoling![10]

Death had recently taken his 'dearest and most beloved friend', Count von Hatzfeld, in his early thirties. Then in September of the same year, Mozart's physician and friend, Sigmund Barisani, died aged 29. Mozart wrote: 'He is at rest! but I, we, all that knew him well – we shall *never* be at rest again – until we have the felicity of seeing him again – in a better world – and *never more to part*'.[11] The experiences of this year caused a reorientation of his mood; from now on, death was never far from his mind, and the thought of it, given his increasingly apparent worldly failure, was perhaps not unwelcome. His presentiment of death finds expression in the spine-tingling music of the stone guest in *Don Giovanni*.[12]

In September 1790 he moved to a new apartment, his last. During his Vienna period he had stayed on average less than a year in a lodging: did his unusually long stay in the Rauhensteingasse result from a premonition that moving was no longer worth the trouble?[13] In December of that year he

[9] Einstein, *Mozart*, 329
[10] *LMF*, 907
[11] *MDB*, 296
[12] Schurig, *Wolfgang Amadé Mozart*, ii, 205, 262; Abert, *Mozart*, 705; Schiedermair, *Mozart*, 329–30, 359; Paumgartner, *Mozart*, 402
[13] Einstein, 34

attended the farewell dinner for Haydn, about to leave for London. According to Haydn's biographer, Mozart, who had had a presentiment of death for some time, said to his friend, tears in his eyes, 'I fear, my father, that this is the last time we shall see each other'.[14] The shimmer of death hung over his last year: perhaps we encounter his longing for it in the letter he wrote to his wife in July 1791: 'I can't describe what I have been feeling – a kind of emptiness, which hurts me dreadfully – a kind of longing, which is never satisfied, which never ceases, and which persists, nay rather increases daily'.[15]

There may be signs of creative exhaustion in the last years, further evidence that his mission was accomplished. He wrote very little indeed in 1790; and when he died, apart from the unfinished Requiem, he had nothing on the stocks – unlike Beethoven, who was working on a number of compositions as death approached.[16] Arguably there was an intermittent falling-off in quality, in such as the 'Prussian' quartets, *La clemenza di Tito* and the last string quintet. Perhaps Mozart was finding composition increasingly difficult towards the end. Ideas were not coming as readily as in the past. He was unable to complete his commission to write piano sonatas and six string quartets for the King of Prussia. The three quartets he did write took him a long time, and he borrowed themes from drafts he had made in the early 1770s.[17] *Die Zauberflöte* is a mass of borrowings, from Handel, Schobert, C. P. E. Bach, Haydn and Clementi, but above all from his own works written when he was twenty.[18] Was Mozart's musical mind like some brilliant mathematical ones, fertile in youth but then exhausted?

[14] Nissen, *Biographie*, 576
[15] *LMF*, 963–4; Einstein, 80–1; Paumgartner, 34
[16] Bayan Northcott reporting the opinion of Hans Keller, on *Music Weekly*, BBC Radio 3, 31 January 1988
[17] The opinion of Einstein and A. H. King, as reported in Tyson, *Mozart: Studies of the Autograph Scores*, 40
[18] Curzon, 270; Ghéon, 320

* * *

This consoling story satisfies narrator and audience in the manner of a theodicy which justifies the ways of God to man. The theodicy has been a perennial narrative mode in the West; it provides pattern and meaning, reconciling us to history. According to the way of thinking which produces a theodicy, if we regard Mozart's death as a bad joke, a demonstration of the futility of human aspirations, we commit not only error, but impiety too:

> All Nature is but Art, unknown to thee;
> All Chance, Direction, which thou canst not see;
> All Discord, Harmony, not understood;
> All partial Evil, universal Good:
> And, spite of Pride, in erring Reason's spite,
> One truth is clear, 'Whatever IS, is RIGHT.'[19]

God, who knows when even a sparrow falls, would not allow a Mozart to die unfulfilled. The more one biographer studied the events of Mozart's life,

> the more they revealed to me a connection of cause and effect so manifestly intentional, so profoundly logical, at all points, that it became impossible to ignore, in the career of this man and artist, the directing will of a higher power.[20]

Only God knew the conditions on which a Mozart could be vouchsafed to us.[21] According to another biography:

> But this very death had something providential about it, closing the drama of a providential life. No other artist, even among the greatest, lived such a life: beneath its mediocrity, even beneath its misery, lay hidden the sign of a unique predestination.[22]

[19] Pope's half-line, 'Whatever is, is right', is set to music at the end of the chorus 'How dark, O Lord, are Thy decrees', in Handel's *Jephtha* (1752)
[20] Alexander Oulibicheff, *Nouvelle biographie de Mozart* (Moscow, 1843), i, p.xi
[21] Oulibicheff, i, 122
[22] Wyzewa and Saint-Foix, v, 301

God allowed Mozart to complete his task, and then took him to himself; at most, the overture to *Die Zauberflöte* and the Requiem suggest that there may have been one last, perfect symphony in him, which he 'would surely have written, had God but allowed him a few more months of life'.[23]

When and how did the consoling story of Mozart's death grow up? There is no hint of it in Schlichtegroll. Niemetschek did not think that he had finished his work: 'What more would his inexhaustible spirit have given the world?', but he did suggest that his titanic efforts in the last year may have burned him out, and he told how Mozart lamented that he was writing the Requiem for himself.[24] Rochlitz does not fully develop this story, but he provides many of its elements. He insists that Mozart worked himself to death, and that his last days revealed a special intensity:

> He had been very ill when he travelled to Prague; but the amount of work had once more excited the power of his spirit and concentrated it. The many distractions vitalized his spirits, cheered his mind to a light joyfulness; the little lamp flared up brightly once more before it was extinguished.[25]

Rochlitz drew an influential parallel between Mozart and Raphael, who also died young; both artists, sensing death was near, in a heightened mood poured their last forces into works of otherworldly significance – Raphael into his *Transfiguration*, Mozart into his Requiem.

Arnold develops at great length the theme of Mozart burning himself out with unremitting work:

> What straining of his imagination, what constant wearing-down of his spirit, what excitement of his brain-fibres! What continuous sapping of his vital forces! In a word: his whole life was –

[23] Georges de Saint-Foix, *Les symphonies de Mozart* (1932), Eng. trans. (London, 1947), 162
[24] Niemtschek, *Leben*, 65
[25] *AMZ*, i (1798–9), 177 (19 December 1798)

the consumption of life. History shows us a host of great spirits who burned themselves out.[26]

Other composers simply recycled the ideas of their youth, but Mozart was constantly original. The achievements of his last years were stupendous in quantity and quality; it is not surprising that *La clemenza di Tito* shows all the signs of exhaustion, and of a melancholy presentiment of death.

All of these themes, from Niemetschek, Rochlitz and Arnold are taken up into Nissen's vast rag-bag of a biography. He also quotes a passage from the *Allgemeine musikalische Zeitung*: 'One might almost say that Mozart when working on his Requiem was already no longer alive, that his soul already was largely separated from his body, and that he worked here on earth as one half-transfigured'.[27] Unfortunately Nissen does not supply a precise reference. Is it perhaps from an unsigned article by Rochlitz? In any event, Nissen provided the raw materials which later biographers could work into fully-fledged theodicies.

The greatest theodicy of the nineteenth century was not an orthodox Christian one. It was the modernized, philosophical theodicy of Hegel. The consoling story of Mozart's death is sometimes given Hegelian echoes, or even a Hegelian frame-work. Hegel argued that the world-spirit works its purpose out through human history, which reveals a clear pattern and direction. The process is teleological, and dialectical; the contrasting achievements of earlier epochs are taken up, synthesized and preserved in later ones. Heroes, geniuses, play an important role in this working-out – for example, Napoleon was the world-soul on horseback – but they rarely live happy lives. The world-spirit uses them, then discards them when its purpose is fulfilled.

> This constant pruning of Mozart's worldly hopes seems as if absolutely intended by a higher power in order to bring to light

[26] Arnold, *Mozarts Geist*, 61
[27] Nissen, 627

a finer bloom and more perfect fruit. It is impossible, I maintain, for any perceptive person to read through this sober and truthful account of Mozart's life . . . not to have the feeling as he reads it of witnessing the action of something like a Greek tragedy, the working out of an inescapable destiny, the destiny of Mozart's genius.

Did Mozart himself ever realize this sacrificial nature of his destiny?[28]

One could say that Mozart the man was only the earthly vessel of his art; indeed that the man was sacrificed to the musician. But every great artist obsessed with his art is sacrificed, as a person, to that art.

It is as though the world-spirit wished to show that here is pure sound, conforming to a weightless cosmos, triumphant over all chaotic earthliness, spirit of the world-spirit.[29]

These may be no more than rather Hegelian figures of speech. But Mozart's significance was assessed within a Hegelian framework in the mid-nineteenth century by A. B. Marx and F. Brendel.[30] Above all, Oulibicheff's book, published fifteen years after Nissen's, is written in the light of 'a new science, the philosophy of history'. [31] Oulibicheff's story is worth retelling.

* * *

A Hegelian approach to any cultural phenomenon – religion, philosophy, music – writes the history of its chosen theme as a necessary process of evolution towards perfection. Early stages are marked by inadequacy or incoherence. For instance the religion of a past epoch will either be too narrow and limited to satisfy the spirit, or it will have branched out luxuriantly in many directions, losing its unity in the process.

[28] Turner, *Mozart*, 158
[29] Einstein, 103, 487
[30] Gudrun Henneberg, 'Der Einfluss der Philosophie Hegels auf das Mozart-Bild in der ersten Hälfte des 19. Jahrhunderts', *MJb 1978–9*, 257–62
[31] Oulibicheff, i, 1

The ultimate goal is the final synthesis, in which diversity and richness of expression form a consistent whole. This unity-in-diversity can alone satisfy the spirit, and so all past time is an unconscious striving towards it.

For Oulibicheff, Mozart is precisely this final synthesis in the domain of music. Previous ages had brought each musical genre in isolation to perfection. Polyphony was perfected by Palestrina, fugue and counterpoint by Handel and Bach, melody by Gluck and Piccinni, the use of instruments by Haydn and Boccherini. 'All the branches of music had borne fruit.' But each was in itself too one-sided; two or three hours of nothing but fugue bores and exhausts the listener. 'You have understood the mission of Mozart. His instructions were explicit: to pacify the warring schools, unifying their colours and emblems into a single flag.' Mozart mastered and unified all previous achievements in music, thereby greatly augmenting its power, attaining a universal style, cleansed of local colouring and particularity, providing models for future generations.[32] So, for example, the quartets he dedicated to Haydn are the eternal types of the genre. Mozart, in fact, achieved the ultimate and most important revolution in the history of music.

All of Mozart's life was marshalled by a divine tactic towards this end. The perfect teacher was provided for him in his father Leopold. His complex, contradictory nature, which brought him so much trouble in everyday life and ruined his worldly prospects, was necessary to his mission. He who was to express everything had to experience everything, and so he was by turn sanguine and melancholy, carefree and hypochondriac, absorbed in work and relaxed in pleasure, devout and clubbable, exalted and libertine. 'As for the terrifying haste with which our hero marched to the accomplishment of his destiny, that cruel haste, we understand it today. Eight centuries had been waiting for him, and

[32] Oulibicheff, ii, 210–11

he was not allowed to delay.'[33] By the end, he had completed his task, and his forces were all used up. His deathbed complaint at the imminent termination of his existence was touching and understandable, but mistaken: 'God was calling his servant to himself'.[34] In his innermost being, Mozart knew this: for he was 'profoundly melancholy. Every day he dreamt of death. At his piano in the watches of the night, he loved to launch himself on the wings of improvisation towards those unknown regions to which death holds the key'.[35]

Two works especially reveal Mozart's dialogue with death: *Don Giovanni* and the Requiem, in the circumstances of which 'all the world has recognized the finger of God'. Mozart wrote the opera

> in his happiest days of pleasure, glory and health; but already the great voice of death came to him periodically. Every night it spoke to him, drowning the thousand enchanted voices of pleasure. Hence *Don Giovanni* is the result of an equally poised conflict, of an equilibrium of contrary influences. The Requiem proclaims the definitive victory of one of these.[36]

The other great theodicy among the studies of the life and works is the five-volume account by the French catholics, Wyzewa and Saint-Foix. Their book was begun before World War I, but in one respect its method is very modern. They explain the evolution of the artist by a detailed study of his relationship to the music he heard, absorbed and transformed. To use the modern jargon, it is an *intertextual* study. Rather less modern is their determination to find the hand of Providence at every turn. As the child prodigy travelled

[33] Oulibicheff, i, 70
[34] Oulibicheff, iii, 423
[35] Oulibicheff, i, 148
[36] Oulibicheff, iii, 419

about Europe, he experienced a succession of musical influences, and these experiences were miraculously arranged in exactly the right order to develop his maturing genius.

Mozart's mission, as they see it, was to master all the resources of his art; to unite the musical craftsmanship of the difficult, 'learned', North German contrapuntal style epitomized by Handel and J.S. Bach with the more approachable grace of the *galant* style of the Italian and Italian-influenced composers such as J.C. Bach (Wyzewa dislikes the *galant*, seeing nothing in it but rococo triviality: Saint-Foix is susceptible to its charm); to renew religious music; and thus open the way to the future. The first great journey, in 1766, took him to Paris and London. In Paris he happily came under the influence not only of the Germanic expressivism of Schobert, but also of the balancing clarity of French music. The trip to England, where a shallow Italianate taste prevailed, might have represented a step back; but perhaps this was a level of attainment peculiarly adapted to the nine-year old, and in any case he learnt how to write operatic arias there. His next great journey was to Italy, where he deepened his knowledge of modern operatic style but ran the risk of falling into elegant superficiality. Providentially, between the return from London and the departure for Milan came a brief stay in Vienna, where he came in contact with a higher ideal of musical expression. In Bologna, by another providential accident, he met Padre Martini, who coached him in the old traditions of counterpoint.

The voyages were punctuated by salutary periods of rest in Salzburg, during which Mozart assimilated what he had learnt on his travels. At Salzburg from 1773–7 his new employer obliged him to compose *galant* and italianate music; but when he visited Paris in 1778, he became acquainted with new developments in music drama associated with Gluck. When he finally settled in Vienna in 1781, he seemed all set to work as a *galant* composer, gratifying the pleasure-loving Viennese taste. But Providence intervened again, in the form of Van Swieten with his enthusiasm for the old North German masters of counterpoint. This influence proved decisive and irreversible.

The Viennese masters of Mozart's time were working unconsciously to create the modern symphony, that synthesis of the learned and the *galant*, which culminated in Haydn, Mozart and Beethoven. Mozart pushed the development on, himself attaining a 'Beethovenian' level in *Don Giovanni* and his last three symphonies. And then, by the end,

> not only is the instrumentation of *Die Zauberflöte*, of its overture for example, already quite 'modern' and quasi-'Wagnerian': it is also the spirit of this music, which has for us a purer, more perfect beauty, clothed with a significance which, going beyond 'Romanticism', anticipates the art of the masters of our contemporary schools.[37]

So Mozart played his allotted part in the divine plan for music, producing compositions which were 'quite angelic and celestial . . . perfumed with a supernatural grace'.[38]

Even the misery of his last years was a necessary part of his destiny. The failure of his worldly hopes concentrated his mind upon the pure demands of his art; no longer would he pander to a popular taste which he could not woo. This withdrawal caused a marvellous transfiguration at the end. Like the great saints, he renounced the world, withdrew from materiality and turned into himself, so as to mount to higher regions.

> We witness, as we study the work of Mozart arrived at the end of his brief span, an ascension which we are compelled to consider from a spiritual, or rather from a completely supernatural point of view; for now external events have no more purchase. Or rather these external events act upon him only

[37] Wyzewa and Saint-Foix, ii, 422
[38] Wyzewa and Saint-Foix, ii, 97

through an obscuring mist of misery. And this misery becomes an element in his withdrawal; for he knows well that success and the desire to please no longer have a part to play in his life.

Mozart's worldly defeat is a spiritual victory, his death a sanctification.[39]

Few biographers follow Oulibicheff, or Wyzewa and Saint-Foix, in explicitly arguing that Mozart's destiny was shaped by supernatural forces. But many regard his career as having meaning in a larger scheme of things. They see the history of Western music as a logical and necessary progression. This commits them to supposing that the composers now regarded as great were working at a common task, pushing on musical progress; that there is a connection and continuity across the generations. Mozart's role, accordingly, was to receive the torch from the hands of Bach and Handel, carry it as far as he could, and prepare the way for the next stage. Jahn, for instance, is critical of Oulibicheff's attempt to find a pattern culminating in Mozart: but he cannot resist a pattern himself.

> But [the influence of Bach and Handel] reaches beyond his compositions in the severe style. The perfection of *polyphonic* composition which characterizes all Mozart's works, and wherein consists one of his chief merits, rests, even in its broadest and freest development, upon the foundations laid by those masters.
> They laid deep hold on his imagination and intellect, giving him a powerful impulse to classical studies, without which his genius would not have arrived at a full mastery of his art.[40]

He thinks that Mozart appropriated all that was good in Italian opera, brought it to its climax, then launched the German opera of the future. *Die Zauberflöte* was accordingly his greatest, opening the way to Weber and Wagner. If one

[39] Wyzewa and Saint-Foix, v, 21, 40
[40] Jahn, *Life of Mozart*, ii, 390, 400

thinks in this way, and many do, it follows that though he died young, nothing was lost, for the next lap belonged to Beethoven.

> Now, at the end of his life, the flight of his genius took him to a new country, no longer ruled by the taste of a single stratum of society, however cultured, but only by the artist's own conscience. On the horizon the dawn of *Beethovenesque* art was already shining.[41]

As Count Waldstein wrote in Beethoven's album:

> Mozart's genius still mourns and laments the death of his charge. With the indefatigable Hayden he found refuge but not employment; through him he now wishes once more to be united with someone. By means of your ceaseless diligence you shall receive: *Mozart's spirit from Hayden's hands.*[42]

This is a theodicy, even if God is left out.[43]

*   *   *

The explicit theodicies of Oulibicheff, and Wyzewa and Saint-Foix, beautiful stories though they are, will not convince anyone who doubts the existence of God, nor the believer who does not think that Providence constantly intervenes to shape the course of history. But we are still left with the quasi-theodicies, the consoling stories which maintain that Mozart was burnt out and ready for death, that he had said all that he had to say and played his part in musical evolution. Are these stories believable?

There is no indisputable evidence for the hypothesis that Mozart was expecting and half-longing for death in his last years. The last letter to his dying father may simply be a

---

[41] Abert, quoted in Hildesheimer, *Mozart*, 40
[42] *MDB*, 467
[43] Kreitmeier, 186; Abert, ii, 117; Tenschert, 93

rather conventional repetition of masonic doctrines, or even, as Hildesheimer has argued, plagiarized from Moses Mendelssohn's *Phädon*, a copy of which was recorded among his possessions when he died. The passage expressing longing in his letter to Constanze of July 1791 begins 'You cannot imagine how I have been aching for you all this long while'.[44] It seems perverse to read this as longing for death rather than longing for his wife. If the last piano concerto expresses intimations of mortality, then those intimations must have begun well before the last year. It was completed and first performed in 1791: but Tyson's study of the autograph score has demonstrated that much of it was written in *particella* – that is to say, sketched out in its essentials – in 1788.[45]

The last letters to his wife, written a matter of weeks before he died, are full of vitality and gusto, and excitement at the success of *Die Zauberflöte*:

> Immediately after your departure I played two games of billiards with Herr von Mozart, the fellow who wrote the opera which is running at Schikaneder's theatre; then I sold my nag for fourteen ducats; then I told Joseph to get Primus to fetch me some black coffee, with which I smoked a splendid pipe of tobacco; and then I orchestrated almost the whole of Stadler's rondo . . . At half past six I went out by the Stuben gate and took my favourite walk by the Glacis to the theatre. But what do I see? What do I smell? Why, here is Don Primus with the cutlets! Che gusto! Now I am eating to your health![46]

Faced with this, those who wish to argue that Mozart was a burnt-out case in 1791 are reduced to the expedient of claiming that it is sham, a brave face put on to comfort his ailing wife. The theory does not fit the evidence, and so the evidence is refashioned.[47]

[44] *LMF*, 963
[45] Tyson, 156
[46] *LMF*, 967
[47] Schenk, *Mozart and his Times*, 434

His so-called late style can be interpreted, not as a sign of fulfilment and spiritual purification in readiness for death, but rather as a vigorous quest for new directions. Its pared-down simplicity will then no longer be an unloading of worldly baggage in preparation for the ascent to heaven, but an adaptation to the neo-classical style which was sweeping the visual arts and literature. The unbridled passion and individual expression of the *Sturm und Drang* gives way to balance and universality in, for example, Goethe and Schiller. In architecture, the exuberance of the rococo is replaced by elemental, undecorated grandeur, ideally represented by the designs of Ledoux. In painting, the voluptuousness and frivolity of Boucher and Fragonard yield to the seriousness and heroism of the half-empty canvases of David. Haydn's *Creation* belongs here, and so does Beethoven's *Eroica*. Perhaps Mozart too was adapting to the spirit of the age. The elevated humanism of the masonic works including *Die Zauberflöte*, the lofty heroism of *La clemenza di Tito*, the comparative plainness of the late chamber music – here, we may think, is the epitome of neo-classicism.[48] On the other hand we may feel that these works are pervaded by a sense of melancholy and inwardness, a special quality to be explained in terms of the state of Mozart's soul rather than in terms of the mood of the time.

The contention that Mozart was suffering from creative exhaustion by the end collapses under scrutiny. It is true that 1790 was an unproductive year, but the output of 1791 was phenomenal. Tyson's analysis of the paper on which the 'Prussian' quartets were written proves that Mozart did not after all supplement a flagging inspiration by using abandoned starts written twenty years earlier; they are entirely new work.[49]

He has also argued that Mozart did in fact have a number of works in progress, apart from the Requiem, at the time of his

[48] Wyzewa and Saint-Foix, v, 165; Paumgartner, 414, 431
[49] Tyson, 41–7

death. In 1800 Constanze listed 98 fragments 'that are of lasting value (for many others have been destroyed on account of their total unusability'. It used to be thought that they were all abandoned starts, abandoned because the commission or concert for which they were intended fell through, or because Mozart found them unsatisfactory. According to Tyson, some of them may represent work in progress. On the basis of his study of the manuscripts he argues that Mozart began his compositions as outline sketches. Some of these were filled in immediately, some abandoned, some – the 'work in progress' – taken up and completed in due course, which might mean as much as one or two years later. Surveying the surviving, datable fragments, Tyson surmises that at the time of his death Mozart was working on a horn concerto, a violin sonata, a contredanse, a work for mechanical organ, a string trio, a string quintet and another mass apart from the Requiem.[50]

As for the claim that a decline in quality can be detected in some of the late works, this is so much a matter of debatable aesthetic judgment that the biographer can build nothing solid upon it. The 'Prussian' quartets have been thought less good than the 'Haydn' ones, the last string quintet judged inferior to those of 1787. But not all have shared these opinions, and some indeed have thought the opposite: 'The late Vienna quartets and quintets are his most adventurous music'; 'But the String Quintet in E flat (K614) dated April 12th, dominates all the other marvels'.[51]

With respect to Mozart's place in the great teleological unfolding of Western music, linking Bach to Beethoven, it has been argued that the influence of Bach and Handel has been overstated. Contrapuntal writing did not go out in the *galant* period. It continued to be important in church music, and Mozart always wrote in that style for the church. It is likely that he learned as much from Michael Haydn, his colleague at

[50] Tyson, 126–57
[51] Burk, p.ix; Ghéon, 309; Curzon, *Mozart*, 257; Boschot, *Mozart*, 216

Salzburg, and from the Italian Padre Martini, as from the two great German baroque composers recognized by posterity.[52] Since the contrapuntal tradition was not dead, destiny did not require a Mozart to revive it.

Many of the issues discussed here converge upon *La clemenza di Tito*, the last large-scale work that Mozart took on and brought to completion. It was commissioned as the official opera for the festivities surrounding the coronation of Leopold II in Prague. Evidently it was a flop: the second performance was sparsely attended, and the theatre director, Guardasoni, petitioned the authorities for compensation for his losses with it. They conceded that 'at court there was moreover a certain prejudice against Mozart's composition'.[53] According to legend, the Empress referred to it as 'German swinishness'. For most of the nineteenth and twentieth centuries *Tito* failed to find a place in the repertory; it is comparatively rarely heard today. A number of explanations have been proffered for this failure.

The simplest explanation is lack of time. The Bohemian estates did not give Guardasoni the commission until 8 July, a mere nine weeks before the coronation; and he tried to persuade Salieri to take it on, before turning to Mozart.[54] According to Rochlitz, 'He recognized that, since he was not a God, he must either produce a wholly mediocre work, or he must concentrate on the main numbers and simply compose the less important ones in a facile manner according to the general taste of the time; wisely he chose the latter course'.[55] Rochlitz adds that because time was so short, he entrusted the simple recitatives to another, and that as each number was completed it was given to the copyist, thereby

[52] Sadie, 86–7
[53] *MDB*, 411
[54] For an up-to-date discussion of the commissioning and composition of *Tito* see Robbins Landon, *Mozart's Last Year*, 84–101. Landon however overstates the proportion of the opera composed during the last eighteen days, if Tyson's analysis is correct; see Tyson, 48–59
[55] *AMZ*, i (1798–9), 151 (5 December 1798)

making revision impossible. Study of the autograph confirms the first statement; but some numbers *were* revised. According to Niemetschek, 'He began the [opera] in his travelling coach . . . and finished it in the short space of eighteen days in Prague'.[56]

Arnold detects not so much haste as exhaustion – sickness unto death – in *Tito*. He has wept when studying the score, so clearly does it reveal Mozart's sad state at the time.

> Mozart wrote this opera as his powers ebbed away. His great genius was bidding farewell to the world. The energy of his spirit ran down as his body sickened. Hence the sparse instrumental accompaniment, the calm sublimity and melancholy in the melodies and in the character of Titus . . . But this very Mozart, who usually composed so willingly, giving himself freely, scattering the treasure of his genius in all directions, all at once became here listless and sparing . . . This opera has a quite distinctive character, and is unlike any other work of this artist. A feeling of a contemplative, sorrowing, tranquil spirit prevails in the arias, and all tender feelings are coloured with melancholy . . . Only in the final choruses does he gather himself up by sheer force from his dying slumber. It is the last flaring-up of the dying light, which gathers up all its forces for one last time, before sinking into utter darkness . . . We sense the emptiness, the exhaustion of the energy of the great master. There is less interplay of the instruments, indeed the scoring as a whole is sparser than in his other works . . . the bar-columns for the wind instruments, ever becoming emptier, seem to indicate the bound wings of his genius.[57]

Many have said in addition that Mozart had lost interest in *opera seria*, an outdated genre. So, the conclusion is that *Tito* is a failure because Mozart took the job only for the fame and

---

[56] Niemtschek, 32
[57] Arnold, 356–9

money, he had too little time, and his creativity was on the verge of exhaustion.

Everything about this assessment of *Tito* – and of Mozart's last days - can be challenged. In the first place, many today would doubt that the opera deserved its long neglect; it is at last returning to the repertory and winning admirers, who find it almost unbearably beautiful and moving. If late nineteenth and early twentieth century commentators found it dull and inferior, that was their fault and not Mozart's, the result of the blindness of Romanticism to Classical aesthetic values. There is absolutely no evidence that Mozart himself had turned against *opera seria*. Arnold is right to draw attention to the sparse, austere scoring; but this may simply be in deference to the known preferences of Leopold II, or in conformity to fashionable neo-classical simplicity. There is no need to think that Mozart was exhausted.

Niemetschek's claim that the opera was composed in a mere eighteen days is almost certainly an exaggeration. It seems probable that what he left to the last eighteen days was most of the arias, for he did not know the cast until then, and he always tailored his arias to the voices in question. But he already knew who was singing Titus and had composed his arias in advance. The biggest aria of all, Vitellia's rondò 'Non più di fiori' may have been composed as a concert aria for Josepha Duschek several months earlier. It is likely that he began work on the concerted numbers and choruses seven weeks before the première. In other words, if 'Non più di fiori' was already written less than half of Mozart's work was left for the last eighteen days. It was a rushed job, but not as crazy as Niemetschek suggests.

The opera was based upon a libretto by Metastasio. It had classic status, and had been set many times. The Dresden court poet Caterino Mazzolà drastically revised it for Mozart, simplifying it and rendering it more dramatic. Mozart and Mazzolà played fast and loose with the conventions of *opera seria*; conservative music-lovers would have been greatly offended, and this may have been the cause of the opera's immediate flop.[58] During the next decades, however, its reputation grew, and enjoyed more international success than any of his other stage works. Arias from it were a staple ingredient of Constanze's benefit concerts. For if *Tito* was ahead of its time in 1791, it soon came to seem modishly up-to-date. There had been a tendency to simplify and speed up Metastasio's librettos, which Mozart simply carried further. The simple scoring and pathos of *Tito* resembles and perhaps imitates Paisiello's *Nina*, which enjoyed a great success in Italy, then in Vienna when it opened in the autumn of 1790.[59] Mozart, who had been criticized for the excessive richness and difficulty of his scores, was adapting himself to the taste of the time, with notable success. If this argument is correct, he was not an exhausted composer at the end of his creative life; he was vigorously embarking upon new ventures. There is no consolation for his early loss.

[58] Marita P. McClymonds, 'Mozart's *La clemenza di Tito* and opera seria in Florence as a Reflection of Leopold II's Musical Taste', *MJb 1984–5*, 61–70
[59] D. Heartz, 'Mozart and his Italian Contemporaries: *La clemenza di Tito*', *MJb 1978–9*, 275–93

Chapter IX

Existentialist scepticism

An existentialist approach to narrative, as in Camus for example, resolutely rejects religious or metaphysical frameworks which discern in events the workings of a divine providence. From this sceptical point of view tragic events are not redeemed when located in a larger context of meaning. Events, indeed, have no cosmic significance at all. This sense of the randomness, the contingency, the pointlessness and futility of things is what existentialists term the absurd. In place of theodicies, which insist that in God's plan nothing is wasted, nothing in vain, existentialists fear that everything may be wasted and in vain.

This depressing insight is almost unbearable; consequently, existentialists warn us, we try to evade or deny it. We find, or rather we impose, pattern and meaning. This is the source of the narrative impulse on which the classic novel is based. Time is without boundaries; the past comes from, and the future is going to, we know not where. In order to feel at home and comfortable in it we cut it into manageable chunks, we give it a shape, we narrate it. In the archetype of the fairy tale, we begin 'once upon a time' and we conclude 'they all lived happily ever after'. Even when we relate tragedies, the ending is a rounding-off, a completion, a catharsis.

> What is the novel, in effect, if not a universe in which action has a shape, where final words are spoken, where humans possess one another and where the whole of life takes on the shape of destiny. The world of the novel is simply a rectification of the real world in accordance with the deepest human desire.

We seek to impose upon our own lives the order, unity and meaning which we achieve in the domain of art. But we are constantly frustrated, for, as Camus explains, human beings are

> foreigners in the world, exiles in their own country. Except in glowing moments of fulfilment, all reality is unsatisfying to them. Their actions melt into other actions, return to judge them in ways they did not expect, run away like Tantalus's water through an unseen opening. To find the opening, to dominate the course of the river, to grasp their lives as destinies, that is their true nostalgia, which they feel at the heart of their native land.

Though we ourselves lack unity, when we contemplate others, we easily fall into the trap of imagining that they are coherent:

> This is the cause of that unfortunate envy which so many people feel for the lives of others. Looking at them from the outside, one imparts to them a coherence and a unity which in reality they cannot have, but which appears obvious to the observer. The latter sees only the framework of these lives, ignoring the worms which gnaw it away. Thus we turn the lives of others into a work of art. We turn them into romance.[1]

From this existentialist point of view all the stories considered so far would be in bad faith, because they impose, unjustifiably, grand unifying patterns on Mozart's life. They give it form and significance, however tragic. From the very beginning, the end is in sight, and Mozart's life is like an unbroken arch, whose supporting pillars are his birth and death. An existentialist account, by contrast, would fracture the arch of the narrative, finding only a succession of events, linked together by causal connections and a complex mass of individual human decisions, but not by any overall pattern of meaning or purpose.

[1] Albert Camus, *L'homme révolté* (Paris, 1951), 314, 306, 311–12

It is not being claimed here that any recent biographers of Mozart have consciously adopted an existentialist perspective. But the way of telling Mozart's history has of late increasingly reflected an attitude of scepticism towards metaphysics and grand theory, an attitude which has become pervasive in our culture and which is articulated in an explicit fashion by existentialism. Hence all larger patterns are doubted. But if all the preceding stories are repudiated, then how does this sceptical approach explain the apparent failure of the last years – the decline in popularity and the growing indebtedness, which may have caused overwork and contributed to his last illness and death?

I shall consider in turn two modern ways of relating the events of Mozart's Vienna years, which ended so tragically at five minutes to one a.m. on Monday 5 December 1791. The first proposes that his decline and fall resulted from an unfortunate coming-together of difficulties. The second suggests that his death came out of the blue; it was random, a bad joke.

* * *

In the chapter of accidents which brought Mozart down, money troubles played an important part. He got off to a bad start in Vienna. He was finally dismissed from the archbishop's service in June and left to fend for himself. But the time for earning money as a musician, whether by performing or by taking pupils, was late autumn, winter and early spring. During the summer the nobility were out of town on their country estates. That first summer must have been his leanest time, probably leaving him in debt.[2] Even when his circumstances improved, his income was inevitably seasonal, and variable from year to year, as Niemetschek remarks.[3] The composition and staging of operas was a further disruptive factor. It involved a considerable and draining expenditure of

[2] Braunbehrens, *Mozart in Wien*, 41–2
[3] Niemtschek, 30

time and effort, for a remuneration which was not in proportion.[4]

Those whose income is seasonal – for example farmers – often bridge the gap with loans. Those whose income is irregular and unpredictable cannot easily plan their expenditure. Mishaps threw Mozart off course, especially illness. Niemetschek refers also to Constanze's illnesses as a cause of the money troubles. Treatment was expensive; of the 918 gulden recorded as owing at the time of Mozart's death, 226 were owed to apothecaries and a surgeon. Then there were doctors' fees, and the considerable expense of sending Constanze for spa cures in Baden. Illness put a stop to work, and therefore to earning. Not only his own illness did this, as the begging letters to Puchberg in July 1789 reveal:

> I need not tell you once more that owing to my unfortunate illness I have been prevented from earning anything . . . Now that my dear little wife seems to be improving every day, I should be able to set to work again . . . At any rate, people are consoling me by telling me that she is better – although the night before last she was suffering so much – and I on her account – that I was stunned and despairing . . . I am indeed most unhappy, and am forever hovering between hope and fear! . . . At the moment she is easier, and if *she had not contracted bed-sores*, which make her condition most wretched, she would be able to sleep. The only fear is that the bone may be affected. She is extraordinarily resigned and awaits recovery or death with true philosophic calm. My tears flow as I write.[5]

Upon the problems caused by personal and family circumstances (we should not forget that four of his children sickened and died during the Viennese decade) were heaped additional difficulties stemming from the policies of the

[4] Steptoe, *The Mozart-Da Ponte operas*, 70
[5] *LMF*, 930, 932

Josephinian state. Joseph II set out to encourage economic growth, with some success. There was an expansion of manufacturing activity, especially around Vienna. But this aggravated the existing housing shortage, pushing up rents. There were problems supplying the capital with wood for heating, which became more expensive.[6] Several of Joseph's policies may have reduced the amount of money available for patronizing music. The emperor was committed to strengthening his state by rigid economies. Court activity was drastically reduced. Joseph virtually abandoned the Hofburg and Schönbrunn, taking up residence in a little house in the Augarten. Staff were dismissed, official salaries reduced and many pensions withdrawn.[7]

All of this happened before Mozart settled in Vienna. For a time, the salons of the nobility made up for the decline in court ceremonial; but Joseph's policies undermined noble incomes too. He was determined to end privilege, and equalize the burdens of the state: consequently the nobles were made liable to direct and indirect taxation. A proposed land tax, and the abolition of manorial dues and services, threatened their incomes still further. Residence in the capital was becoming less attractive to them. With the ending of their judicial privileges, they might suffer the indignity of witnessing members of their order in the pillory, or sweeping the streets with shaven heads and placards announcing their crimes. It seems that many gave up their private orchestras and concerts, and even their town houses.[8]

A nadir was reached in 1788. The harvests of that and the preceding year had been short; bread prices soared and there were riots in Vienna. And now the empire was at war with the Turks. Not only did this take the emperor and many of the nobility away to the front; it led to inflation and increased

---

[6] H. Wagner, 'Das Josephinische Wien und Mozart', *MJb 1978–9*, 5
[7] Wagner, 2
[8] Braunbehrens, 335

taxation. It is not surprising that Mozart's affairs reached crisis point in that year, the year when the begging letters to Puchberg began. Most of his publications of his compositions occurred between 1785 and 1788, before the setback of the Turkish war.[9] The economic climate did not improve until after the accession of Leopold II in 1790. Given the illnesses of 1789, the fact that Mozart's finances did not return to an even keel before 1791 is understandable. There is no need to explain his plight in terms of social rebelliousness, depravity, incompetence or semi-autism.

1788 was a bad time to turn to moneylenders. A considerable part of the available credit was loaned to the state, whose needs increased in wartime. When in 1786 Joseph seized capital assets in private foundations such as monasteries the shortage of credit available to individual borrowers was aggravated. Then in 1787 he took the lid off the interest rate by repealing the usury laws.[10] Nissen tells that Mozart had recourse to pawnbrokers because of the high interest charged for ordinary loans, and a letter of 1790 refers to interest at 20 per cent.[11] In the light of this, the abject begging letters to Puchberg should probably be read not as if they were twentieth-century requests to a bank manager for a loan, but as pleas for assistance at a low rate of interest or even interest-free.

A further cause of Mozart's deepening plight was the fact that his music did not win him immediate and unreserved fame and fortune. One of the best known stories about Mozart, for which our earliest version is Niemetschek's 1798 biography, concerns the first performance of *Die Entführung*. Joseph II is said to have commented: 'Too beautiful for our ears and an enormous number of notes, dear

---

[9] Braunbehrens, 149–50
[10] Ernst Wangermann, *From Joseph II to the Jacobin Trials* (Oxford, 1969), 26–7
[11] Nissen, *Biographie*, 683; *LMF*, 945

Mozart'.[12] There is a version in Kelly's memoirs of 1826, and Kelly says he heard it from Mozart himself.[13]

A good story, at best second-hand, and first recorded sixteen years after the alleged event, should not be taken too seriously; but it reflects what was widely thought about his music in the 1780s and early 1790s. It cannot be doubted that many found it too rich and complex, above all too difficult. The instrumental parts were more independent than was usual in *galant* music, producing an elaborate texture which could not be appreciated at a single hearing. In that pre-gramophone age, when the fashion was to perform absolutely new music, a single hearing was all that most of his works would get. *Idomeneo* received four performances during Mozart's lifetime. It is easy to imagine how that opera, loaded with riches, which so repays repeated listening, might have had less immediate appeal than simpler, infinitely less rewarding stage works. His mature music is complex in expressive terms, emotionally ambivalent and ambiguous, shifting from mood to mood within a single movement, just as it constantly shifts between major and minor.

The difficulty of Mozart's music for the listeners was matched by its difficulty for the players. Given the complex part-writing, accurate timing and intonation were essential. Evidently not all orchestras and chamber players were sufficiently skilled. Niemetschek was convinced that these were the reasons for Mozart's failure to obtain due recognition during his lifetime.[14] At about the same date, the composer Dittersdorf recorded the opinion of Mozart he had delivered, so he said, in conversation with Joseph II:

> Indisputably he is a great genius, and I have yet to find any composer possessing such an astonishing richness of new ideas. I could wish that he were not so spendthrift with them. He

[12] Niemtschek, 23
[13] King, *Mozart in Retrospect*, 3
[14] Niemtschek, 46–7, 70

does not allow the hearer to pause for breath; for the moment one relishes a beautiful idea, along comes another, driving away the first, and immediately that leads on to yet another, so that in the end one can retain none of these real beauties in the memory.[15]

The same story is reiterated in contemporary newssheets and memoirs. A discussion of *Die Entführung* in Knigge's *Dramaturgische Blätter* of 1788 is interesting because the critic finds much of the music wonderful:

Next, the composer has been too loquacious with the wind instruments. Instead of only reinforcing the melody where that is required, and supporting the harmony as a whole, they often darken the former and confuse the latter, prevent simple, beautiful singing and disturb the singer's delivery . . . No less does too artful a texture obscure the fluency of song in many places. The expert knows the value of such passages, but for popular delivery this kind of thing is of no use. The same is true of the frequent modulations and the many enharmonic progressions, which, beautiful as they sound on the pianoforte, have no effect in the orchestra, partly because the intonation is never pure enough either on the singers' or the players' part, and especially is this true of the wind instruments; and partly because the resolutions alternate too quickly with the discords, so that only a practised ear can follow the course of the harmony. This awkwardness is especially noticeable in the many arias in minor keys which, because of their numerous chromatic passages, are difficult to perform for the singer, difficult to grasp for the hearer, and are altogether somewhat disquieting.[16]

Such opinions persisted for some time after Mozart's death. One critic wrote in 1794 of 'An almost unadulteratedly spicy diet, which spoils the palate if one's taste for it continues'.[17]

[15] *AMZ*, i (1798–9), 380 (13 March 1799)
[16] *MDB*, 328
[17] *MDB*, 472–3

It was not only the operas which left Mozart's contemporaries hesitating and confused. Rochlitz tells the following stories about the quartets dedicated to Haydn:

> After the late Artaria had sent them to Italy, they were returned 'because the engraving contained so many mistakes' – that is to say the many strange accords and dissonances were thought to be engraver's errors . . . The late Prince Grassalkowich (for example) once had these very quartets performed by some players from his orchestra. Again and again he called out 'You are not playing correctly'; and when it was proved to him that this was not so, he tore the parts up on the spot.[18]

Cramer's Hamburg *Magazin der Musik* referred to them in 1787 as 'too highly seasoned'.[19] As with the operas, so with the chamber music, there is evidence to suggest that the occasional failure of these works to please may have been due to the inability of players to perform such difficult music.[20]

Mozart's failure to gain recognition in his last years, therefore, may have stemmed from his very originality, and from the difficulty experienced by contemporary music lovers in coming to terms with his art. Careful and knowledgeable Mozart scholars have long been aware of this.[21] Extra difficulties may have come along towards the end. The early death of Joseph II was a misfortune for Mozart, if not for the empire. It was not just that the run of *Così fan tutte* was prematurely cut off by the mourning. The new emperor, Leopold II, was not especially interested in music. His consort was, but her taste was rather conservative and moralistic. Her dismissal of *La clemenza di Tito* as 'German swinishness' may be apocryphal, but she did find 'the music very bad so that almost all of us fell asleep'.[22] The appreciation and

[18] *AMZ*, i (1798–9), 855 (11 September 1799)
[19] *MDB*, 290 (see also 349)
[20] *MDB*, 317–9
[21] For example Schiedermair in his biography of 1922
[22] *NMD*, no.109

recognition of Mozart's genius took time to develop. His fame became firmly established during the 1790s, and this is the measure of the cruel tragedy of his early death.

          *   *   *

Now for the second modern telling of Mozart's death in relation (or rather non-relation) to his life. Throughout the book up to this point stories have been recounted which fit within the long-accepted trajectory of his career. Let us remind ourselves of it, for the distinctive feature of the second 'existentialist' account is that it rejects it. It begins with the rapid ascent to fame of the boy and the youth. There is then a dip, a period of marking time, when Mozart was in his late teens and early twenties, the period under Colloredo at Salzburg. Within this interval falls the disastrous trip to Paris. After Mozart's migration to Vienna in 1781 there comes a brilliant rise to celebrity and fortune, culminating in 1785. Then Mozart's star begins to wane, with brief bursts of brilliance, however, when he visits Prague. His concert series, which brought him so much money, runs into the sand. According to one recent calculation, he gave one public concert in 1781, three in 1782, five in 1783, seven in 1784 and no fewer than fifteen in 1785.[23] That was the year in which his father informed Nannerl that Mozart had made 559 gulden at a single concert of which not much had been expected by way of profit, and that 'If my son *has no debts to pay*, I think that he can now lodge two thousand gulden in the bank'.[24] In the remaining six years of his life, however, only five public performances in Vienna are recorded. Mozart wanted to play, but the Viennese public no longer wanted to hear. In July 1789 he wrote to Puchberg:

[23] Steptoe, 57
[24] *LMF*, 888–9

> But I must mention that in spite of my wretched condition I decided to give subscription concerts at home in order to be able to meet at least my present great and frequent expenses . . . But even this has failed. Unfortunately Fate is so much against me, *though only in Vienna*, that even when I want to I cannot make money. A fortnight ago I sent round a list for subscribers and so far the only name on it is that of the Baron van Swieten![25]

Legend has it that the three great last symphonies, composed in 1788 in the hopes of a subscription series, were not performed in Mozart's lifetime.

Up to 1785 we hear of Mozart frequenting the salons of the nobility and the rich bourgeoisie resident in Vienna and performing in their houses. There is a list of distinguished names – Thun, Rumbeke, Cobenzl, Esterházy, Galitzin, Trattner, Zichy, Palffy, Auersperg, Jacquin. After 1785, reference to such contacts progressively dries up. Mozart's career plunges downwards. His reputation then revives, quite rapidly, after his death in 1791.

This trajectory makes for a suspiciously good story; the gentle reader can lament the sufferings of the neglected genius, and marvel at the obtuseness of the Viennese. He or she can feel superior to Mozart's heartless, philistine contemporaries. Our last account begins by challenging this framework,[26] which, it argues, results in part from the elementary historical blunder of mistaking an absence of documentary record for an absence of events. It then provides an alternative trajectory.

* * *

We cannot be confident that Mozart's public performances dried up so dramatically after 1785. Our knowledge of Viennese concert life in this period is utterly dependent upon

[25] *LMF*, 930
[26] It is challenged especially by Braunbehrens.

chance: the chance survival of a ticket or programme, the chance of a reference in a letter or diary.[27] The German periodical press of the time was remarkable in the amount of attention it gave to music, but by no means every concert was reviewed or noticed. In a letter of 13 January 1786 Leopold Mozart informed Nannerl that Mozart had given three concerts in December to 120 subscribers. No other record of these concerts has survived. The police records, which would have listed every concert, were destroyed in a fire in 1927.

The period of known concert activity corresponds precisely with the period for which documentary evidence is good. Mozart's letters to his father are extant up to the summer of 1784; all of the remaining letters, with the exception of the last one in 1787, just before Leopold's death, are lost. For the missing period there are scraps of information about Mozart's doings in Leopold's letters to Nannerl. For some years there are very few letters from Mozart to other correspondents – merely four from 1786, and five from 1788. Our knowledge is especially rich for the spring of 1785, when Leopold was staying with his son in Vienna and sending back detailed reports to Salzburg; correspondingly, this time has the appearance of being Mozart's busiest in terms of performances, both public and in noble households.[28]

The thesis that he stopped giving concerts gains some support from the fact that he stopped composing piano concertos: after 1786, there were two new ones only. K595, the last one, remained uncompleted probably from 1788 until 1791. But this is not conclusive evidence against concerts. In 1785, when he gave at least fifteen, he composed only three new concertos and no new symphonies. Evidently he was using the stock he had built up in 1784; and it may be

[27] Otto Biba, 'Grundzüge des Konzertwesens in Wien zu Mozarts Zeit', *MJb 1978–9*, 132–43; Mary S. Morrow, 'Mozart and Viennese Concert Life', *Musical Times*, cxxvi (1985), 453–4
[28] Braunbehrens, 160, 174

that after 1786 he felt that his repertory was large enough. Two public performances are recorded for spring 1786, and a letter from Leopold to Nannerl suggests that there was an Advent series in that year as well.[29] In 1787 Mozart was in Prague at the beginning of both the spring and autumn concert seasons, which may have made it impossible for him to arrange concerts in Vienna.

In June, July and August 1788 the three last symphonies were composed. In all likelihood they were performed at a series of academies in the autumn. In a letter to Puchberg Mozart mentions that his concerts at the Casino are to begin next week; he sent two tickets.[30] Traditionally it has been assumed that these concerts did not take place, but this is absurd. Mozart must have known whether he had enough subscribers when there was only a week to go. That he had had tickets prepared, and was sending them to his friends, is surely conclusive. There were in fact several occasions when one or more of the three last symphonies could have been performed: on the tour via Dresden and Leipzig to Berlin in 1789, on that to Frankfurt in 1790, and at the Vienna Tonkünstler-Sozietät benefit concerts in April 1791.[31] Symphony no.40 was almost certainly performed at least twice, for there is a second version with clarinet parts added.

1789 was the year when his subscription list came back with only Van Swieten's name on it. Too much should not be made of this; he was trying to mount a series in the dead summer period, when most of the nobility were in the country. It does not prove that he gave no concerts at other times. Two of his letters of 1790, in May and October, refer to plans for concerts. We just do not know whether any of these took place. In any case he was away on a trip to Frankfurt at

[29] *MDB*, 280
[30] *LMF*, 915. This letter was formerly thought to date from June but was probably written in autumn: Braunbehrens, 345
[31] Neal Zaslaw, *Mozart's Symphonies* (Oxford, 1989), 421–31

the end of that year. The end of 1791 was taken up with the two last operas and with a trip to Prague.

If a reduction in concert-giving cannot legitimately be inferred from the gaps in the documentation, neither can a diminution in Mozart's contacts with Viennese high society. The Trattners, for example, are rarely mentioned in his correspondence, never after February 1785. But it would be a mistake to conclude that relations ceased. They were godparents to four of Mozart's children, including Franz Xaver Wolfgang, born in July 1791.There is no reason to suppose that Mozart was singled out for neglect when the nobility contracted their patronage of music in the difficult late 1780s. Mozart continued to get opera commissions. From 1788 he played a central part in the ambitious concerts of Handel oratorios promoted by Van Swieten and the Gesellschaft der Associirten Cavaliers, an association of noblemen.[32] He must have been paid for arranging and directing the Handel. A performance of *Acis and Galatea* was given for his benefit in November 1788. After his death it was this association which mounted the first performance of the Requiem for the widow's benefit.

Mörike's little novel, *Mozart on the Road to Prague*, depicts him as a lionized celebrity. So do Rochlitz and Niemetschek, inconsistently combining this view of him with the story of his neglect in Vienna. It cannot be disputed that some of his contemporaries had difficulty in coming to terms with his music; at the same time it seems likely that he *was* a celebrity in his lifetime, and not only in Prague, Leipzig and Berlin. Loschenkohl printed his silhouette, as one of the notables of Vienna, in his Calendar for 1786. More tickets were sold for the première of *Così fan tutte* in 1789 than for any other opera that season; the revival of *Figaro* in 1789 was a success according to the same criterion.[33] At the Prague coronation of 1791 the opera impresario Guardasoni put on

[32] Braunbehrens, 340–1
[33] According to the findings of Dexter Edge.

not only *La clemenza di Tito* but also *Così*, and *Don Giovanni*, which played to an overflowing house. Mozart's death was reported in many newspapers throughout Europe.[34]

If the tale of his neglect by his contemporaries is a myth, have his financial difficulties also been exaggerated?[35] The highest estimate of his income in his best years, at 11,000 gulden p.a., comes from Kraemer. Kraemer's figure has generally been dismissed. It is based upon an inflated estimate of the sums received for performing in noble households and for public concerts. But Robbins Landon estimates that Mozart earned 5763 gulden in 1791. Braunbehrens claims that his documented income for that year was 3725 gulden. For his last six years Braunbehrens puts it 13,122, that is, an average of almost 2200 per annum. In addition to the documented income, Braunbehrens is certain that he earned other undocumented sums, for concerts, teaching and publication of his compositions.[36] The larger figure, so it is claimed, would not disgrace a nobleman, the smaller was a good middle-class income. On either estimate, Mozart was by no means poor.

The official document which listed his debts also valued his goods and chattels at 592 gulden. This has been cited as evidence of his miserable poverty when he died. But according to Robbins Landon the valuation was conducted by an official who was a fellow mason, who obligingly put in a low figure so as to save the widow from estate tax;[37] it was in fact normal practice to estimate the value of the chattels of the

---

[34] Braunbehrens, 287, 411, 429
[35] On Mozart's finances see Kraemer, 'Wer hat Mozart verhungern lassen?', *Musica*, xxx (1976), 203–11; Bär, 'Er war . . . kein guter Wirth'; Angermüller, '*Auf Ehre und Credit*'; Steptoe, 'Mozart and Poverty'; and Moore, 'Mozart in the Market-Place'. See also the discussions in Braunbehrens, Steptoe (*Mozart-Da Ponte Operas*) and Robbins Landon, *Mozart's Last Year*.
[36] Braunbehrens, 152; Robbins Landon, *Mozart's Last Year*, 61
[37] Braunbehrens, 133

dead well below market prices.[38] Accordingly, this figure represents only a fraction of the real value of Mozart's possessions. For example, the clavier was listed as worth 80 gulden; its purchase price would probably have been 900.[39] Mozart's house was luxuriously furnished, and he had an expensive wardrobe.[40] The report in a Vienna newspaper of 13 December 1791 that 'this man's widow sits sighing on a sack of straw amidst her needy children' is Romantic nonsense.[41]

What we know of Mozart in his last years, then, according to this version, is not consistent with a view of him as a poor man. When he travelled, he had his own carriage, either purchased or hired. He kept a horse for exercise. He had a large first-floor apartment in the centre of Vienna, with a billiard room. He sent his wife to a fashionable watering-place for her health. He put his son into a boarding school which charged 400 gulden p.a.[42]

*

Our second 'existentialist' telling of Mozart's life, having criticized the received trajectory, substitutes an alternative map of his career. The fullest delineation of this alternative map is to be found in the recent book by Braunbehrens.

*

Here is an image of Mozart powerfully, clear-sightedly and successfully shaping his own destiny. His decision to settle in Vienna and make his living as a freelance was a gamble, but not a rash one. He could have tried the life of a travelling

---

[38] Moore, 31
[39] Bär, 'Er war . . . kein guter Wirth', 37
[40] Braunbehrens, 133–5
[41] *MDB*, 423–4
[42] Braunbehrens, 391

virtuoso, but that ran the risk of low status, of being thought of as little better than a gipsy or travelling circus performer. An appointment as a Kapellmeister in a noble or princely household would have committed him to much administrative routine, and his letters show that he thought of himself as a composer, not an administrator. A Kapellmeistership offered security, but low pay and dependent status. Jomelli's 4000 gulden plus perks at Stuttgart, and Holzbauer's 3000 at Mannheim were quite exceptional. Haydn received only 1000 from Prince Esterházy, and was not allowed to take on outside work. His prosperity only began when he left Esterházy service to go to London and compose for publication. Mozart was coolly and sharply aware of financial realities, as his correspondence demonstrates.[43] In 1782 he explained to his father why he did not want to be tutor to Princess Elizabeth of Württemberg:

> You write that 400 gulden a year *as an assured salary* is not to be despised. What you say would be true if in addition I could work myself into a good position and treat these 400 gulden simply as an extra. But unfortunately that is not the case. I should have to consider the 400 gulden as my chief income and everything I could earn besides as an extra, the amount of which would be very uncertain and consequently in all probability very meagre. For you can easily understand that you cannot act as independently towards a pupil who is a princess as towards other ladies.[44]

What he wanted was an honorific, salaried but not tying court appointment. None was vacant in 1781, but he guessed he would get one if he waited, and he was right. The salary of 800 gulden which he was awarded in 1787 only seemed small by comparison with the extravagant generosity of Maria Theresa's time; by Joseph II's standards it was not ungenerous. In the meantime, Vienna was 'a splendid place – and for

[43] *LMF*, 799–800
[44] *LMF*, 827

244

my métier the best one in the world'.[45] Vienna had a population of 200,000; all the other towns in the Habsburg lands
of Germany and eastern Europe were small (except Prague
with its 70,000), far too small to support a freelance musician. Vienna was rich; as well as the court there were wealthy
noble households, some of them having private orchestras,
and a growing stratum of prosperous merchants. Moreover, it
was a city uniquely devoted to music.

Mozart's gamble paid off; by 1785 he was celebrated and
highly paid, living in the spacious and splendid Camesina
house. His subsequent house-moves should not be read as a
steady decline; he took a large house with a garden in the
suburbs for a time, and his last apartment was scarcely inferior to the Camesina house. He rapidly raised his standard of
living to the level of his high income, but this was policy
rather than extravagance. Mozart wanted to be treated not as
a lackey but as a social equal in the noble and bourgeois
households where he played and gave lessons. Only thus
could he command generous payment. His concern for dress
was part of the same strategy. He had already explained this
to his father in 1781:

> At the time of my affair with the archbishop I wrote to you for
> clothes, for I had nothing with me but my black suit. The
> mourning was over, the weather was hot and my clothes did
> not arrive. So I had to have some made, as I could not go about
> Vienna like a tramp, particularly in the circumstances. My linen
> was a pitiful sight; no house-porter in Vienna wore shirts of
> such coarse linen as mine . . . One must not make oneself cheap
> here – that is a cardinal point – or else one is done. Whoever is
> *most impertinent* has the best chance.[46]

Mozart was not neglected by the imperial court under Joseph
II. Not only was he given a salaried post which left him free
for other activities; he was also commisioned to compose

[45] *LMF*, 721
[46] *LMF*, 764

four operas between 1781 and the emperor's death. For the last of these, *Così fan tutte*, he was promised, according to his own letter to Puchberg, twice the standard payment. He was in financial difficulties at the time: was the Emperor trying to help him out? Considering the 'enlightened' message of *Die Entführung* and the social progressiveness of *Figaro*, it may be that Mozart was being employed as a mouthpiece for the reform politics of the Josephinian court. In a letter to Puchberg, Mozart refers to Salieri's plots in connection with *Così*; but perhaps this should not be taken too seriously. Salieri esteemed Mozart's music and had it performed. A week before the aforementioned letter Salieri had arranged the première of Mozart's Clarinet Quintet at the Tonkünstler-Sozietät concert.[47] He conducted a considerable amount of Mozart's music at the three coronation ceremonies in Frankfurt in 1790, Prague in 1791 and Frankfurt in 1792.[48]

Mozart's bid for fame and fortune ran on to the rocks in 1788, for reasons already cited - the Turkish wars, economic recession, inflation, high interest rates, the collapse of noble patronage, his wife's and his own illnesses. But he did not bow fatalistically to ill fortune. He was on the lookout for new ways of earning, and had already thought of a trip to England. He sought, and found, outlets. Van Swieten's Gesellschaft der Associirten Cavaliers, which mounted the ambitious performances of Handel oratorios, was one of these. The nature of musical patronage was changing. Instead of noble households hiring a staff of musician-servants, rich nobles and bourgeois were banding together to support musicians thought of as artists. Beethoven was to be succoured in this way. This is the context for understanding Constanze's declaration that certain Hungarian nobles had promised him an annual subscription of 1000 gulden, and

[47] *LMF*, 935; Braunbehrens, 358
[48] Robbins Landon, *Mozart's Last Year*, 103–4

that an even larger sum was promised from Amsterdam.[49] After 1787 he had ceased to compose the cassations and serenades which were performed at entertainments in noble houses. He began to compose and publish dances for balls, music suited to a wider audience.

The letters to Puchberg requesting loans dry up at the end of the summer of 1790; his letters become more cheerful and it looks as if his affairs had taken a turn for the better. Evidently he had resolved to make a supreme effort to attain financial stability:

> I am firmly resolved to make the best of my affairs here and then return to you with great joy. What a glorious life we shall have then! I will work – work so hard – that no unforseen accidents shall ever reduce us to such desperate straits again.[50]

This is exactly what he did in 1791; all the signs suggest that he amassed a good income and made progress in clearing his debts. He had been invited to go to London, but was now doing so well in Vienna that he did not take up the offers. He attempted a simpler style of opera in *La clemenza di Tito*, which eventually achieved considerable popularity. *Die Zauberflöte*, aimed at a broader audience, was a triumph. In his last letter but two he wrote to his wife in terms which suggest that he had overcome his money problems:

> Why must it rain just now? I did so much hope that you would have lovely weather. Do keep very warm, so that you may not catch a cold. I hope that these baths will help you to keep well during the winter. For only the desire to see you in good health made me urge you to go to Baden. I already feel lonely without you. I knew I should. If I had had nothing to do, I should have gone off at once to spend the week with you; but I have *no facilities for working at Baden*, and I am anxious, as far as possible, to avoid all risk of *money difficulties*. For the most

[49] *MDB*, 421–2
[50] *LMF*, 942

> pleasant thing of all is to have a mind at peace. To achieve this,
> however, one must work hard; and I like hard work.[51]

Two months later, out of the blue, came the meaningless,
absurd accident of illness and premature death.

*   *   *

From a human point of view, these 'existentialist' ways of
telling Mozart's death are distressing: to a professional historian, mistrustful of imposed patterns, their brutal contingency
is tempting. Furthermore, it is not difficult to imagine how a
contrary myth might have grown up, a myth falsely depicting
the composer dying in neglect and poverty.

Constanze Mozart would have been a prime source of it;
and indeed she was left a widow without an income, for
Mozart had neglected to insure with the Vienna
Tonkünstler-Sozietät. Six days after his death she petitioned
for a pension, claiming that she had been left 'in circumstances which border upon indigence and want'.[52]
According to Niemetschek, rumours were circulating that
Mozart had left debts of 30,000 gulden. The widow sought an
audience with the emperor and assured him that 3000 would
suffice to clear them. For two hundred years this figure of
3000 has largely been believed – after all, by contrast with
the 30,000, it sounds reasonable – and the story proposes to
us the image of a widow defending her dead husband's
reputation against charges of profligacy. But the official
inventory of his estate lists debts of 918 gulden only. Even if
we suppose that the 1451 gulden borrowed from Puchberg
were still outstanding in full, this is still less than 3000. Did
Constanze exaggerate the debts to improve her case for
assistance? Did she add in the 900 gulden dowry promised to

[51] *LMF*, 968
[52] *MDB*, 421

herself in the marriage contract in order to reach the figure of 3000?

Schlichtegroll's *Nekrolog* of 1793 declared that he had had a considerable income but 'in consequence of his exceptional sensuality and domestic disorder [he] left his family nothing beyond the glory of his name'.[53] But perhaps Schlichtegroll is simply reflecting prejudiced gossip from the Salzburg sources on which he drew. According to Niemetschek in 1798:

> Even though his talent was so well known, as much as his compositions were sought after: so little thought was given to rewarding him accordingly and to supporting him. He had often indeed made considerable sums; but because of the uncertainty and irregularity of his receipts, because of the frequent confinements and long drawn out illnesses of his wife, in a town like Vienna, in all conscience it follows that Mozart was bound to be in want. Therefore he decided to leave the city where no position for a genius like Mozart was to be found.[54]

This, which was incorporated verbatim into Nissen, is a key document in the story of the starving genius. Niemetschek's drift is strongly anti-Viennese; not only did that city fail to appreciate him, its musicians conspired against him and, it is hinted, may have poisoned him. From Niemetschek comes the story about *Figaro*, 'that at the first performance Italian singers, out of hatred, envy and low intrigues made every effort to ruin the opera by making intentional mistakes'.[55] He was much better esteemed in north Germany and his widow was deeply moved by her reception in Leipzig, Halle, Hamburg and Berlin.[56] Above all, Niemetschek combines a neglected genius story with a Bohemian nationalist one

[53] *MDB*, 469
[54] Niemtschek, 30
[55] Niemtschek, 25,
[56] Niemtschek, 42

which has echoed through the literature of the ensuing two centuries. No city appreciated Mozart so well as Prague. The day of his concert there in Spring 1787, when he was rapturously received, was one of the happiest of his life.[57] His crowning masterpiece, *Don Giovanni*, was written for Prague, which proves what respect he had for the musical perception of the Bohemians.[58] Their excellent orchestral players were able to do full justice to his difficult music, and even played the overture to *Don Giovanni*, composed at the last minute, at the first performance without any rehearsal whatsoever.

Can this story be trusted? In a letter to Gottfried von Jacquin Mozart himself described the success of his visit to Prague. He also wrote that he was longing to be back in Vienna, and there is nothing in his correspondence to confirm the alleged special relationship with the Bohemian capital.[59] The story of the singers sabotaging the first performance of *Figaro* does not accord with his known friendship with some of them, nor with the reminiscences of Kelly, who sang Don Basilio and Don Curzio.

The story of Viennese neglect and poverty was gladly and uncritically accepted by subsequent biographers. According to Schurig, Mozart's last year was unspeakably sad and impoverished; when he died he counted as no more than a poor minor musician, scarcely of local significance, a poor devil for whom no person of power or importance in Vienna showed any real concern.[60] Schiedermair thought that he was no more esteemed in Vienna than dozens of second-rate contemporaries; his financial situation at the end was catastrophic.[61] Even Bär maintains that when Mozart was given a

---

[57] Niemtschek, 27
[58] Niemtschek, 27–9
[59] *LMF*, 902–4
[60] Schurig, *Wolfgang Amadé Mozart*, ii, 262, 380, 392
[61] Schiedermair, *Mozart*, 328, 394

third-class burial, he was a long-faded star; few if any would have recognized his greatness at that time.[62]

There are amusing parallels to the Bohemian nationalist story. At times it appears that Vienna was the only city which could have failed to appreciate Mozart. If only his Viennese friends had united to support him, he would have lasted longer, laments Henri de Curzon. If only Grimm had not forced him to leave Paris against his will when he was on the verge of success, he would have become a French composer.[63] 'London was the place in which he had been happiest and to which he always longed to return', writes Haldane.[64]

*

Should we then conclude that all of this is a myth, the most pervasive and misleading myth of all about Mozart? Should we embrace the rival version of Braunbehrens and Robbins Landon, the depiction of Mozart lionized and triumphant, in temporary difficulties in the late 1780s, but overcoming them in 1791, only to be defeated by the ultimate bad joke, the cruel and unexpected catastrophe of his early death? The careful historian must insist that this new picture is by no means proved, that indeed it is a selective reading and interpretation of the evidence.

Mozart's great ambition was to compose opera, but during his lifetime he was far from the most popular in this field in Vienna, ranking seventh on one estimate; the works of Paisiello, Salieri and Martín y Soler all scored many more performances.[65] *Don Giovanni* and *Così fan tutte* disappeared from the Viennese stage after their first runs. It may be that during his lifetime he was thought of above all as an

---

[62] Bär, *Mozart: Krankheit – Tod – Begräbnis*, 139, 144
[63] Curzon, *Mozart*, 130–2, 236–7
[64] Charlotte Haldane, *Mozart* (London, 1960), 101
[65] Steptoe, *Mozart-Da Ponte Operas*, 45–7

instrumental composer and performer: but this raises the problem of whether he continued to give public concerts after 1786. The fact that he stopped composing piano concertos gives cause for thought. According to King he was less published during his lifetime than Handel, Haydn and Beethoven during theirs – though it may have been Mozart's deliberate decision to publish only a relatively modest amount of his music, so as to retain financial control over the rest.[66] It is by no means obvious that everything was coming right for him in 1791. One of a group of men who were thinking of approaching Mozart to compose an opera based on Shakespeare's *The Tempest* wrote that 'He is in very straitened circumstances and supports himself by teaching'. A letter of September from Count Rasumovsky to Prince Potemkin advises that the latter could employ Mozart, who was 'somewhat discontented here'.[67]

He himself complained constantly about conspiracy and neglect in Vienna. A recent assessment of the growth of his fame argues that he was held back by his reputation as a *Wunderkind*: it was difficult for his contemporaries to accept a different, mature Mozart, difficult for him to recognize that as a mature man he could not expect instant success, praise and help from all sides. He wanted to please, but was not as clever as Haydn in meeting the taste of the public.[68] There is a mass of documentary evidence to prove that his music did not immediately win universal acclaim.

The stories of financial chaos began immediately after his death. It is impossible to come to a firm conclusion about his financial circumstances in 1791; the evidence is lacking, or obscure, or contradictory. Much ink has been spilt over this in recent years, with the result that we now know more

[66] King, *Mozart in Retrospect*, 2. I am indebted to Stanley Sadie for the suggestion that Mozart kept works back by deliberate policy.
[67] *NMD*, no.106; *MDB*, 406–7
[68] Gernot Gruber, 'Mozart und die Nachwelt', *Acta mozartiana*, xxxii (1985), 53–8

clearly that we will *never* be sure about Mozart's income, expenditure and indebtedness. These three factors will now be reviewed in turn.

Where Mozart's income is concerned, Braunbehrens (and Robbins Landon) persistently choose the most optimistic interpretation in order to support their picture of a successful Mozart. For example, in a letter to Puchberg of 25 June 1791, Mozart writes that the latter will receive 2000 gulden in a few days on his behalf.[69] This may have been borrowed money rather than income; but Braunbehrens guesses it is to be interpreted in the light of a remark in Contanze's petition to the emperor for a pension in December 1791:

> He was assured shortly before his death of an annual subscription of 1000 florins from a number of the Hungarian nobility; while from Amsterdam he was advised of a still larger annual sum, for which he would have had to compose only a few works for the exclusive use of the subscribers.[70]

There is absolutely no evidence to back up this guess, and we should probably dismiss it.

A more cautious estimate of Mozart's income is provided by Bär; he reckons that Mozart received no more than 11,000 gulden for the whole of the six-year period from December 1785 to December 1791, that is to say an average of 1833 gulden p.a. Even this figure is higher than what is yielded by adding together the known receipts. Into this category fall his official salary, sums he received for operas, his share of his father's estate, and other receipts precisely specified by him in his correspondence. The following table is based upon these known sums.[71] It includes a figure of 1000 gulden for Mozart's concert earnings in Prague in 1787, even though the

[69] *LMF*, 957
[70] *MDB*, 421–2; Braunbehrens, 153
[71] It is based upon Moore's table in 'Mozart in the Market-Place', but I have incorporated the correct sum for *Così*, 450 gulden for his Dresden performance and have omitted any figure for the Requiem, since the precise sum cannot be established.

Existentialist scepticism

evidence for this is very indirect. Nissen gives it in his biography, but he may have obtained it from a letter of Leopold Mozart to his daughter. Leopold himself had received the information from Mozart's English friends, the Storaces.[72] For 1789 it includes no more than 450 gulden for the composition of *Così fan tutte*. In spite of Mozart's own testimony that he had been promised 900, the researches of Dexter Edge into the theatrical ledgers have shown that in the event Mozart received no more than the standard payment. He was paid in the very week of Joseph II's death; perhaps the emperor had promised double payment, but the promise had not been recorded in writing.[73] But it does include a payment of 450 gulden for playing before the Dresden court. Mozart does not mention this in his letter home to Constanze, saying instead that he received a very fine snuff-box. But a contemporary newspaper quotes this sum, and so, in spite of the doubts of some scholars, it should probably be accepted.[74]

year	gulden
1786	756
1787	2417
1788	1025
1789	2400
1790	935
1791	1700
Total	9233

It cannot be doubted that there were further receipts for which no precise figure can be given. During his visit to Prague in autumn 1787, the fourth performance of *Don Giovanni* was given for his benefit. In 1788 came his benefit performance of Handel's *Acis and Galatea* in Vienna; he may

[72] *LMF*, 906
[73] In a paper 'Mozart's fee for *Così fan tutte*'.
[74] *NMD*, no.90

well have earned other money from Van Swieten's Handel concerts. He had both composition and piano pupils during these years. He gave public concerts in Vienna in 1786 and 1791 and almost certainly in 1788. He gave concerts on his trips to Frankfurt and Berlin. As already argued, Mozart may have given public concerts of which no record has survived. But we cannot even begin to estimate what sums, if any, he made from known and unknown concerts. For example, on 3 March 1784 Mozart wrote to his father about a series of three concerts. He expected 130 subscribers, each paying 6 gulden, that is to say an income of 780.[75] Unfortunately there is absolutely no information on the vital matter of expenses. An orchestra might cost one or two hundred gulden per concert; then there was rent, heating, transport of instruments and copying of parts to pay for. Bär speculates that Mozart may have given up public concerts simply because they made so little money at the end of the day. It is not beyond the bounds of possibility that Mozart, like Beethoven, sometimes gave concerts on which he actually lost money.

There will have been income from publishing; Robbins Landon estimates 739 gulden from this source for 1791 alone. This figure rests upon no documentary evidence. It is based in part on the sums Haydn requested from publishers. But we do not know whether Haydn regularly got as much as he asked. Beethoven often received much less.[76] In 1791 Mozart also received a down payment on the Requiem, apparently; the sources give various figures for this.

The list of possible sums is still not complete. In 1789 in a letter to Hofdemel he referred to a mysterious 450 gulden from abroad.[77] According to legend, Schikaneder paid him nothing for *Die Zauberflöte*, but this should perhaps be doubted. These additional unrecorded sums very probably brought Mozart's receipts for his last six years up to the total

[75] *LMF*, 869
[76] Moore, 24–5
[77] *LMF*, 919

of 11,000 gulden estimated by Bär; he may well have exceeded that figure.

Bär also attempts an estimate of Mozart's expenditure. He bases this in part upon a contemporary Viennese commentator, Johann Pezzl. According to Pezzl it was possible to maintain a middle-class living standard in Vienna on an income of 500–550 gulden per annum. But Mozart, Bär argues, a court employee seeking noble patronage lived, and had to live, at a higher level than that. He rented good and sometimes luxurious apartments in the inner city, and spent a good deal on clothes to keep up appearances. Travel was expensive and he made six major journeys during his Vienna years. He sent his wife for cures at Baden, he lent money to friends, and he probably started out with debts. On top of household furnishings, he bought two luxury items – a clavier and a billiard table. Bär reckons an expenditure of 12,000 gulden for the period from December 1785 to December 1791. Given his estimate of Mozart's total income at 11,000 gulden for that period, there would have been a deficit of 1000 for the last six years.

Others have concluded from this, and from comparison of Mozart's estimated income with that of civil servants and musicians in noble service, that Mozart had a middle-middle class income or better. If it is then argued that his income suffered a temporary dip in the late 1780s but was picking up strongly in 1791, it follows that the prognosis was good; Mozart's course was set towards worldly success. Recent research, however, strongly suggests that this account of Mozart's situation and prospects is at best ill-founded in the evidence, at worst excessively optimistic.[78]

In the first place, the methodology employed here is faulty. An estimated income is compared with an estimated expenditure. Both estimates have a substantial margin of error: therefore the comparison is utterly unreliable. Secondly,

[78] The opinion of Moore, 'Mozart in the Market-Place'

Pezzl's opinion that 550 gulden would suffice to maintain a single man in a middle-class living standard has been misunderstood. Pezzl is not proposing that this is enough to enable a man to live in comfort. It is just sufficient to keep a man above the level of the impoverished masses.

Without doubt Mozart's income, and wealth as represented by his possessions, put him firmly in the middle classes – perhaps in the top 10 per cent of the Viennese population. But this does not mean that he was comfortably off. For the income structure of Viennese society described a very sharp pyramid. The mass of the population, the bottom 80–90 per cent, was very poor indeed. The middle class was small, but even so there was a vast difference in wealth between its top and its bottom.

Comparisons with other salaries are not meaningful. Mozart had to live on his; others in government or noble service often did not. A nobleman's Kapellmeister might receive much of his remuneration in kind – firewood, clothing, housing, carriage and so on. His money salary, therefore, would be pocket-money. In that underdeveloped economy, nobles might be rich in land and possessions but relatively poor in cash – hence Mozart's complaints when he was rewarded with yet another watch or snuffbox, instead of ready money. Civil service salaries were mostly very low, not intended as living wages. In the light of all this, it has to be concluded that the evidence at our disposal does not entitle us to believe that Mozart, were it not for his debts and temporary misfortunes, would have been prosperous.

A fair amount of information has survived about Mozart's debts, but not enough, or not reliable enough, to enable the historian to construct a complete and coherent account. Beginning in 1788, the letters record a loan of 100 gulden from Hofdemel and a string of loans from Puchberg. The chance survival of the begging letters to Puchberg, endorsed by the recipient with a note of the sums he sent, has given a decisive direction to the stories written about Mozart's end.

Mozart evidently used Puchberg as a banker, on occasion having large sums (for example the 1000 gulden from his father's estate) paid to the Viennese merchant. The letters indicate that Mozart was short of cash in the summer of 1788; requests for loans then resume in the summer of 1789 and continue to the summer of 1790. Mozart tried to persuade Puchberg to lend him a large sum, of one or two thousand gulden, on a medium-term basis so that he could get his head above water; but Puchberg usually gave only modest sums, perhaps intended to be short-term. The letters record a total of 1451 gulden. Some of this was probably paid back. In some of his letters requesting aid, Mozart designates specific sums he is about to receive, from which Puchberg can be reimbursed. Other letters reveal that he often found it impossible to repay Puchberg as soon as he had promised, and that the debt accumulated. According to Nissen, 1000 was still outstanding at Mozart's death: the widow repaid this some years later.[79]

Mozart's reliance upon Puchberg appears to have ended in the autumn of 1790. At that time he obtained the large loan he had wanted, from the moneylender Lackenbacher, who supplied 1000 gulden for two years at 5 per cent.[80] He wrote to his wife, probably about this transaction, that 1000 would clear his debts, and leave a little over; but not long after he was writing about borrowing 2000, paying off 1000 and 20 per cent interest, and leaving himself with 600.[81] Finally, in June 1791 comes the obscure reference in a letter to Puchberg to a sum of 2000 gulden, which may have been another loan.

All of this is confusing; worse is to come. On 7 March 1792 an official notice was placed in the *Wiener Zeitung* asking that Mozart's creditors come forward, so that his estate might be settled. The official assessment of his estate lists unpaid

[79] Nissen, 686
[80] *MDB*, 371–2
[81] *LMF*, 942, 945

debts of 918 florins, all to tradespersons. There is no mention of a sum of 2000 gulden, no reference to Lackenbacher or Puchberg, no debt to any moneylender.[82] The possibility that Constanze later exaggerated his debts has already been mooted; but these are the realms of the uncertain and the unknown.

Perhaps the best piece of documentary evidence about Mozart's finances at the end is the official assessment of his estate.[83] Even this is problematic, because of its oddity. What is unusual about it is that it reveals substantial debts and little cash, side by side with luxurious possessions. For example, a billiard table appears to have been virtually unknown outside the homes of the aristocracy. If the debts are ignored, and the value of Mozart's assets is compared with that of other musicians, it appears that Beethoven was worth 11 times as much as Mozart when he died, Haydn 22 times and Salieri 36 times. Obviously these men lived longer, had time to overcome their early difficulties and accumulate wealth. But this is beside the point when estimating Mozart's situation in 1791. Mozart's debts make his situation relative to them much worse. Yet his furniture was worth as much as Haydn's, and much more than Salieri's or Beethoven's. His clothes, though much less valuable than Haydn's, were worth as much as Salieri's and more than twice as much as Beethoven's. This supports the traditional story of a period of prosperity, when the luxurious possessions were acquired, followed by a catastrophic decline. That Mozart's fortunes had turned for the better in 1791 remains a possibility, but not a certainty.

All of this drives us towards the first 'existentialist' version, which accepts the received trajectory of the life, explaining his downfall as a chapter of accidents. In the light of the ill-documented and often mythical nature of stories recounted in earlier chapters, this telling gains in plausibility. But as long as one or more of the earlier stories remain possible, the

[82] *MDB*, 443, 592
[83] See Moore's excellent discussion in 'Mozart in the Market-Place'.

'chapter of accidents' is not a knock-down winner. For it involves a series of interpretative decisions. The uninterpreted evidence is not decisive for or against the hypothesis that Mozart was hounded to death by intrigue and gossip, nor against that he had finished his work. By itself it cannot decide whether he was ostracized as a social rebel, destroyed by sensuality and irregularity, or a tragic lonely genius. An 'existentialist' version, a 'chapter of accidents', decides to reject these: but what it offers is a plausible alternative, not a refutation.

CONCLUSION

Conclusion

The preceding chapters have presented a series of stories about Mozart's death. It is fitting that two very different conclusions should now be offered.

*

The first is a sceptical one. An argued case can be made out for each of the stories. Each one makes the life – and the death – intelligible. Some evidence, however circumstantial, can be marshalled for each one. Conversely, it is impossible conclusively to decide between them. Why is this?

To begin with, there are too many gaps in the evidence. Documents, including letters, have been lost or destroyed, much important information was never recorded – for example, Mozart's complete performing schedule. The eye-witnesses failed lamentably to provide an accurate record for posterity immediately after the events concerned, and they are long dead, unavailable for questioning. Those eye-witness accounts we have, preserved in the early biographies, must be approached with great caution. No intelligent, cultured and self-critical observer who knew Mozart well left an extended account of his Vienna years.

It is always difficult to know an individual; even true self-knowledge is rare. Obviously the problem is greater where out-of-the-ordinary mortals are concerned; we ordinary ones have to struggle to understand them. It gets worse once they are dead, for memory is selective. The famous come to be remembered, not as they were but as survivors think they ought to have been. The reader feels that this process affected the memories, for example, of Rochlitz, Kelly, and increasingly of Constanze and Sophie.

Consequently the traditional picture of Mozart is partly founded upon gossip, which quickly blossomed into legend and myth. It really *is* a tradition, which has fed upon itself, resolving problems it has itself created, building ever higher and further from the reliable data concerning Mozart's life and death. For example, very early on he came to be viewed as a paradigmatic genius, according to contemporary conceptions of genius. This implied strangeness and alienation. The alienness of Mozart was incorporated into the tradition, and in due course, psychological and sociological explanations of that tragic characteristic were added. Each age understood him in accordance with its own ideas, and so anachronism steadily accumulated. Successively he was a Romantic genius, a German nationalist, an expression of the Nietzschean will-to-power, a Marxist rebel.

It is to be feared that these difficulties can never be overcome. They will always deprive us of the truth about what Mozart was like, how he lived and why he died. To be sure, if we had a time machine and could go back, some of the outstanding questions could be cleared up. If we could send a doctor, we could obtain a secure diagnosis of the last illness and cause of death. For the problem here is simply that information is lacking. If we could interview Mozart, we might get a clear picture of his income and liabilities – on condition that he did not give evasive or misleading answers. If we could observe him in his social and professional life, we would be able to form our own opinion as to whether he was disorderly, or a bad colleague, or difficult, or socially rebellious.

'We would be able to form our own opinion': already the issue is not mere matters of fact. Judgment, interpretation is required. Can it really be believed that a time machine would make it possible to establish with certainty how popular

Mozart was as performer and composer, and what were the causes of his neglect if he *was* neglected? Similar questions today would be matters of conjecture and dispute.

The inevitability of judgment and interpretation can be illustrated with reference to the best evidence we have about Mozart, namely his own letters. Here, as it were, we have it from the horse's mouth. But is he always telling the truth? More profoundly, does he always know the truth about himself? At the extremes are starkly opposed opinions of the letters. Some have thought that they are delightfully exuberant, charmingly frank, perhaps a touch naïve in their openness; Mozart reveals his heart in a tumultuous outpouring. Others have thought the reverse. Hildesheimer thinks that the letters present a series of masks, behind which Mozart hides; not only from others, but also from himself. Which is the correct interpretation of the letters? How could we ever know?

Take, for example, his letters from Paris, sending back to Salzburg the news of his mother's death in a foreign land. Jahn thought that they exhibit great sensitivity and affection for his father, filled as they are with information about Mozart's doings in the hope of distracting the father from his grief. Hildesheimer was impressed instead by Mozart's indifference to his mother's death, his callous matter-of-fact preoccupation with his own affairs. Another writer thinks that they show that Mozart had gone into a deep, paralyzing depression.

Or take that famous letter of 1791 in which Mozart says: 'I can't describe what I have been feeling – a kind of emptiness, which hurts me dreadfully – a kind of longing, which is never satisfied, which never ceases, and which persists, nay rather increases daily.' This has variously been interpreted as proof of his manic depressive tendencies, of his longing for death, of his realization, all too late, of his total isolation from other human beings, and of his companionate marriage with his Constanze.

Conclusion

It is tempting to plan a cleansing of the Mozart portrait, removing the accretions of myth and legend. This is the task Braunbehrens set himself in his recent study. But a pristine portrait cannot be attained; the predilections of the writer interfere. Braunbehrens's book has its own interpretative slant. He depicts Mozart as a social progressive, even though most of the evidence for this is merely circumstantial. He arranges the evidence so as to depict a determined and successful Mozart. A shake of the kaleidoscope could re-arrange the same evidence into a different pattern. The reader of an old biography of Mozart – say Schurig's – immediately notices the flavour of the period in which it was produced, the aroma of past philosophies. It would be at once arrogant and naïve to suppose that we can escape the same fate. No historian can approach the past with entirely innocent eyes, bracketing off the assumptions and attitudes of the present, surrendering to the texts.

The ambition to get behind the stories to the actual events is doomed from the outset. In this instance, stories and events cannot be disentangled. What is striking is how far back the stories go. Immediately after the death, Mozart's family and friends, reporters and music lovers who barely knew him if at all, began to weave narrative patterns. The poisoning story, for instance, was circulating within a matter of days. Indeed, unless Constanze was lying, Mozart himself was telling that story a few weeks before he died. The story-telling about Mozart began during his lifetime – began when he was a child prodigy. His contemporaries, including his father, perceived him, his character, his sayings, his doings, through narrative webs; they made sense of him by means of themes and concepts which fitted together into patterns. Patterns, not pattern; there are a number of narratives in play, which do not always match, and which were, no doubt, simplifications and distortions.

Furthermore, it seems that Mozart perceived himself in the same way. Often in the letters we catch him writing about himself, as a novelist or dramatist would write about a key character, relating the moments of his existence, the successes and the failures, to a larger scheme. He and his father discuss what he should do to fulfil his divine mission. They correspond endlessly about the conspiracies directed against him. There are times when Mozart depicts himself as misunderstood. He casts himself as a victim of, and a rebel against, aristocratic privilege. Sometimes he is the virtuous German bourgeois, shocked by the superficiality, the excess, the viciousness, of Frenchified court society. He even writes about his life as governed by unintelligible fate.

The sources we have, even the original letters, therefore make it appallingly difficult to separate out the events and the narratives. Maybe it is even worse than this. For the stories that Mozart, and his contemporaries, told about him, may have affected the way he behaved, and the way they reacted to him. It was not the case that first there was the life, and afterwards, the stories; life and stories were always interwoven, not so much interacting as indistinguishable. As historians, therefore, we are not only asking about how several different stories were shaped to fit the life; we are also studying how the life was to some extent shaped to fit several different stories. To recoin a phrase: 'I am narrated, therefore I am'. But the narratives, and the self they produce, are not consistent, nor are they the whole story. The life spills out of their contrived framework.

What story did Mozart tell himself as he lay on his deathbed? Did he see himself as a genius who had fulfilled his mission, as a failure, as a victim of conspiracy, the social order, or fate?

*

The alternative conclusion is more positive. It argues that the portrait can be cleaned, with the aid of a vigorous application of historical method. The myths can be cleared away and the reality revealed. Above all it is necessary to adopt a critical attitude to the tradition, and the sources upon which it is based. Early testimony needs to be checked wherever possible. One witness can be checked against another, provided that it is remembered that an apparent confirmation is no confirmation if one 'witness' has stolen the other's story. Checking against documents, such as those amassed by Deutsch, is better still. Always it must be asked: was this witness in a position to know, did he or she have a motive for distorting the truth? Hence a question mark will always hang over the memoirs of Da Ponte and Kelly; their reminiscences cast such a favourable light upon themselves. Some legends have been destroyed by scientifically ascertained facts. Plath's investigation of the handwriting, and Tyson's of the paper-types of the autograph scores, provide elegant examples.

The portrait-cleaner will have a sharp eye for anachronism, and will take great care to understand documents and events in the contexts, economic, social, political and cultural, of Mozart's own day. Bär's study of the death and burial is a model in this respect. All of these historical techniques were too rarely applied before the mid-twentieth century. Biographies like Jahn's are honourable exceptions; for the first 150 years, scholarship was outweighed by romantic myth-making. By contrast the last fifty years have seen solid and considerable advances in knowledge and understanding.

A sceptical attitude often results from making an un-realistic and unneccessary demand for certainty. The human sciences deal in probability more than certainty: for practical purposes, probability is usually sufficient. This book's exposition and discussion of the stories about Mozart's death can end with some conclusions – most of them probable, some of them certain. Mozart was certainly not poisoned, and his last illness was almost certainly rheumatic fever and/or infective endocarditis; he probably died of heart failure resulting from those illnesses and the treatment. The evidence for self-destruction by dissipation is poor; but he may well have put obstacles in his own path. He had a sharp tongue, he did not always meet deadlines, he lived up to his income and beyond it. Constanze Mozart was not a bad wife who ruined him. He may have been something of a social rebel, but the theory that this played a major part in his destiny is a possibility rather than a probability. The notion that he was so odd as to be incapable of normal human relations is improbable. There is little to be said for the thesis that he was burnt out and ready to die.

The real Mozart is not forever hidden behind gossip and legend; for the letters are a wonderful source. Hildesheimer's distrust of them in their entirety rests upon a prior commitment to a particular, and implausible, account of Mozart's personality. The natural approach is to trust the letters, except in those instances where there are specific grounds for mistrust. To be sure they must be read with care, and a sensitivity to layers of meaning; for Mozart was a sophisticated man – certainly not the naïve child of legend. The reader must then avoid the mistake of trying to find a perfectly coherent and consistent personality. This mistake afflicts many biographies, such as Ghéon's or Paumgartner's. All too often the author goes imaginatively beyond the evidence, in an attempt to reconstruct an inner core of personal identity unifying the moments of the life. Real people are not like that.

Bearing this in mind, what sort of man do the letters reveal? They reveal a complex man: sometimes a snob, sometimes a social rebel; torn between sharp, ironic perception of others and sentimental sympathy; sensual and usually given to hilarity, but on occasion moralistic and straitlaced; intermittently tactless, generally well-socialized. He was not having thoughts of death in 1791.

✳

Conclusion

Here then are two radically different conclusions; it cannot be proved that one is right and the other wrong. The historian is unable to prescribe: gentle reader, you must choose.

Select Bibliography

Abbreviations used

AM   *Acta Mozartiana*
AMZ   *Allgemeine musikalische Zeitung* (Leipzig)
MISM   *Mitteilungen der Internationalen Stiftung Mozarteum*
MJb   *Mozart-Jahrbuch*
MT   *Musical Times*

1. Documents

Anderson, Emily, ed. and trans.: *Letters of Mozart and his Family* (London, 1938, 3/1985) [*LMF*]

Bauer, Wilhelm A., Deutsch, Otto Erich, and Eibl, Joseph Heinz: *Mozart: Briefe und Aufzeichnungen*, 7 vols. (Kassel, 1962–75)

Deutsch, Otto Erich: *Mozart: Die Dokumente seines Lebens* (Kassel, 1961, suppl. 1978); Eng. trans., *Mozart: a Documentary Biography* (London, 1966) [*MDB*]

Eisen, Cliff: *New Mozart Documents: a Supplement to Otto Erich Deutsch's 'Mozart: Die Dokumente seines Lebens'*, (London, 1991) [*NMD*]

Leitzmann, Albert: *Wolfgang Amadeus Mozart: Berichte der Zeitgenossen und Briefe* (Leipzig, 1926)

Schurig, Arthur: *Konstanze Mozart: Briefe, Aufzeichnungen, Dokumente 1782–1842* (Dresden, 1922)

2. Works purporting to contain original testimony

[Arnold, I. T. F. C.:] *Mozarts Geist* (Erfurt, 1803)

Belmonte, C.: *Die Frauen im Leben Mozarts* (Augsburg and Berlin, 1905)

Genast, A.: [memoir], *Acta mozartiana*, xxvii/4 (1980), 83

Holmes, Edward: *Life of Mozart* (London, 1845, 1912 edn.)

Jahn, Otto: *W.A. Mozart* (Leipzig, 1856–9): Eng. trans., *Life of Mozart* (London, 1891)

271

Select Bibliography

——: *Gesammelte Aufsätze über Musik* (Leipzig, 1866)

Kayser, J.F.: *Mozart-Album* (Hamburg, 1856)

Marignano, Nerina Marignano di, transcr. and compiled: *A Mozart Pilgrimage: Being the Travel Diaries of Vincent and Mary Novello in the year 1829*, ed. Rosemary Hughes (London, 1955) [Novello]

Neue Zeitschrift für Musik, xii, no.45 (Leipzig, 2 June 1840), 180

Niemtschek, Franz: *Leben des K.K. Kapellmeisters Wolfgang Gottlieb Mozart, nach Originalquellen beschrieben* (Prague, 1798); Eng. trans. (London, 1956)

Nissen, Georg Nikolaus von: *Biographie W.A. Mozarts* (Leipzig, 1828)

Rochlitz, Johann Friedrich: 'Verbürgte Anekdoten aus Wolfgang Gottlieb Mozarts Leben', *Allgemeine musikalische Zeitung*, Leipzig (i, 1798–9), 17, 49, 81, 113, 145, 177, 289, 480, 854; iii (1800–01), 450, 493, 590) [*AMZ*]

——: 'Raphael und Mozart', *AMZ*, ii (1799–1800), 641–53

——: 'Ein guter Rath Mozarts', *Für Freunde der Tonkunst*, ii (Leipzig, 1825), 281–304

Schlichtegroll, Friedrich: *Mozarts Leben* (Graz, 1794)

Schlosser, J. A.: *Mozarts Biographie* (Prague, 1828)

3. Secondary works: books

Abert, Hermann: *W. A. Mozart* (Leipzig, 1919–21; 10/1985)

Angermüller, Rudolph: *'Auf Ehre und Credit': die Finanzen des W. A. Mozart* (Munich, 1983)

Autexier, Philippe A.: *Mozart et Liszt sub rosa* (Poitiers, 1984)

Bär, Carl: *Mozart: Krankheit – Tod – Begräbnis* (Salzburg, 1967, 2/1972)

Blom, Eric: *Mozart* (London, 1935, rev. 1962)

Blümml, Emil Karl: *Aus Mozarts Freundes- und Familienkreis*, (Vienna, Prague and Leipzig, 1923)

Boschot, Adolphe: *Mozart* (Paris, 1935)

Braunbehrens, Volkmar: *Mozart in Wien* (Munich, 1986); Eng. trans., *Mozart in Vienna 1781–1791* (London, 1989)

Breakspeare, E. J.: *Mozart* (London, 1902)

Brophy, Brigid: *Mozart the Dramatist* (London, 1964, 2/1988)

Burk, John Naglee: *Mozart and his Music* (New York, 1959)

Carr, Francis, *Mozart and Constance* (London, 1983)

Chailly, Jacques: *La flûte enchantée, opéra maçonnique* (Paris, 1968); Eng. trans., *The Magic Flute* (London, 1972)

Cotte, Roger: *La musique maçonnique et ses musiciens* (Braine-le-Comte, 1975)

Curzon, Henri de: *Mozart* (Paris, 1920)

Dalchow, Johannes, Duda, Gunter, and Kerner, Dieter: *Mozarts Tod 1791–1971* (Pahl, 1971)

Daumer, G. F.: *Aus der Mansarde*, iv (Mainz, 1861)

Davies, Peter J.: *Mozart in Person. His Character and Health* (New York and London, 1989)

Deutsch, Otto Erich: *Mozart und die Wiener Logen* (Vienna, 1932)

Ehrenwald, J.: *Neurosis in the Family and Patterns of Psychosocial Defence: a Study of Psychiatric Epidemiology* (New York, 1963)

Eibl, Joseph Heinz: *Wolfgang Amadeus Mozart: Chronik eines Lebens* (Kassel, 1965)

Einstein, Alfred: *Mozart: his Character, his Work* (London, 1946, /1971)

Favier, Georges: *Vie de W. A. Mozart par Franz Xaver Niemetschek précédée du nécrologe de Schlichtegroll* (St Étienne, 1976)

Forbes, Elliot, ed.: *Thayer's Life of Beethoven* (Princeton, 1967)

Ghéon, Henri: *Promenades avec Mozart* (Paris, 1932), Eng. trans. as *In Search of Mozart* (London, 1934)

Grosser, J. E.: *Lebensbeschreibung des k.k. Kapellmeisters W. A. Mozart*, (Breslau, 1826)

Haldane, Charlotte: *Mozart* (London, 1960)

Haas, Robert: *Wolfgang Amadeus Mozart*, (Potsdam, 1933, 2/1950)

Hildesheimer, Wolfgang: *Mozart*, (Frankfurt, 1977), Eng. trans. (London, 1983)

Hoffmann, E. T. A.: 'Don Giovanni' in *Six German Romantic Tales*, trans. R. Taylor (London, 1985)

Hutchings, Arthur: *Mozart: the Man: the Musician* (London, 1976)

Hussey, Dyneley: *Wolfgang Amadé Mozart*, (London, 1928, 2/1933)

Keller, Otto: *Wolfgang Amadeus Mozart. Sein Lebensgang nach den neuesten Quellen geschildert* (Berlin and Leipzig, 1926)

Keys, Ivor: *Mozart: his Music in his Life*, (St Albans, 1980)

King, Alec Hyatt: *Mozart: a Biography with a Survey of Books, Editions and Recordings* (London, 1970)

——: *Mozart in Retrospect: Studies in Criticism and Bibliography*, (London, 1955)

Kreitmeier, Josef: *W. A. Mozart: eine Charakterzeichnung des grossen Meisters nach den literarischen Quellen* (Düsseldorf, 1919)

Levey, Michael: *Life and Death of Mozart* (London, 1971)

Ludendorff, Mathilde: *Mozarts Leben und Gewaltsamer Tod* (Munich, 1936)

Massin, Jean and Brigitte: *Wolfgang Amadeus Mozart* (Paris, 1959)

Select Bibliography

Maunder, Richard: *Mozart's Requiem: On Preparing a New Edition* (Oxford, 1988)

Moberley, Robert B.: *Three Mozart Operas*, (London, 1967)

Mörike, Eduard: *Mozart auf der Reise nach Prag* (Stüttgart and Augsburg, 1856); Eng. trans., *Mozart's Journey to Prague* (London, 1957)

Neumayr, Anton: *Musik und Medizin am Beispiel der Wiener Klassik* (Vienna, 1987)

Nettl, Paul: *Mozart and Masonry* (New York, 1957)

——: *Mozart in Böhmen* (Prague, 1938)

Nohl, Ludwig: *Mozarts Leben* (Leipzig, 1877); Eng. trans. *The Life of Mozart* (London, 1877)

Ottaway, Hugh: *Mozart* (London, 1979)

Oulibicheff, Alexander: *Nouvelle biographie de Mozart* (Moscow, 1843)

Paumgartner, Bernhard: *Mozart* (1927; Zürich, 1945)

Pushkin, Alexander: *Mozart and Salieri* (1830), trans. A. Wood (London, 1982)

Rau, Heribert: *Mozart: ein Kunstlerleben* (Frankfurt, 1858; Leipzig, 5/1887)

Robbins Landon, H. C.: *Mozart and the Masons: New Light on the Lodge 'Crowned Hope'* (London, 1982)

——: *Mozart: The Golden Years* (London, 1989)

——: *1791: Mozart's Last Year* (London, 1988)

Sadie, Stanley: *Mozart* (London, 1965)

——: *The New Grove Mozart* (London, 1982)

Saint-Foix, Georges de: *Les symphonies de Mozart* (Paris, 1932), Eng. trans. (London 1947)

Schenk, Erich: *W. A. Mozart: eine Biographie* (Zürich, Vienna and Leipzig, 1955); Eng. trans., *Mozart and his Times* (London 1960)

Schiedermair, Ludwig: *Mozart: sein Leben und seine Werke* (Munich, 1922)

Schmid, E. F.: *Wolfgang Amadeus Mozart* (Lübeck, 1934)

Schurig, Arthur: *Wolfgang Amadé Mozart* (Leipzig, 1913, 2/1923)

Sitwell, Sacheverell: *Mozart* (London, 1932)

Stendhal, [Beyle, M.-H.]: *Vie de Mozart* (Paris, 1814; 1970)

Steptoe, Andrew: *The Mozart–Da Ponte Operas* (Oxford, 1988)

Tenschert, Rudolf: *Wolfgang Amadeus Mozart* (Salzburg, 1952)

Thayer, A. W.: *Salieri* (Kansas City, 1989)

Thomson, Katharine: *The Masonic Thread in Mozart* (London, 1977)

Turner, W. J.: *Mozart: the Man and his Works* (London, 1938)

Select Bibliography

Tyson, Alan: *Mozart: Studies of the Autograph Scores* (London, 1987)
Wangermann, Ernst: *The Austrian Achievement* (London, 1973)
Wyzewa, Théodor de and Saint-Foix, Georges de: *W. A. Mozart: sa vie musicale et son oeuvre* (Paris, 1912–46)
Zaslaw, Neal: *Mozart's Symphonies: Context, Performance Practice, Reception* (Oxford, 1989)

4. Secondary works – Articles

Bär, Carl: 'Er war . . . kein guter Wirth: eine Studie über Mozarts Verhältnis zum Geld', *AM*, xxv (1978), 30–53
Barraud, J.: 'A quelle maladie a succombé Mozart?', *La chronique médicale*, xxii (15 Nov 1905), 737–44
Biba, Otto: 'Grundzüge des Konzertwesens in Wien zu Mozarts Zeit', *MJb*, 1978–9, 132–43
Boissevain, Willem: 'Neue Erklärung der Todesursache Mozarts: "Hitziges Frieselfieber" war bakterielle Herzklappenentzündung', *MISM*, xxxviii (1990)
Curl, J. S.: 'Mozart considered as a Jacobin', *Music Review*, xxxv (1974), 131–41
Davies, Peter J.: 'Mozart's Illnesses and Death', *MT*, cxxv, (1984), 437–41, 554–61
——: 'Mozart's Illnesses and Death', *Journal of the Royal Society of Medicine*, lxxvi (1983), 776–85
——: 'Mozart's manic-depressive tendencies', *MT*, cxxvii (1987), 123–6, 191–6
Deutsch, Otto Erich: 'Die Legende von Mozarts Vergiftung', *MJb 1964*, 7–18
Dittersdorf on Mozart, *AMZ*, i (1798–9), 379–82 (March 1799)
Eibl, Joseph Heinz: 'Süßmayr und Constanze', *MJb 1976–7*, 277–80
Greither, Aloys: 'Mozart und die Ärzte, seine Krankheiten und sein Tod', *Deutsche medizinische Wochenschrift*, lxxxi (27 Jan and 3 Feb 1956), 121–4
——: 'Noch einmal: Woran ist Mozart gestorben?', *MISM*, xix/3–4 (1971), 25–7
Gruber, Gernot: 'Mozart und die Nachwelt', *AM*, xxxii (1985), 53–8
——: 'Die Mozart-Forschung im 19.Jahrhundert', *MJb 1980–83*, 10–17
Heartz, Daniel: 'Constructing *Le nozze di Figaro*', *Journal of the Royal Musical Association*, cxii (1986–7), 77–98
——: 'Mozart and his Italian contemporaries: *La Clemenza di Tito*', *MJb 1978–9*, 275–93
Henneberg, G.: 'Der Einfluss der Philosophie Hegels auf das

Select Bibliography

Mozart-Bild in der ersten Hälfte des 19. Jahrhunderts', *MJb 1978–9)*, 257–62

Heuss, Alfred: *'Das dämonische Element in Mozarts Werken'*, Zeitschrift der Internationalen Musikgesellschaft, v (1906–7), 175–86

Hormayr, J.: 'Mozart', *Österreichischer Plutarch*, viii (1807), 129–40

Kerner, Dieter: 'Mozarts Todeskrankheit', *AM*, x (1963), 5–10

——: 'Probleme einer Mozart-Pathographie', *Der Deutsche Apotheker*, xxiii (1971), 589–92

Kraemer, Uwe: 'Wer hat Mozart verhungern lassen?', *Musica*, xxx (1976), 203–11

Kramer, K.: 'Strittige Fragen in der Mozart-Biographie', *AM*, xxxiii (1976), 75–84

McClymonds, Marita P.: 'Mozart's *La clemenza di Tito* and opera seria in Florence as a reflection of Leopold II's musical taste', *MJb 1984–5*, 61–70

Moore, Julia: 'Mozart in the Market-Place', *Journal of the Royal Musical Association*, cxiv (1989), 18–42

Morrow, Mag S.: 'Mozart and Viennese Concert Life', *MT*, cxxvi (1985), 453–4

Münster, Robert: 'Nissens "Biographie W. A. Mozarts" ', *AM*, ix (1962), 2–14

Price, Curtis: 'Italian Opera and Arson in Late Eighteenth-Century London', *Journal of the American Musicological Society* xlii (1989),

Schefer, L.: 'Mozart und seine Freundin', *Orpheus* (1841), 273–339

Schickling, Dieter: 'Einige ungeklärte Fragen zur Geschichte der Requiem-Vollendung', *MJb 1976–7*, 265–76

Schuler, Heinz: 'Freimaurer und Illuminaten aus Alt-Bayern und Salzburg und ihre Beziehungen zu den Mozarts', *MISM*, xxv/1–4 (1987), 11–39

Smyth, F.: 'Brother Mozart of Vienna', *Transactions of Ars Quatuor Coronatorum*, lxxxvii (1974), 37–73

Staehelin, Martin: 'Zum Verhältnis von Mozart- und Beethoven-Bild im 19. Jahrhundert', *MJb 1980–83*, 17–22

Steptoe, Andrew: 'Mozart and Poverty: a Re-examination of the Evidence', *MT*, cxxv (1984), 196–201

Wagner, Hans: 'Das Josephinische Wien und Mozart', *MJb 1978-9*, 1–13

Select Bibliography

5. General

Abrams, M. H.: *The Mirror and the Lamp: Romantic Theory and the Critical Tradition* (New York, 1958)

Balazs, E. H., Hammermayer, L., Wagner, H., and Wojtowicz, J.: *Beförderer der Aufklärung in Mittel- und Osteuropa: Freimaurer, Gesellschaften, Clubs* (Berlin, 1979)

Bernhart, F.: 'Freemasonry in Austria', *Transactions of the Ars Quatuor Coronatorum* (1963), 1–7

Burke, P.: *Tradition and Innovation in Renaissance Italy* (London, 1974)

Camus, Albert: *L'homme révolté* (Paris, 1951)

Dean, Winton: *Handel* (London, 1980)

Dickson, P. G. M.: *Finance and Government under Maria Theresa 1740–1780* (Oxford, 1987)

Fauchier-Magnan, *The Small German Courts of the Eighteenth Century* (London 1958)

Fischer, F. *Germany's Aims in the First World War* (London, 1967)

Langsam, W. C.: 'Francis II and the Austrian Jacobins', *American Historical Review* (April 1945), 471–90

Ligou, D., ed.: *Histoire des francs-Maçons en France*, (Toulouse, 1981)

Lindner, D.: *Ignaz von Born, Meister der Wahren Eintracht: Wiener Freimaurerei im 18. Jahrhundert* (Vienna, 1986)

Murray, P., ed.: *Genius: The History of an Idea* (Oxford, 1989)

Roberts, J. M.: *The Mythology of the Secret Societies* (London, 1972)

Sagarra, E.: *A Social History of Germany 1648–1914* (London, 1977)

Schiller, F.: *Über naïve und sentimentalische Dichtung* (1795)

Taylor, R.: *The Romantic Tradition in Germany* (London, 1970)

Trousson, R.: *Le thème de Prométhée dans la littérature Européene* (Geneva, 1964)

Wagner, H.: 'Die Freimaurer und die Reformen Kaiser Josephs II', *Quatuor Coronati Jahrbuch* xiv (1977), 55–73

Wangermann, E.: *From Joseph II to the Jacobin Trials* (Oxford, 1969)

Index

Index

Index

Index